Printed in the United States of America
ISBN 978-194482000-8

Copy Editor: Deborah Paddison
Design and Layout: Ruth E. Thaler-Carter
Cover photo: Jim Morrison –
   F-86Ds looking for playtime with the Canucks over Germany
Publisher: A Flair for Writing
Printing: Book1One

Dedication

To my family and friends,
all of whom undoubtedly saw things differently than I did.
"As Luck Would Have It."

and To Jack and Leslie

my Life PRE-PAT

by her devoted Groom

9-14-2017

Acknowledgments

I wish to acknowledge the contribution of Deborah Paddison
(for the second time) for her work as my copy editor
and for recommending Ruth E. Thaler-Carter to handle
the layout, arrange the photos and oversee the printing.

The cover photo is of an acrylic painting by James Scott Morrison of
three F-86Ds titled "Looking for Canucks," one of several he painted of
his time as a pilot with the 496th Fighter Interceptor Squadron.
His military paintings and those of Western North Carolina
have won several awards.

And finally, my love and thanks to my wife, Patricia,
who patiently reviewed innumerable drafts of
every happening, story, adventure in my life before her arrival.

Dedication

To my family and friends,
all of whom undoubtedly saw things differently than I did.
"As Luck Would Have It."

and To Jack and Leslie

my Life PRE-PAT

by her devoted Groom

9-14-2017

Acknowledgments

I wish to acknowledge the contribution of Deborah Paddison
(for the second time) for her work as my copy editor
and for recommending Ruth E. Thaler-Carter to handle
the layout, arrange the photos and oversee the printing.

The cover photo is of an acrylic painting by James Scott Morrison of
three F-86Ds titled "Looking for Canucks," one of several he painted of
his time as a pilot with the 496th Fighter Interceptor Squadron.
His military paintings and those of Western North Carolina
have won several awards.

And finally, my love and thanks to my wife, Patricia,
who patiently reviewed innumerable drafts of
every happening, story, adventure in my life before her arrival.

Contents

Introduction

In 2002, I wrote a book titled *Weeden & Co.: The New York Stock Exchange and the Struggle Over a National Securities Market*. It was an esoteric subject; difficult to explain, harder to make interesting. Telling it correctly was a challenge. Those who might read it knew the subject as well as I did. The feedback was slim, but generally positive. So far, it stands as the only definitive account of that struggle.

It was followed by *Dog Days*, written for the 2004 reunion of the officers and men of the 496th Fighter-Interceptor Squadron, in which I served as a pilot from 1953 to 1956.

These efforts encouraged me to do more writing. I decided to write a memoir.

I have had an interesting life—a lucky life. I enjoy recounting stories about it if someone will listen: hiking in the Sierras, life on a Norwegian freighter, flying fighter planes, running for Congress. Some are funny. Some are scary. There are near-misses and foreign adventures.

I also realized that I knew very little about my four grandparents, all of whom found their way to California in the 1870s. They started out from England or Sweden, all but one on their own. None kept a diary. There are no letters written to loved ones. There are a few vague stories about them passed on by my parents. As a result, they will all but disappear as my generation dies. I am uncomfortable with this happening to me.

I grew up in a house on St. Charles Street in Alameda, California, very close to San Francisco Bay. Three of my grandparents died before I was born. Only my father's mother was alive until I was seven or eight. There are photos with the two of us standing together in the backyard of her house on Sherman Street in Alameda. She looks old and tired but has a pleasant face that must have been quite beautiful. I remember the short walk from our house to hers to have tea together. Her Danish maid, Gertrude, would prepare it with thinly sliced white toast that curled and had trouble holding the honey. Grandma would come downstairs and we would sit, just the two of us, I with my legs neatly crossed, carefully holding my teacup, having a grownup conversation. I felt very proud, for Grandma seldom came downstairs for anyone. That memory is still with me.

The memoir includes the family I grew up with and the family I helped create. It also introduces you to a number of unusual and interesting people I met along the way. You will come to know them all, albeit through my imperfect lens.

I describe my life mainly in an anecdotal manner. The adventures, challenges, disappointments and rewards chosen are those that I best remember and include my reactions at the time and upon later reflection. They are not meant to misstate nor mislead the reader, or myself, as to who I am. My title, As Luck Would Have It, might sound whimsical, even frivolous, but it is not meant to be. Luck was by my side all the way. I have led a lucky life.

Most of my writing took place in my office on our property near Danbury, Connecticut. The office is attached to our horse barn, reachable by outside stairs, and overlooks a riding ring where Pat, my second wife of 30 years, works out on her "Mister Big." The office is cluttered with boxes, open file cabinets, overstuffed bookshelves—the normal accumulations of someone my age.

The walls are splattered with photographs of family, including an old photogravure of Captain Weeden's ship, the S/S Marion Chilcott, and a photo of him standing solidly by a ship's wheel box. They include parents, children and other family members. There are several shots of me that remind me of some past place, event or experience in my life. It is the perfect atmosphere for reminiscing about the past.

I have spent an undue amount of time thinking about my life, how I behaved, how I appeared to others, how I come off to myself in the cold light of honest appraisal. It is not a particularly pleasant experience. What stands out are the adventures, for sure, but also the obvious mistakes and the near-misses. There have been enough of the latter that I decided on the title As Luck Would Have It as reflecting not only the physical dangers I encountered, but everything else about my life. In the writing, I have learned a great deal about myself.

I take the risk that no one will be interested, but, hey! I've been a risk-taker all my life.

Don Weeden
Danbury, Connecticut
June 2017

Chapter 1
Childhood to Boyhood

They told me I arrived quietly and without damage, courtesy of a Caesarean birth, on the morning of June 7, 1930, "from my mother's womb untimely ripped." I suppose it was a precursor to further unusual things awaiting this fifth child of Mabel Lillian Weeden, née Henrickson.

In Mother's birthing room, the hope was high for a daughter to replace Barbara, her second child, who died suddenly of meningitis at the age of eighteen months. Frank, my father, would have been pacing the floor of the waiting room, hoping the same. He would also be wondering whether Dr. Loomis, my mother's obstetrician, was doing the right thing in agreeing to perform a hysterectomy, a procedure ordinarily not allowed at that time unless the life of the mother was in jeopardy. Mom had insisted this was to be her last child, whatever the outcome. She was 33 years old, beautiful and shapely at 108 pounds, and fed up with bearing children.

The stock market had crashed in October of the previous year. It was spreading its pain further and deeper than anyone could imagine. The society in which Mom and Dad traveled was being badly hurt. Some close friends, partners of now-ruined brokerage firms, had taken their own lives, unable to face their friends and customers who were losing everything. Fortunately, my father's firm, Weeden & Co., had not dealt in stocks, only bonds, and had remained profitable. I have speculated that had the Crash come a month earlier, I might not have been conceived.

The arrival of a fourth son was not what my parents had wished for, and it appears they had some difficulty in adjusting. There is a lost photograph of me at the age of three sitting on the steps of our front porch at 1236 St. Charles St., waiting for my father to arrive home. My cheerful face is adorned with long golden curls that reach down to my white party dress. Soon after, I am told, my father and close friends decided to make me into a boy. The golden curls were shorn, clothes from my brothers' closet replaced the dress, and I joined the masculine world.

My earliest remembered trauma has me returning home from playing with my pants full of "doo-doo" (not the first time) and our maid putting diapers on me before allowing me out to play again. Fear of public embarrassment has stalked me ever since.

A similar incident occurred in the third grade when Miss Frost, my teacher (we called her "Frosty ball"), refused to excuse me from class 5 minutes early at noon break. The humiliation was terrible, but the bicycle ride home was even worse.

I was subject to temper tantrums during these early years, caused, according to my brother Alan, from having fallen out of my crib early on. I don't remember the falling, but I do remember my brothers sitting on me until I stopped my tantrums.

The girl/boy thing raises the question of whether I was subconsciously scarred by being unloved or unwanted by my parents. It might apply in theory, but there is nothing I can remember, felt or thought to support such a conclusion. I remember the parents as being busy, less than fully attentive, but always available whenever I needed them. They were protective, encouraging and fair. If anything, it was I who, in taking for granted their interest and support, went about growing up on my own terms. I seldom asked for their help. Being cute, a bit precocious, quick and anxious to please, I was loved by almost everyone. First in line were our live-in servants, who adored me; in particular, Gussie Eckstein. Gussie was our live-in cook, who arrived when I was five and remained as part of the household for many years after my departure for Stanford. There also was my peer group from the neighborhood, who accepted me as one of their leaders. There were my two older brothers, Jack and Alan, who included me in many of their activities. I enjoyed having the freedom to do most anything I wanted to do that parental absence and a safe environment allowed.

That environment begins with our house at 1236 St. Charles St. It was the only home my parents lived in from 1926 until 1988, when my mother died. In 1947, I left for Stanford. I returned often, but never for any length of time. Until the end, the house, the garden, the interior, the very pictures on the wall remained as they were when we were growing up. Mom and Dad (especially Mom) insisted that it continue as the primary gathering place for the family as long as they were alive. This was important to me as a reminder of my youth.

As the picture suggests, it was a solid, unpretentious house, situated on a quarter-acre lot neatly placed between similar homes. It was well built and comfortable, but tight for our family of six (plus a live-in cook). The property included a garden in the rear shaded by five oak trees and a spacious gardener's shed in one corner. A garage, barely able to accommodate our 1937 Buick Roadmaster, was squeezed in along one side of the lot.

The interior was straightforward: a downstairs that included a living room and formal dining room (both sparsely used); a breakfast room overlooking the garden, with a large map of the world on one wall (the British Empire was colored in red); a kitchen, laundry room and pantry; plus a rather small servant's room. The upstairs was accessed by an interior staircase and upper hallway that led to five bedrooms, an open sleeping porch and two bathrooms. The basement was used by my oldest brother, Bill, 10 years my senior, for stuffing birds. Alan, six years older, created a darkroom in the corner for developing his photos.

The combination of four active boys and parents often traveling made our home the neighborhood headquarters for many unsupervised activities.

During the 1930s, all of us lived at home. We ate dinner with our parents in the breakfast room and ended the evening, after homework, doing our individual thing or playing cards in Dad's bedroom upstairs. There was the normal rough-necking exemplified by a bedroom door permanently pockmarked by a handful of marbles thrown by Jack at Bill, who closed the door "just in time." A typical after-dinner sport involved the stairs, which took two 90-degree turns on their way to the second floor. It became our internecine struggle, waged often over Mother's objections. We brothers would space ourselves on different stairs, I on the highest. On the signal "Go!" we scrambled and tumbled over each other to see who would reach the second floor first.

Another game, also popular with our friends, was "Socks." We would space ourselves at various corners of the upstairs hallway (at night it was totally dark), each with two rolled up socks as weapons to lob at one another. We would very quietly move around until hit by a sock, putting the "hittee" out of the game. The house was also subject to water fights and other confrontations between Alan's and Bill's gangs, which caused some damage, outrage from Gussie and resignation from Mom, if she were not away on a trip. These fights were known to me only through their recounting of them years later.

One thing sticks indelibly in my memory: the numerous times Mom told me to leave the dinner table and go up to my room. I had a habit of laughing uncontrollably, especially when encouraged by one of my brothers. They would make a funny face or wave their middle finger at me when Mother wasn't looking, then put on an innocent face while Mother ordered me to "stop giggling or go to your room." As soon as I managed to control myself, one of them (it was usually Bill) would make another face and start me off again. I would still be giggling as I traipsed up the stairs, depending on Gussie to save something for me to eat after dinner was over.

It was in the breakfast room, with its large world map, that I first learned my geography. One of us would think of a country or city or river; the others would ask him questions requiring a "yes" or "no" answer. After seven questions, the others had to guess the object in mind. We played the game often, especially after World War II started.

On Sunday evenings in the 1930s and '40s, we would gather in Dad's sitting/bedroom and listen to the radio. The broadcasts included Jack Benny, Fred Allen, Charlie McCarthy and the "Manhattan Merry-Go-Round." Dad's bed was nestled in one corner with ample pillows to lean against. The room was large enough for several comfortable chairs and a permanent table for playing cards.

A favorite program was "Double or Nothing." A member of the studio audience would be chosen to answer a series of questions on a subject of his or her choice. If the first question was answered correctly, the prize would double until it reached $64. One evening a sailor was chosen who picked food as his subject. He answered the first two questions correctly, and then, for $8, answered "beans" to the question, "What is the noisiest food in the world?" The audience erupted in laughter, which continued at a high-decibel level until the half-hour show went off the air.

When the program resumed the following Sunday, it began with the new audience laughing uproariously. Finally, the moderator was able to explain over the noise that the answer to last week's question was "celery."

I tell this story to point out how much inflation has occurred between then and the $64,000 prize money needed to gain attention on a similar quiz program in the Fifties, but also to dramatize how constrained we were in acceptable public communications at the time.

Card-playing and dominoes were favorite family pastimes. Even my Uncle Norman, my dad Frank's younger brother, participated. He lived two blocks away on Sherman Street in the house of his parents, Henry Frank and Alice Marie Weeden. He would walk over after dinner and on the weekends. The three of them could play dominoes for hours together and never grow bored.

From the moment I could sit in a chair and hold my own cards, they would include me. They knew all the games popular at the time, but with us children they mostly played hearts. Mom insisted that we play for money, even if it were only for pennies.

At the beginning, someone had to stake me for any losses but would split the winnings. It was a good deal until I earned some money and learned what it felt like to lose. I was 11 and had just come home from earning $1.10 on the weekend as a stock boy at Lewis's Market. I asked to be included in a game of dominoes my parents and Uncle Norman were playing. Mom insisted that I put up my own money now that I had earned it working. I readily agreed. Several games later, I had lost my entire $1.10 in earnings. I excused myself, went to my room and cried myself silly.

My three brothers and I often played a game called "Hell." It involved four decks of cards in which each player tried to get rid of a pile of 13 cards, either by placing them on four other piles in front of him or by placing them on piles in the center of the table that were available to all four players equally. The name "Hell" referred to the excitement when two or more players tried to place a card onto a newly formed pile at the same time. My reaction time was faster than the others, and I won more than my share, even when I had to stand to reach the center piles.

When I was four, Mom had tried sending me to a pre school several blocks away, but I cried the first day and she never sent me back. The same happened later during my first public performance at Mrs. Lattick's piano classes.

It was around that time when I began to venture out on the street without close oversight. Our house was near the end of a dead-end street with little traffic. There was a sea wall at the dead end separating us from the San Francisco Bay.

There was one other boy my age living on the block, Bobby Flint. His father was a detective with the Oakland police force and his mother seemed as relaxed as mine regarding his whereabouts during the day. Most days we had the block to ourselves, except for the daily delivery of groceries, ice and other essentials. We were friendly to the postman, stayed clear of the Chinese gardeners and made faces at the autos that intruded onto our block. We knew all the backyards and the fences that allowed easy access to the neighboring streets with the names of Bay and Hawthorne. Our street was shaded by chestnut and sycamore trees, and the backyards were filled with gnarly old live oaks with prickly leaves. In a vacant lot, there was a fig tree and a couple of scraggly redwoods. There we dug ourselves a hole in the moist sand and covered it with plywood, dirt and stones. It was there that Bobby and I enticed Phyllis Mehrtens into showing us the difference between boys and girls.

Bobby was my closest friend. In the summers of our seventh and eighth years, his parents took me with them up to a summer home they had on the south fork of the Trinity River in Northern California.

To get there, we drove in Mr. Flint's Model T up the Sacramento Valley to Red Bluff, past Redding, then turned west through Hay Fork, Peanut and Forest Glen to a layout on the side of State Highway 12. We left the car and hiked the last three miles along a dusty trail. The house was ample with a big veranda on three sides, nestled among a variety of evergreens and oaks and a large apple orchard. There wasn't another house within two miles. For more than a month, Bobby and I had the run of the area. The Flints pretty much left us to ourselves to swim in the river, fish for trout, roam the area and pick apples, with a stern warning each morning to keep an eye out for rattlesnakes and black widow spiders.

One summer we all hiked upriver to the deep, quiet pools from whence the salmon had started their four-year journey to the Pacific Ocean and now were returning to lay their eggs and perish. The Indian tribes were the only ones allowed to take the fish, but only through spearing them from logs tied together as they quietly floated down from upstream. The salmon were over 2 feet long, fat with pink meat and slabs of red eggs ready to be laid. The Indians would cut them open on the shore and share the meat with us, either cooked or raw.

We would play cowboy and Indians; we were the Indians. Mrs. Flint would take the tops of her silk stockings and sew them into sashes for us and make a headdress out of the remains of hawk feathers found here and there. We made bows and arrows and went hunting all day long.

For fifth grade, Bobby and I went to different schools. St. Charles Street was the dividing line between districts. From Sadler Primary School, he went to Haight with the rest of our class, and I went to Washington Grammar School. His father got a new job and they moved away. When I was in high school, I learned that he had had rheumatic fever, which weakened his heart. We talked together once on the telephone, but I never saw him again. I have always wondered what happened to him but never made the effort to find out.

I continued to hang out with the boys I met at Sadler. They lived on the streets bordering mine. They had names like Butch, Fritz and Peewee. They became my buddies all the way through high school. After graduation, we scattered off to college, the military or working for one's father. Our "territory" included Franklin Park, with a basketball court, baseball diamond, tennis courts and a grass area for playing football. It had the usual swings, merry-go-round and slides. In between there were four blocks of tree-lined dead-end streets, backyard fences easily scaled, and vacant properties with jungle-like growth—perfect for kids looking for adventure.

It also included the Encinal Yacht Club, located at the foot of Grand Street five blocks to the south. It was reached by a 200-yard-long wooden walkway supported on pylons embedded in the mud. We could also walk there by way of the mud flats when the tide was out.

After school we would congregate at Franklin Park or the Yacht Club. In the summer and weekends we were together from dawn 'til dusk. We used the dead-end streets to play football or hockey on roller skates or "one-foot-off-the-gutter." We yelled at autos that dared to interfere. We must have been a pest to the neighbors who occasionally would call the police or our parents. There were those evenings when we unscrewed the light bulbs in the street lamps reachable by standing on someone's shoulders. We waited for the police cars, with their low, wide headlights, to appear at the top of the block. We would then scurry over back fences until we were several blocks away. We owned the streets and the neighborhood. We were devilish but not destructive; mischievous yet innocent—qualities that fit me to a T.

My parents were around less than the other parents. The country was deep into the Depression. Business was slow. Dad was busy traveling to Weeden's five offices: San Francisco, Los Angeles, Chicago, Boston and New York. Mom often accompanied him, leaving me with older brothers and Gussie. School was easy, and the little homework didn't require help or encouragement. I even managed to skip three half-terms before leaving fifth grade.

These times were not incident free. Mishaps and accidents happened. Some were near-misses; others caused permanent injury. My brother Jack was sitting with others on the roof above a target used for bow-and-arrow practice. Eleanor Neff wanted to try it out, and before anyone could move she shot an arrow high and wide, hitting Jack squarely just below his left eye (he still has a slight scar). Ray Lewis brought his .22-caliber pistol to the Yacht Club one day where it accidentally went off, the bullet skipping off the water and going all the way through Johnny Gorman's chest—without hitting anything vital. The real tragedy happened to Bob Christie, who dove off the raft at the club while playing water tag and hit the bottom with his head. The accident left him paralyzed for life from the neck down. He was well liked and we visited him for years, but then everyone who knew him moved on.

After finishing the fourth grade at Sadler and a year at Mastick Elementary School, I was transferred to Washington Grammar School, 10 blocks away in another part of town. I knew none of the other students. Wanting to impress my new teacher and classmates, I recited the poem "Captain Courageous," which I had memorized. It was a mistake. I had already been marked as the kid from the fancy part of town. In the schoolyard after school, I was confronted by an unfriendly group of classmates led by Jackie Brodie. I told him I didn't like fighting, but if he wanted to fight, let's do it one-on-one. After some back and forth, nothing happened. Not long after, Jackie Brodie and I became good friends.

Four or five years earlier, Art Alwyn and I had been walking together out on the mud flats. When we returned to the Hawthorne Street steps, there was an older boy standing at the top holding a rubber blackjack. Beside him lay our shoes and socks, which we had left behind. He said, "I won't let you up unless you give me something." We knew him only slightly. He was from outside our neighborhood. He was older than we, and much bigger. He twirled the blackjack in a menacing way and kept threatening to use it.

I became afraid. I didn't know what to do. Art said nothing. Finally, I offered to pay him a nickel to go away. He didn't take the nickel, and after a while he left. I was relieved, but I also was humiliated that I had offered him the nickel not to hurt me. He was the first bully I had ever encountered. I have never forgotten how he intimidated me and how I reacted. I have hated bullies and bullying ever since.

Our neighborhood consisted mostly of boys. I was a leader of those my age. Jack was part of a group three years older. Sometimes we joined up and roamed the neighborhood together. Jack was quieter than I, more laid-back and relaxed. We got along well together. Sometimes he would slow me down. Sometimes he would have to protect me. Sometimes he would alibi for me. He was great.

You might ask, "Where were the girls?" Actually, there were not a lot in our neighborhood. Those that were, were not included in our street activities. The exception was Alexine Garland, who told dirty jokes, none of which I understood at the time.

Sometimes, I was asked to play touch football with Alan's friends from Alameda High, who thought I was cute, quick and could catch a pass. I remember once when two of them, members of the Alameda High football team, practiced their blocking on me. One hit me high and one hit me low, knocking me out just as Mom showed up to witness it. Alan got into a lot of trouble.

Alan was my first hero. He was six years older, smart, good looking and popular. He would always include me when playing with his buddies. He would also use me as his gofer. It was OK with me, but it upset Mom when she learned of it.

The San Francisco Bay was part of the neighborhood. It was only four houses down our dead-end street. There was a small stand of trees and brush; then concrete steps that led down to the mud flats when the tide was out. When the tide was in, I would sit on the wall with my feet dangling over the edge. It was fun to sit there all by myself thinking about all the countries on our world map that were out there over the horizon. When the wind was up and the weather nice, the sailboats from the Encinal Yacht Club would be out cavorting among the waves. Occasionally, Pan American's China Clipper would take off from its base about a mile down the shoreline, bound for Hawaii and farther west. It would lift off the water right in front of me. I would think about my dad when he was my age, sailing on his father's freighter through the China Sea. I dreamed of doing the same someday.

If the tide was out, I might go down the steps, staying close to the sea-wall, and jump from rock to rock, or take my shoes and socks off and walk way out on the mudflats. Every now and then I would step near a clam buried in the mud and watch the water squirt up from his hiding place. I would end up at the Encinal Yacht Club and join others in a game of tag. We would chase one another all around the deck, leaping over the railing into the water and out to a raft anchored nearby. The water was always cold. Afterwards, we would all crowd into the shower room and get warm again. There was a Swede, named Uno, who worked there. He would yell at us that we were using up all the hot water. We were a constant irritant to him. I was an active child. Sometimes my exuberance would get me into trouble. Whenever discovered, I would immediately repent and promise not to do it again.

As I grew older, my neighborhood expanded to include all of Alameda and downtown Oakland. A map shows Alameda as a sausage-shaped city, joined to Bay Farm Island on the southwest and bordering Oakland along its northern edge. There was an estuary separating the two cities and the only access points were the same three bridges and an underwater Tube that exist today.

I spent three years at Washington School. My new classmates eventually accepted me. Their last names included Brodie, Peralta, Friedman and Heineker. These were different from those in my neighborhood: Richards, Davis, Wright and Lyons. We were friendly, but not close, like the ones I grew up with. Except for Jackie Brodie, I don't remember ever going into their homes. In school, I continued to do better than most, became captain of the Junior Traffic Reserve and was given responsibility for the school's museum.

It was during this time that the Japanese bombed Pearl Harbor. (After that, we referred to them as "Japs"). I was playing touch football at Franklin Park when I heard the news. I remember turning to someone and telling him not to worry because I just read that Admiral So-and-So said recently: "If the Japs start a fight with us, we will beat them in three weeks."

President Roosevelt made a speech to Congress the next day citing December 7th as "a day that will live in infamy." I heard him while I was in my woodworking class. We listened in silence, understanding little about what it would mean over the next few years. The first to feel its effects were the two Japanese kids in our class who would soon be shuttled off to Utah along with all Japanese living in states along the Pacific Coast. It was justified by the nation's fear that they might cause harm to our war effort.

Nothing, and everything, changed with Pearl Harbor. While the normal routines of school and family life continued, the war was always on our mind. The newspapers and radio were filled with news of the war's progress. At the beginning it was all bad. Dad joined the Civilian Air Patrol. They had the job of watching the sky for incoming enemy aircraft. Blackout curtains were installed. Mom spent her days at the American Red Cross headquarters on Central Avenue and every week drove out to the Naval Hospital near Livermore. She was part of a group called the Gray Ladies. They visited the wounded, many of whom were badly burned during the naval battles in the Pacific. Mom would write letters for them and try as best she could to cheer them up.

There was plenty for kids to do. We collected tin foil and rubber from the neighborhood. We participated in paper drives through the schools and churches. We saved our pennies and bought savings stamps of $0.10, $0.25 and $0.50 denominations. The stamps were sold in the schools and in theaters. We pasted $7.50 worth into booklets, took the booklets to the post office and received a United States Treasury bond worth $10 after 10 years. Everyone wanted to do their bit.

Many staples of life were rationed: sugar, salt, coffee, tea and, most important, gasoline. Special stickers were issued to every automobile, truck or piece of farm equipment with coupons entitling one to differing amounts of gasoline depending on the purpose of the vehicle. Vacation trips were planned based on how many coupons you had saved up. Occasionally, even the best of us would, "in an emergency," turn to siphoning someone else's gasoline tank.

The war created a strong feeling of togetherness because everyone was involved in some way. At its core was the military draft which involved all able-bodied men from 18 to 42 years of age (and women who volunteered for service). Several from our neighborhood were called up immediately for the Army while others volunteered for the Navy, Marines and Air Corps. My brother Bill had already started medical school and was given a commission allowing him to finish before serving four years in the Army. Alan was at Stanford when he volunteered for the Navy Officer Candidate School; he eventually ended up in the Navy's Underwater Demolition Teams, stationed on Hawaii. Uncle Norman, who was almost 45, served out the war as a sergeant in the Army Intelligence Corps. He could have a gotten an exemption from being drafted on the argument that he was critical to Weeden & Co., but he and Frank didn't think that would be proper. He ended up spending

As Luck Would Have It

the war in an office on New Montgomery, just across Market Street from Weeden's office on Montgomery Street.

The war was soon made real when telegrams began arriving from the War Department reporting those killed in action: Eddie Fry, John Parker, Bud Robards. The only one I knew personally was Bud Robards.

Bud Robards had joined the Marines. He was Alan's age. He was the one who hit me "low" when I was knocked out just as Mom arrived. The Robards lived down the street in a house overlooking the bay. On election night in 1940, I was at their house to hear the results. Dad still supported FDR. I wanted Wendell Willkie to win, thinking no one should run for a third term. The Robards were Republicans, kindred spirits. I had no clue about these matters, I just wanted to be different from Dad. The early returns had Roosevelt the overwhelming winner.

While in the seventh grade, I won third prize in the Donald D. Lum Essay Contest, open to Alameda grammar school students. It was not mandatory, but I was encouraged by my teacher to submit something. Life Magazine had included an article without pictures titled "The Men of Bataan." I happened to read it, liked it and thought it would make a good essay. I translated it into seventh-grade language and added my own foreword and ending. I had forgotten all about it when I was told that I was the winner from Washington School and had come in third overall. This was not the result I expected. I struggled with the issue of plagiarism. Upon advice, I remained silent. I rationalized that a great deal of creative effort went into presenting the material as seen through the eyes of a seventh-grader.

My next surprise came when, shortly before the end of the school year, they told me I would be receiving a medal at the graduation ceremonies for the eighth-graders. This was bad enough, but I had, as a lark, just the day before, had my head shaved along with my friend, Smith Anderson. Chagrin and public embarrassment suggested illness. "Nothing doing," said the parents. I ended up walking down the center aisle of a packed school auditorium with a sailor's gob hat (also called a "Dixie cup" hat) hiding my bald head.

S/S Marion Chilcott; Henry F. Weeden, captain (right); Captain Weeden behind the wheelbox (left).

Frank and Norman on deck upon reaching Hawaii.

Don's father, uncle, grandfather and grandmother: Captain and Mrs. Weeden with sons Norman, Frank and Dexter.

Christina Henrickson, née Nelson, mother of Mabel, known as Gaga.

Formal portrait of Mabel.

Mabel Weeden (left) on board ship, 1930s.

Charlotte Henrickson, (right) Mabel's sister.

Mabel in uniform of a Gray Lady with the American Red Cross, WWII (left) with Elizabeth Virgin (right), former wife of Mabel's brother-in-law, Dexter Weeden.

FRANK WEEDEN.

Norman, Mabel and Frank
at Soda Springs, late 1920s.

Frank as coach and
founder of Alameda
Swim Association.

Frank and Norman, 1922,
on founding Weeden & Co.

Norman visiting
Don Weeden's
family on Pond
Brook.

1236 St. Charles
Street in Alameda,
with map location
via Google –
the neighborhood
social center.

Don in early years.

With Bobby Flint.

Sadler School kindergarten class, June 1936: Don (front row, second from left), Smith Anderson (back row, far left); Bobby Flint (back row, far right).

As Luck Would Have It

Chapter 2
High School Days

In February 1943, when I was 12 years and 8 months old, I finished grammar school and entered Alameda High School. I was considered advanced as a child, and I skipped three half-year terms before entering high school. (Of course, it may be that I was restless and tended to disturb others in the classroom.) I found it to be a disadvantage for my burgeoning high school social life, as I was shorter than most of the girls in my class.

Jack was in his junior year. He was a role model for me and a great older brother; he was the one who talked me out of smoking. He was a very good swimmer. He had already won the 100-yard backstroke competition at the North Coast Championships in his sophomore year. In the summer of 1944, he went to the National AAU Outdoor Swimming Championships, where he won the gold medal in the 100-meter backstroke. He returned a hero and was elected president of the student body.

Alameda High was located two miles from my house, easily reached by foot, bike or bus, depending on the weather. At high school, I was now back with the neighborhood gang full-time. We all ended up joining the same fraternity, Phi Lambda Epsilon. It had all the Greek ritual jargon that is part of grownup organizations like the Masons and Shriners: "The love of brothers binds us closer and closer." Our leader was called "Alpha."

One had to be initiated into the brotherhood. A memorable part of the initiation was "paddling," where the initiate bends over and grabs his ankles while one of the "seniors" smacks his bottom with a flat piece of oak or ash. I was 13 when I was initiated into Phi Lambda Epsilon. It began at 5 a.m. at the Bay Farm Island Bridge, a desolate spot where the initiation ceremony would not be interrupted or observed. I was determined to be brave and not to cry.

Through the day, we were subjected to various physical challenges that we were unable to complete. Each failure was met with a paddling. By day's end, we had severe black-and-blue marks on our behinds. That evening, Mom helped me into a warm bath while expressing shock and anger at what she saw. I begged her to say nothing about it.

There was also the "Round Table," where each member was subjected to "helpful" comments submitted anonymously by his "brothers." They focused on character, attitude and conduct in public. A lot of stupid comments were submitted, but on balance we learned something about ourselves that needed correction.

Phi Lambda Epsilon was a national fraternity. Most of its chapters were in community colleges. Two were located in Santa Rosa and Sacramento. It was on weekend trips to their frat parties that I was introduced to the world of naked women and excessive drinking. I was 14 but not yet ready for either.

My academic record at Alameda High was a solid B-plus. Math and science courses were my strong suits, while languages, including English, were a drag. In Latin, and especially Spanish, I was awful. Besides Sí and Buenos Días, I have retained little from those classes. One thing I do remember was learning not to cheat, even when you get away with it. It happened in Miss Weisenborn's Spanish class. Miss Weisenborn had had a moderate case of infantile paralysis and could not monitor the students when giving a test. I had made use of some notes that were not permitted.

After turning in my paper, I began thinking about how clever I was—and then how uncomfortable I felt. The next day, I went back to admit what I had done. Before I could say anything, she complimented me on my paper. Now I felt even worse. When I told her what I had done, she smiled and said, "I thought you might have had a little help. Why don't you sit down now and rewrite the essay without any help?" I now knew the subject very well and wrote as good a paper as the first one. I can't remember ever cheating again.

Another one of those lessons learned occurred in Mrs. Anderson's course in advanced algebra. She had left the classroom. While she was absent, a few of us started fooling around and ended up throwing chalk-covered erasures at one another. When she returned and saw what had happened, she asked a few of the "usual suspects," including me, whether or not they had participated. We all said no, until she asked Butch Richards, who confessed that he had. Mrs. Anderson said nothing more. The class continued, and no one was reported, except I left the room having lied. I remember it to this day and feel some shame when I do. I saw Butch recently when five of the "old gang" gathered for lunch and to reminisce. The incident did not come up.

In athletics, I tried to follow in my brothers' footsteps and maintain the family's regional dominance in the backstroke. Bill had won the 100-yard backstroke at the North Coast Swimming Championships, followed by Alan and Jack, who won it four and three times, respectively, making it eight consecutive years of gold medals. When my turn came, I gave it my best effort, but fell short by a hand slap to my competition from Palo Alto High School.

Much credit goes to Frank (Dad), who was our principal coach. My talents were elsewhere, more in the field of racquet sports, where a stretched-out physique with long arms and legs was not a necessity.

Frank had made coaching his major avocation. He began with his sons in the Thirties. After the war, a swimming pool was built in a vacant lot just behind our property. The pool became the property of the five adjacent property owners and became their social center. At first, Frank used it to teach the neighborhood kids how to swim. Eventually it included children from all over Alameda. The program was formalized into a "make every Alameda five-year-old water safe." Frank then financed the building of two swimming pools in city parks. The program even took children as young as two years and gained national recognition. Frank was still actively involved when he passed away at 91.

After my silver-medal finish in 1946, I sensed that my father was disappointed, although I wasn't sure whether it was about him or me. I was happy having done better than expected and was soon on the bus to Yosemite National Park. I had a job waiting for me and a lot of old buddies to see from the previous summers.

The summer of 1946 was my fourth year of working in Yosemite. In 1943 I was 13 when I first visited Yosemite Valley with my mother. We used a good bit of the family's ration of gasoline to get there. We stayed at Yosemite Lodge in one of the single-family cabins. It was late July. The war had been going for a year and a half, and Yosemite Park and Curry Company was having a hard time attracting employees. Their normal supply of college-aged kids were going into the military or working in factories producing goods for the war effort.

My brother Jack had been lifeguarding at Yosemite Lodge since the beginning of the summer. He thought the company was desperate enough for employees that they might even take me. Mom said OK, and I went over to their personnel office. They were interested if I was 14 years old. I immediately said I was. They had an opening for a dishwasher at the dining room at Camp Curry. Mom was leaving the next day, so I moved into a tent in Dodge City where all male employees were housed. It was early August and I planned on working through Labor Day when the season ended. Jack and I could take the bus home together.

I didn't last more than week and had to take the bus home alone. My story goes something like this: When I started, there had been a fight going on between the busboys from the dining room and the guys in the dishwashing room. It had started when the busboys would dump the dirty dishes onto the steel tables, causing the dishes to scatter. This created more work for the dishwashers.

The dishwashers began to retaliate by throwing garbage at the busboys as they dropped off the dirty dishes. The busboys then saved all the dishes until the very end of the meal and dumped them all at once, making a real mess of things. It kept the dishwashers working long after everyone else had left. We were making less than $0.16 an hour, so the extra pay meant nothing, but it cut into the time between meals when everyone wanted to go swimming.

I sized up the situation pretty quick: You sit around for two hours doing nothing and then work like hell, sorting out the dishes and glasses and silverware that have been dumped in a big pile by the 10 or 12 bus boys all coming in at one time. After a couple of days, I suggested someone should tell the chief chef, by the name of Reagan. Everyone encouraged me to do it. Unfortunately, my timing was bad. When I went to tell him, he was in the process of berating someone for doing something he didn't like. Instead of coming back at a better time, I just stood there listening to him chewing out this person. Chef Reagan finally interrupted himself, told me to go back to work and chastised me for listening in on something that was none of my business.

The next day, I brought some cards to work and started a little game of 21 with the other dishwashers. We weren't doing anything until the busboys decided to bring in some dirty dishes, so why not? This got the attention of Chef Reagan, while the skirmish between the busboys and dishwashers had not. So there I was, in the process of dealing another hand, when he comes over to me and says, "I knew you were a troublemaker. You're fired." I tried to explain, but he would have nothing of it. My paycheck barely paid for the bus rides down to Merced and then to Oakland, where I took another bus over to Alameda. That ended my first summer working in Yosemite.

In spring of 1944, I wrote a letter to Mr. Ouimet, the personnel manager of Yosemite Park and Curry Co. I explained that it had been my first real job and that I had made mistakes from which I had learned a great deal and that I would like to have another chance to prove that I can be the kind of employee he expected me to be. Mr. Ouimet answered that they would rehire me as soon as school ended in June. It might have been my letter, or it might have been that they were still desperate for workers.

The job turned out to be "Assistant Garbage Man" at Camp Curry. My boss and I handled all the garbage created by the dining room, the cafeteria and the grill. The garbage cans were brought out to the platform behind all three eating areas. We then transferred them onto a big truck that came in twice a day. Empty garbage cans were returned and were steam washed. This was my job. There was a small enclosed area where I would pile the cans three high, eight across, tilted slightly down. I would direct a high-pressure volume of near-boiling water into each of the cans until they were clean and "smell free."

After two sets of 24 cans, it was I who smelled to high heaven. In fact, no matter what I did afterward, I seemed to carry around a faint but noticeable scent. As Jane Racicot, another employee, explained, "You're a nice guy, Weeden, but you really smell awful."

I can't say it affected my love life because I was barely 14, but it did interfere somewhat with my social life. Between lunch and dinner, we would bike down to El Capitan Beach and swim for two or three hours until we had to go back to work. Occasionally, someone would throw me a bar of soap and tell me to use it.

There was one girl, somewhat older, named Nancy Taylor, who took a liking to me. Having turned 14 in June, I wasn't ready for what she wanted.

Finally, I got a break from cleaning garbage cans. By mid-July, the snows in the High Sierra melt sufficiently to open the Merced Lake Camp, located at an elevation of 7,800 feet. They needed two volunteers to clean up the tents and lavatories left untouched from the prior season. Tommy Witter, whom I had known from Mt. Diablo Country Club, worked in the kitchen dishing out mashed potatoes. We both wanted a job change and quickly raised our hands. The work was not much better than before. Tommy came from a wealthy family and was not used to cleaning up after himself, much less others. We both worked hard and had a ball at the same time, as the old-timers, who stayed for the season, included us in their evenings around the campfire singing old songs and telling tall tales from past years.

I graduated to my old job as a dishwasher and became a model employee. My only contact with Chef Reagan was his comment when he first spotted me: "How come you're back here?" I wanted to explain, but he really wasn't interested. By the time the summer ended, I had moved up to busboy in the main dining room. I was already looking forward to the following summer.

Working at Yosemite was a big step in my learning process. The next summer, I was still the youngest employee in the valley. Except for brother Jack, who worked at the lodge, two miles from Camp Curry, I was on my own. I was among a completely new group of older kids from all over California. There was a lot of similarity among us, but also enough difference to make meeting them exciting. There was even a group of kids from the Deaf and Dumb Institute. They had trouble interacting with the rest of us, and I remember a touch football game on the Camp 16 beach involving them. At first there was some extra shoving and minor fistfights, but finally everyone became quite friendly.

All the while, there was the beauty, the uniqueness, the majesty of our surroundings that visually dominated our daily lives. There was no way to escape the overpowering presence of Yosemite Valley: its waterfalls, vertical walls of raw granite, forest trails shadowed by tall redwoods and stately Douglas firs. We climbed to the top of all the major points of interest—El Capitan, Yosemite Falls, Half Dome, Sentinel Rock, Glacier Point—and gazed down on this unbelievable scene from every angle. We hiked up to Tenaya Lake and Little Yosemite on our way to Tuolumne Meadows and Merced Lake. After the dinner shift, we would bike down to a deserted beach somewhere along the Merced River. We would spend the evening around a fire, roasting marshmallows, singing songs and doing a little cuddling.

I was there during the four summers of war, gasoline rationing and minimum tourists. The Yosemite Park and Curry Co. had the concession for the whole park. Included in the Curry Co. management was Donald Tresidder, who soon became president of Stanford University. They ran the operation as though it were a family business. They viewed the valley as their home. For the visitors, they offered a wide range of facilities that fit most everyone's pocketbook. They kept the services simple and in harmony with the surrounding nature. This was easy during the war years, as the number of visitors was modest.

I found that the absence of parental and school oversight fit my desire for independence. I had a lot of confidence and little fear of being on my own. Yosemite was perfect in this regard. I adjusted quickly to the disciplines of the workplace and found a way to integrate into the various employee groups. By the fourth summer, I took on an important role, helping management resolve a growing unhappiness by the employees. This led to the creation of a permanent committee of employees and management and my serving as its first chairman.

Others in my neighborhood got jobs as well: Warren Musser, Smith Anderson, Pete Jordan and Jim Stroube. We remained together and all found girlfriends to pal around with. Warren's girl, Beryl Calhoun, was really cute and looked a lot like Audrey Hepburn. She came from Lindsay, just south of Fresno, the home of Lindsay Olives. Unfortunately, in the summer of '45, they found that she had been stealing things out of the other girls' tents. She was the first kleptomaniac I ever knew and remains the only one.

My girlfriend was Chris Gilmore from Whittier. She was two years older than I and a bit taller. She was not a beauty but she had a great sense of humor. I was still a bit slow in the romance category, which is probably why I think of those times as being quite innocent. She had a problem with lactic acid; if she didn't watch what she was eating, it could be very embarrassing. I once visited her at the University of Arizona, which ended the relationship. Dating someone who was still in high school might be OK in Yosemite, but it didn't go over well with her sorority sisters.

My career path continued upward. In mid-summer of 1945, I became a waiter in the Camp Curry dining room. I was eventually assigned to a station called the Four-Miler. A typical station served 16 seats, usually two tables of four and one of eight. The Four-Miler was located at the farthest point from the kitchen. It required dexterity plus concentration to balance a tray with eight hot cups of soup sitting under their saucer with a plate full of salad on top while weaving through a maze of tables on your way to your destination. The trick was to balance the tray off your shoulder with one hand. While your body was moving to avoid tables, chairs and customers' heads, the tray would remain level and undisturbed. I never had an accident of my own doing.

I did have one incident that could have ended my career in Yosemite. It happened like this: The same Beryl Calhoun mentioned above had preceded me toward the two sets of heavy swinging doors that separated the dining room from the kitchen. These doors are 8 to 10 feet apart and hide the sounds and smells of the kitchen from the diners.

Beryl was returning a few dirty dessert dishes, used coffee cups and little creamers to the dishwashers. It was of sufficient weight that she rested the tray on her shoulder while holding it with two hands. This caused it to bounce a bit as she walked toward the kitchen. As she pushed open the first swinging door, the tray was jostled so that one of the little creamers toppled over, spilling some cream onto the floor. Shortly after, I came flying through, twisting my shoulders as I flipped the door open on my way toward the second swinging door. Just as I was pushing the second door open, the heel of my shoe slipped on the spot of cream. This threw me totally off balance while my momentum continued forward into the kitchen. The tray was now ahead of me as I tried to regain my footing. The tray shot forward and upward throwing the contents of eight sets of dirty dishes outward and then down, crashing onto the concrete floor.

This attracted the attention of those in the kitchen and everyone throughout the dining room. I was immediately on my knees picking up the mess, when I gaze into the feet, then the legs, and then the full 6-foot-3 body (plus chef's hat) of Chef Reagan, who was standing over me with his hands on his hips and a menacing expression on his face. As I returned to my new role, he continued to look at the broken crockery that had spread far and wide across the kitchen floor and then back at me. Finally, he gave a sigh and said, "Weeden, I don't know what to do about you. Clean up the mess and get back to work."

Chef Reagan and I developed a reasonably friendly relationship, which continued through the next season when I ended my working days in Yosemite.

I often reflect on those days: climbing down into the caves near Mirror Lake, where we almost lost one of the girls when she slipped and fell and our flashlight stopped working; swimming in the near-freezing water at the base of Bridalveil Fall; participation in the employee boxing competition and suffering through three rounds before losing, never to box again; the nightly ceremony of the "Fire Fall," where, after an exchange of hellos between Camp Curry and Glacier Point (4,000 feet above), burning cinders were pushed over the rock edge to drift 2,500 feet down the near-vertical section of the valley wall. There were memories without a story: day after day rain free, warm days, cool at night, open meadows and forest trails, the snowy waters of the Merced River and hot sandy beaches along its shore; all to be enjoyed with friends or quietly alone. They are hard to forget, and impossible to recreate.

In 1946, I turned 16 and returned to Yosemite. By this time, I was an old-timer and friendly with the people in personnel. The war was over and the labor shortage had eased. Mr. Ouimet mistakenly over-recruited and was soon faced with letting people go. I, along with Warren Musser and Noel Daniels, another "old-timer" from Lindsay, California, went to Mr. Ouimet and suggested that we could ease his problem by taking a one-month sabbatical, then returning when the usual attrition began. He thought it a terrific idea.

The three of us began a 1,000-mile tour of California by hitchhiking rides along the highways. We were on the road for more than three weeks, returning at the end of July. I recorded 47 times that someone stopped and gave us a ride. We headed for the San Francisco Bay area, avoiding Alameda, then down the coast past Santa Cruz to Monterey. We arrived in Monterey at the height of their Centennial Celebration of Monterey's becoming the capital of California (1846). The Bear Flag flew from every window, and the main street was painted gold.

Then on to Carmel, the art colony and its pure white beaches. We got lucky when a black Buick convertible (top down) stopped and the driver said he was driving as far as Santa Monica. "That's just where we're going!" we all cried while piling in before he could change his mind. What caused him to stop were our signs made on panels from an orange crate with the words, "MAY WE" – "HAVE A" – "RIDE." We would space ourselves along the side of the road in a manner similar to the Burma Shave ads along America's highways.

When we stopped at Tommy Powell's home in Pomona, south of Los Angeles, he hitchhiked with us to the beaches holding a panel with "BURMA SHAVE" on it. One car stopped with four guys inside; they were going all the way to the beach. They insisted on making room for us.

Another day we went to Laguna Beach. It was famous for waves that were perfect for body surfing. The wind was up and the waves were menacing. They did not feather the normal way, but came in hard, breaking only at the last minute. They sucked up all the water in front of them. Red danger flags had been posted, but I wanted to try anyway. Finally catching an incoming wave, I was swept forward on its front edge and then suddenly dumped onto the exposed sand as the wave broke over me. I protected my head with my arms and then found myself being tossed this way and that for what seemed to be an eternity. I ended up on the beach, out of breath and scared shitless. It was stupid to have even thought about trying, what else can I say? It was one of many bullets dodged over the years. I thought later about Bob Christie.

Our odyssey was a great exposure to California, the diversity of its terrain and the variety of people met. Just the characters that picked us up were as varied as their vehicles: the talkative dude in his Buick convertible, the farmer hauling a load of hay, the truck driver who nodded off at the wheel. There was the guy in the Santa Monica shelter for homeless men who propositioned me in the lavatory. He backed off when I threatened to yell to high heaven if he touched me.

One of our better housing facilities was a giant pile of baled hay, eight bundles high. We moved a few of the bales, making a space to sleep where nobody could see us. It was a bit scratchy, and there were little grasshopper-type bugs that shared the space. Peering over the parapet of hay, I felt like Gary Cooper in the movie Beau Geste.

We stopped off at Noel Daniel's home in Lindsay and stayed a couple of days. Noel had his buddies and their girlfriends over for hot dogs and Cokes, and Warren played the piano. Beryl was there, but the "klepto" incident had put a damper on the relationship. Warren's impersonation of Fats Waller playing boogie-woogie was the hit of the evening.

We got back to Yosemite and found that the employee exodus was as we predicted. I was back waiting on tables. Dinner at Camp Curry cost $1.50; tips were extra. We would share the tips with our busboy or busgirl. They averaged out at $0.10 per person, or less than 10 percent. If you had a good night, you could handle 40 settings and take home $2.00. That equaled my wage of $2.00 a day, plus room and board.

Finally, my day of departure loomed, and Warren, Pete Jordan and I decided to celebrate. We also wanted to test what hard liquor was really like. Our exposure to alcohol up to then had been limited to beer consumed at beach parties, mainly because beer was easy to buy. We enlisted a sailor, who was convalescing at the Ahwahnee Hotel, to buy us a fifth of Schenley's. We stashed it in a grove of oak trees in the middle of the meadow outside Camp Curry.

After work, we went to the grove and began to pass around our first experiment with hard liquor. Each of us took a swig and waited. Nothing unusual happened. Again, we passed the bottle around. Nothing unusual.

The nightly "Fire Fall" was about to commence. We became impatient. The next round of swigs came quicker and deeper. The "Fire Fall" came and went. The bottle was empty. Nothing had happened to any of us. Disappointment reigned. In anger, we tossed the bottle far into the meadow and began to walk back toward Camp Curry.

The path was narrow and hard to follow. The moon showed itself above Half Dome. Pete began to weave, stumbled and veered off the path into the tall grass, laughing as he disappeared. We left him to find his way alone. Suddenly, Warren stopped and said, "I'm going to take a little nap," which he proceeded to do. I pushed on, reaching the employees' Recreation Center, which had been my brainchild the summer before. I made it to a couch and picked up a recent copy of *Life* magazine with a picture of General Malenkov of the Soviet Union on the cover.

I woke up in my bed in Dodge City. I was in a very sorry state. I had lost all control of my bodily functions and smelled to high heaven. I got up; took off all my clothes; gathered all sheets, pillowcases and other affected items, and ran through the tents looking for a garbage can. I returned and showered, and then I found another place to sleep.

I was not a happy camper the next morning. I sat in the dining room in my white-and-gold Alameda High block sweater listening to my co-workers sing "For He's a Jolly Good Fellow." Another trip to the latrine and I was on the bus going home. If there was a lesson in this experience, it was soon forgotten. The only permanent fallout is my abhorrence of Schenley's to this day.

During my last semester at Alameda, I served as president of the student body. The previous semester I had been the recording secretary. Kathy Moore, who lived next door, had been elected vice president. Both of us had run unopposed. We were also going steady at the time. What can I say?

At our graduation ceremony in February, I spoke about the need for improved athletic facilities. I emphasized the need to improve them for all students, not just for those playing varsity sports. It was a pragmatic speech, nothing lofty or inspiring. I read from my prepared speech rather than memorizing it. My two older brothers had also been student body president and had memorized their shorter but inspiring speeches about patriotism, the future and our responsibilities to be good citizens. I had some very specific points to make, and I didn't want anyone worried (especially me) that I would stumble and forget what to say.

Academics had been easy for me, with the exception of foreign languages. I spent a minimum amount of time studying, just enough (B-plus) to get into Stanford. I admit to having been complacent. I figured that an I.Q. of 135, varsity letters in two sports and president of the student body would make up for any academic shortfall. The fact that my three older brothers went to Stanford was also in my favor.

Don and Warren Musser
at Camp Sixteen.

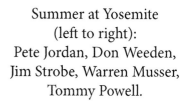

Summer at Yosemite
(left to right):
Pete Jordan, Don Weeden,
Jim Strobe, Warren Musser,
Tommy Powell.

Don (front row, right)
with neighborhood
gang at
Encinal Yacht Club.

Don (left) with
Smith Anderson
and Warren Musser.

As Luck Would Have It

Tom Powell (back) holding Burma Shave sign on Pomonoa-Laguna Beach leg; orange-crate signs resulted in 47 rides over four weeks.

Planning hitchhiking trip around California, 1946 (left): Noel Daniels, Don, Warren Musser.

Overnight accommodations in "Haystack Suite" outside Bakersfield.

Don and next-door neighbor, Kathy Moore. In senior year,
they became "pinned" and were elected president and
vice president of Alameda High School student body.

Zoe Ann Olsen—trained at
Athens Athletic Club, Oakland;
national low and high board
diving champion—earned
silver Olympic medal in
London, 1948.

Don as Caesar and
Diane Musser as Cleopatra.

Chapter 3
Introduction to Weeden & Co.

Graduation turned out to be the end of my active involvement in Alameda. From now on, my mind and body were elsewhere. February through August 1947 was spent working in San Francisco, traveling around California as part of a touring Aquacade and, finally, three weeks with my brothers, Jack and Alan, hiking the John Muir Trail.

Stanford had accepted me for the quarter beginning in September. My father, Frank, said I could work in Weeden's San Francisco office in the interim.

Frank and Uncle Norman talked a lot about their business, but I seldom listened. Now I was eager to learn. On the Monday after graduation, I took an early bus to San Francisco and walked to Weeden's office at 315 Montgomery Street, where I was introduced to Jack Baldwin and Esther Tighe, Weeden's two cashiers. Both had been with the firm for many years. Jack, as he insisted I call him, had taken leave during the war, where he had lost his left hand in combat. They were very nice to me and willing to answer any question I pestered them with.

They explained that Weeden's business was that of a dealer specializing in tax-exempt municipal bonds and shares of California utility companies. Pacific Gas & Electric common stock and the City and County of San Francisco bonds were examples. The stock traders, also known as dealers, made net markets upon request (no added commissions) to financial institutions and securities brokers.

These markets were normally two-sided; that is, a "bid" price ($32) at which Weeden was prepared to buy for its own account, and an "offering" price ($33) where Weeden was prepared to sell from its own inventory (or go "short" if it didn't have any in inventory).

Weeden dealt only with professionals who knew what they wanted and did not rely on Weeden for advice. Weeden used its capital to finance its inventory and took a risk that the value of the inventory might go down before it was sold. The firm's objective was to turn the inventory over as quickly as possible and earn the spread between what it paid and the price at which it sold.

This required an understanding of the trend in interest rates, the condition of the economy and something about the individual security it was quoting. Uncle Norman was especially good at all three.

Weeden had several traders who were very smart about the market value of specific securities. They were critical to Weeden's profitability. I was fascinated watching them make bids and offers. I did this when I wasn't doing my assigned job of learning all about confirming, clearing and settling trades.

I also acted as delivery boy. My daily route included the Bank of America across the street; Wells Fargo Bank and Trust Co., located where Montgomery Street ran into Market Street; and dozens of other banks and brokerage firms located in the "financial district." I found that everyone thought very highly of Weeden and the efficient way we operated. I would hurry down to the Pacific Gas & Electric headquarters building on Market Street close to the Ferry Building. They handled the transfer of their securities when ownership changed. The gentleman there with whom I became friendly (who happened to be the treasurer of the entire company) said, "Weeden did more business in PG&E shares than anyone, including the big brokerage firms Dean Witter and Merrill Lynch."

This was impressive to a 16-year-old son of the founder. I began to think seriously about working at Weeden after finishing my education.

I would also take the cable car uptown and deliver securities to the big insurance companies. Jack Baldwin told me a story about an earlier delivery man (they were also called runners) and my father. There was a big delivery to be made uptown and not much time until the delivery windows closed. The runner asked for 10 cents so he could take the cable car. My father gave him a nickel and said, "You're in a hurry to get there, but there's no hurry on the way back."

After a few weeks, there came the day when we were very busy. It involved a new offering of East Bay Municipal Utility District Bonds (East Bay MUDs). Weeden was a major underwriter and had sold all the bonds it was allocated from the syndicate to its customers. After the offering price was set, Weeden and others began to quote an "aftermarket" for investors who wanted to sell what they had just purchased or wanted to buy additional bonds. A lively demand ensued, and the bonds immediately traded at a premium to the original offering price.

Because the date for delivery was still to be determined, all the trades from the underwriting and the aftermarket trading were confirmed WAII (When As and If Issued), reflecting the fact that until they were actually delivered and paid for there was some slight (ever so slight) chance that they wouldn't be issued. Once the delivery date was set, accrued interest was set for that date on all syndicate sales and aftermarket trades. Normally, delivery date would not be set for several weeks, which allowed considerable time in which trades could occur, all for delivery on the same day. Weeden's allotment in the original underwriting was several million dollars of bonds, while our "aftermarket" trading totaled many times that number.

On delivery date, we had to pick up our allotment from the manager of the syndicate and redeliver them by 1:00 p.m. to receive the funds needed to cover our payment to the syndicate. This was a momentous job for our modest back office. Everyone at Weeden was there to help out. In addition, we had to process the bonds that we had bought and sold during the aftermarket, which, as I explained, amounted to many times our initial allotment. It was a lot of bonds to receive and deliver in one day.

It was important to make deliveries on the same day we received bonds; otherwise, we would have to borrow from our bank to cover the checks we had just written. The overnight interest charge could be significant. Everyone on the street had the same problem and was trying to do the same thing.

Someone had to be in charge of this monumental task of receiving in and turning around literally foot-high piles of bonds before the delivery windows around the street closed down. Jack Baldwin was willing, but he had only one good hand. Esther Tighe knew what to do, and I was eager to do it.

After picking up and delivering our syndicate allotment, bonds began to arrive in lots of 10, 25, 50 and even hundreds. Because all the bonds were issued as $1,000 certificates, a $100,000 trade involved a stack of certificates 2 inches high. These deliveries began to arrive at the window so fast there was no neat way to stack, confirm and repackage. Bonds were piled everywhere there was space.

On each delivery, we had to be sure the number of bonds was equal to the delivery ticket, record the certificate numbers, check that all the coupons were still attached, and then put them together with a sales ticket of our own and get them delivered before 1:00 p.m. Some of those bonds would come back to us a second and even a third time, as the other cashiers on the street also hustled to meet the deadline.

The three hours between 10:00 a.m. and 1:00 p.m. were bedlam. We had hired extra runners who were certified to do the actual delivery and redelivery. I was responsible for receiving, counting, checking and repackaging for delivery out. It was like being in a fast-moving ping-pong game, where as soon as you hit the ball it was coming right back at you. I felt like Charlie Chaplin in that wonderful scene in Modern Times. It also reminded me of the games of Hell I played with my brothers; the quicker you were, the more games you won.

This was my cup of tea. I couldn't slow down for a week, which was lucky because the bonds kept coming in and going out almost as fast as on the first day. I think it was this experience, rather than the trading, that got me hooked on working at Weeden.

Then I had a chance to see some more of California. The Athens Athletic Club in Oakland organized an Aquacade and took it on tour to various towns in California, from Eureka in the north to San Luis Obispo down south. The main attractions were a women's synchronized ballet team—à la the Esther Williams movies—and Zoe Ann Olsen, the reigning national AAU low-and high-board diving champion.

I was part of a three-man comedy act; we would cavort around the pool and diving boards dressed up in old-fashioned swimsuits that covered everything above the knees and elbows. We would act like drunken sailors, wrestling, pushing and tripping each other, and end up doing flatirons off the high board, drenching those sitting along poolside.

It was during the long bus rides that Zoe Ann and I would cuddle up on the back seat and do a little innocent necking. We came to like one another a lot. This was happening while Kathy, whom I had been dating, went off to Manila for six months. Her father had just reopened a branch of the Bank of America that was closed when the Japanese occupied the Philippines in 1942. Zoe Ann would come over to our neighborhood pool and practice her diving, and the relationship became more serious.

The day Kathy returned from Manila, Frank invited her over for dinner. Zoe Ann happened to be practicing at the pool when she arrived, and Frank suggested Zoe Ann join us as well. It would have been a tricky situation for me if she had accepted. I never challenged my father as to whether his invitation was deliberate or innocent on his part, but I've always suspected his motives.

Kathy and I had both changed in those six months, and we agreed to enter Stanford free and clear of any lingering obligations. We did date a couple of times, until the Palo Alto police appeared at a bar near Stanford and arraigned us for drinking while underage. Added to that downer was her recent addiction to scotch at 50 cents a drink while I was drinking bourbon at 35 cents. On my meager allowance, an evening of drinking placed her financially out of reach.

Chapter 4
Along the John Muir Trail

Beginning in early August of 1947, Jack, Alan and I decided to hike the John Muir Trail, which runs along the crest of the Sierra Nevada range. It would be just before the start of fall quarter at Stanford University. It would be Alan's senior year at Stanford, Jack's sophomore year, and I would be entering as a freshman.

Jack and Alan would have just finished swimming at the national AAU outdoor meet at Tyler, Texas. They would also be qualifying for the 1948 Olympics in Helsinki, Finland. Unfortunately, they placed third and fourth in the 100-meter backstroke behind their nemeses, Harry Holiday and Alan Stack, so they didn't qualify.

We started our journey at Whitney Portals, the southern end of the Muir Trail, and hike north to Yosemite National Park, where it terminated. The trail ran 220 miles and crossed 12 passes, all of which were above 10,500 feet in elevation. I was to deposit a cache of food at Reds Meadow, the only point along the trail that could be reached by car.

The Spaniards had named the mountain range that ran along the eastern edge of California "Sierra Nevada," or "snow-clad mountains." When John Muir first saw it, he called it a "Range of Light" and spent the rest of his life exploring, writing about and working to protect his "Range of Light" from intrusion by the roads and vehicles of modern-day life.

As a family, the Weedens had visited the mountains of California many times: skiing at Soda Springs, swimming in Lake Tahoe, traveling north into the Trinity Alps. My brother Bill had fished in the Sierras, including one trip all the way up to Muir Pass. The three of us were familiar with its lower elevations from summers at Yosemite and trips into its middle-level lakes. But this three-week trip, most of which would be above the tree line, was something quite different.

I was excited about the trip because it would be my first chance to be with Alan and Jack by ourselves and away from family and other distractions. Jack and I were close, but Alan was six years older, had been away during the war and was the recipient of my hero worship. Jack's diary of the trip referred to me as "Donnie," a small indication of the relationship even with him.

Jack kept a diary while I took photos with a standard Kodak camera. From the beginning, the trip proved more challenging than we had anticipated. By starting from the south, we were faced with the most difficult hiking of the whole trip. Almost immediately we were above timberline on a narrow trail pointing straight up with switchbacks every hundred yards or so. Jack's boots were new and not quite fitting. Soon he changed to tennis shoes, which lacked the proper support on the rocky, uneven path. The air was thinner than we were used to, and my brothers, supposedly in great shape, were resting every second switchback as we closed in on Whitney Pass (13,600 feet).

This set the tune for the hike until Evolution Valley, five miles past Muir Pass. It was a daily grind of early rising; consuming dehydrated eggs and other unappetizing dried foods; a morning slog up to Forester, Glen, Pinchot, Mather and Muir passes; and lunch of dry foods with high sugar content on the way up or down, depending on the mileage and our condition. The few photos I've included show the desolation of the terrain and the grandeur of the mountains in the distance. In the one with the body sprawled on the ground, that is Jack resting his blisters and wondering whether he could reach Forester Pass (13,200 feet) in the distance.

Some interesting sidebars: On the sixth day we crested Glens Pass (11,978 feet) at 1030 after a five-and-a-half-mile, 2,500-foot vertical rise from Bubbs Creek. We rested just beyond the pass and then descended into to Rae Lakes. When I unshouldered my pack, I discovered that my bright blue and yellow jacket was missing. I questioned why neither one of my presumed bright-eyed and observant brothers had not noticed its absence before we completed our 1500-foot descent over slabs of slippery metamorphic slate. No answer from either one. I found it just below the pass.

The next day, Alan forgot his sunglasses and had to go back two miles before he found them. I must admit that, despite the delay, it gave me a little silent pleasure. Jack was certain that it was his turn tomorrow.

This brings up one of the more frustrating parts of the trip. Our U.S. Geological Survey maps had no way of translating into miles the actual ups and downs plus switchbacks. We relied on Starr's Guide to the John Muir Trail. Unfortunately, it had its own errors and deviated many times from Forest Service signs located along the trail. In one case early on, we thought we had covered six miles in two hours only to find a sign saying it was only three miles back to where we had started. We calculated that if the sign were correct, we would never get to Yosemite before school began.

Our day had now become routine: Jack arose at dawn, followed by me and then Alan. Breakfast was courtesy of Jack; then we hit the trail after everybody finished his private chores. In this regard, Alan was the most fastidious. Sometimes we lost sight of him, even ranging out of shouting distance, as he searched for that perfect tree or boulder.

Lunch was the highlight of our day. It came at a warm and lazy hour. Our outlook was positive and relaxed. The menu was varied from day to day but always contained lots of sugar: Kool-Aid, chocolate bars, cookies, and raisins or dried apricots.

The dried apricots were popular but had a serious side effect. It appears that the method for drying apricots involves sulphur. With the afternoons normally warm and wind-free, the dust from the trail and unpleasant odors remained close to the ground. This gave a heightened interest in being the lead hiker. The problem was soon solved by limiting the apricots to only one of us, who would then hike at the end of the line.

About this time, there began to form some distinct impressions among the three of us about one another. I was considered the feisty one, Jack was laid-back, and Alan was conscious that he was the elder.

Pinchot Pass (12,130 feet) followed by Mather Pass (12,100 feet) brought us to Muir Pass (11,900 feet), the sixth of 12.

Muir Pass was special. The approach and descent were longer and the altitude change greater. The pass topped out at 11,900 feet. From the south, we began our climb at 8,020 feet, where the Middle Fork of the Kings River and Palisade Creek converge. Our guidebook describes the ascent:

"The JMT turns north at LeConte Canyon, staying well above the Middle Fork and begins some long switchbacks and passing just north of a double cascade. The ascent continues past a series of falls and chutes to Grouse Meadow, a serene expanse of grassland.

The trail climbs gently to turbulent Dusy Branch. The route up-canyon ascends between highly polished granite walls past lavish displays of a great variety of wildflowers. The trail passes beside the sagebrush-clothed Little Pete and Big Pete Meadows and swings west to assault the Goddard Divide and search out its breach, Muir Pass. Up and up the rocky trail winds, passing the last tree before you reach desolate Helen Lake. This east side of the pass is under snow throughout the summer in some years. Finally, after five fords of the diminishing stream, you head up to Muir Pass, where a stone hut honoring Muir has been built."

In the visitor's book in the hut, we found inscribed the name "Bill Weeden, the Alameda Stinker, Stanford '41."

If one breaks down the more than 500 lines of text in Jack's diary, a description of what we ate for breakfast, lunch and dinner dominated the list, followed by such interesting subjects as the number of fish caught and miles traveled. The ever-changing panorama of mountain peaks, the flora and fauna along the way, the brilliance of the sky, the quiet of the night, and the gentle gurgle of the nearby creek found only occasional mention.

Jack was reporting what was happening to us: fatigue, hunger, cold, irritation.

The nature around us spoke for itself: the overwhelming grandeur of the scenery, changing with each pass encountered and conquered. Another hardy mountain stream, a meadow filled with late-blooming wildflowers, craggy peaks, and glacier-worn granite was waiting with each turn in the trail.

After the Big Six, the ups and downs became less violent. We were hiking below the timberline more frequently. The creeks became rivers; the Goldens were bigger and easier to catch. Our backpacks were lighter and our muscles were tuned to the daily routine.

Reaching Evolution Valley was the turning point of the trip. With only 110 miles to go and the six highest passes behind us, we felt we had broken old JMT's back, so to speak.

The valley ran slightly east to west for five miles at an elevation of 9,630 feet. Straddling Evolution Creek were three picture-perfect meadows: Colby, McClure and Evolution. Stands of sugar and lodgepole pine, some spruce, and patches of blueberry and currant spread themselves out from the meadows, filling in along the creek and edging out the granite walls that towered nearby. As we settled in close to sundown, Alan and I caught the limit of eager Goldens, which seemed to jump right out of the creek onto our dry flies and soon into Jack's frying pan. Plenty left over for breakfast.

(It was to this place where I returned, 25 years later, with my son, Frank, and two school friends from my Alameda days. Then in 1986, it became the destination of a second trip into the Sierra with my wife-to-be, Pat Cawley, while we were courting.)

From McClure Meadow, we shouldered our packs for an easy downhill trek to the Diamond D dude ranch and the prospects of a sumptuous dinner. As we started down toward the south fork of the San Joaquin River, we stopped and looked back, up past our pristine valley, over desolate Evolution Basin to the rocky crags named for our evolutionists. Out of sight were Muir Pass and the hundred miles of the most rugged landscape in America.

After lunch we and a thunderstorm raced down the San Joaquin at a terrific pace, arriving at Blaney Meadows simultaneously.

The meal at the Diamond D was truly sumptuous and served family style. Alan had two helpings, I had three and Jack managed four. (Jack also threw up afterwards, but only a bit, he said.)

Breakfast was equally sumptuous. The weight we were carrying as we began a short, steep hike out of the canyon seemed more in the stomach than on our backs. Then a thunderstorm hit with all its fury. We crowded under a large pine and watched some girls from the camp ride by in the drenching rain. We observed the glacial tracks at Heart Lake, reached Selden Pass by 1500, dropped down to Marie Lake (10,564 feet) and made camp. I finally finished reading Wuthering Heights, thank God, which had made me increasingly irritable the last few days.

The day started bad when I discovered that one of my socks was burned to a crisp, the result of Alan trying to replenish the fire from his sleeping bag. The night had been bitterly cold and our sleeping bags were drenched with dew. This, along with Alan's unsuccessful effort to catch one of the 14-foot brook trout said to inhabit Marie Lake, delayed our departure.

We Crested Silver Pass. Beautiful view of Ritter and Banner, four days' hike to the north. Dropped down past Lake of the Lone Indian to Fish Creek. Here we ran into people amazed that we had come all the way from Whitney. One couple offered us breakfast with fresh eggs and bacon. I died a thousand deaths when our cook's ego told them, "No thanks, we just had breakfast" (of dehydrated eggs and no bacon).

By this time, a little tension was developing between Jack and me on one hand and Alan on the other. An incident on our way to Virginia Lake from Fish Lake helped bring it to a head. We came to a rather steep portion of the trail, with long, tiring switchbacks. It was mid-afternoon and the sun was blazing down. There were almost no trees on the way except for one shady spot about halfway up, just where the trail made a 90-degree turn toward the top of a moraine behind which lay beautiful Virginia Lake. The vista before us was breathtaking, and Alan, with a good eye for such things, decided to capture it on film. I happened to be the carrier of the camera and passed it over to Alan. He took the picture, of which we no longer have a copy, and then the camera was returned to me. Or it wasn't, depending on who was telling what happened.

Unfortunately, the discussion took place some 1500 feet higher in altitude at the top of the moraine. The issue discussed was whether the responsibility for the camera had shifted to Alan or whether I had the responsibility to make sure that someone had it in his possession.

Alan finally said, "Look, I'll go down then and get it." This offer immediately elicited an "OK" from Jack and me, which caught Alan by surprise. Similar situations along the way, such as when Alan would say to the two of us, looking up from the book he was reading, "I'll get some wood for the fire," or "I'll fill the canteen" would find one of us saying, "Relax, I'll do it." Not this time.

While Alan was making his way down and back, Jack and I determined to our satisfaction that the responsibility for the camera had transferred to Alan and the fact that he had put it down somewhere near my backpack was not enough to shift the responsibility back to me. We also had time to mull over all the times that Alan did, or did not do, that tended to irk one or the other of us. They were nothing outrageous, just those little irritating things that get under the skin when everyone is tired, hungry and sore.

When Alan finally arrived, he was not a happy camper. He was moody and non-communicative throughout our evening on the shore of beautiful Virginia Lake. His silence lasted through most of the next morning, when he finally blurted out that we were both assholes which he had suspected for a long, long time. This broke the tension and began a roundtable discussion about what was wrong with each of us. This kept our mind off the lava-strewn trail of vesicular basalt for several miles. In the end, we had ironed out most of the sore points and had cleared the air. At lunch break, we were extremely chummy.

(This was the first of many roundtable discussions among the three of us. They mostly occurred during our time together at Weeden & Co. These early impressions of one another never quite disappeared. Over time our differences were adjusted for and respected, with the result that we are more closely aligned to one another today – almost 70 years later.)

We arrived at Reds Meadow and retrieved the cache of food I had left on the way to Lone Pine. Nearby was an unusual rock formation called Devil's Post Pile. It is made up of columnar basalt rocks between 2 and 3 feet in diameter, with some rising over 60 feet high.

Rose at 0900. Eight down and four to go.

Our next camp was at Shadow Lake, the most picturesque one we've seen, with Ritter, Banner and the Minarets in the background. It was then we stepped off at a fast pace with Jack leading the way. He had decided that we could reach Yosemite in two days, but wiser heads prevailed. We sped over Island Pass and down to Thousand Island Lake, where for some unknown reason we all became silly and laughed all the way to Rush Creek. We attributed it to the low altitude and higher level of oxygen in the air. We met some doctors from the Stanford Clinic who shared their 200-proof alcohol they had packed in by mule. We got silly again and Alan fell into the creek when returning from communing with nature. Later, Alan burnt his jeans while drying them before the fire and then melted the flashlight.

The next morning we practically ran up the 1,600 feet to Donahue Pass. Donahue was our eleventh pass and the gateway to Yosemite National Park. We immediately experienced a change in the trail construction, like going from a dirt road onto macadam. The trail provided a great view of the Lyell Glacier and meadows far below. A long debate ensued between Jack and Alan over which peak was Mt. Lyell. Alan boasted of his A- in map reading, but Jack turned out to be right. The stream was milky white with granite dust churned out by the glacier ice polishing the granite underneath.

Vogelsang Pass turned out to be higher (10,700 feet) than we thought and no slam-dunk. We stayed the night at Merced Lake High Sierra Camp and enjoyed a great dinner, followed by songs around the campfire. Some of the employees were old-timers whom Jack and I had known from prior summers working at Yosemite Valley. Then off to bed and a pleasant sleep, but not before the girls we had known rolled stones against our cabin.

After a hearty breakfast, we left, leaving two dead fish behind in Jack's bed as a parting goodbye to the rock-rollers. While walking through Little Yosemite Valley, I felt as though I was walking down the center aisle of a grand cathedral. The pine and redwoods were the tallest trees we'd seen on the whole trip.

At Nevada Falls, we stretched ourselves out toward the edge and gazed straight down 600 feet to the pool at the bottom. Vernal Falls was next, and then down the slippery steps below known as the Mist Trail. Jack counted 645 steps while Alan counted only 627. I was making sure I didn't slip.

At the bridge below Vernal, we asked someone to take a picture of the three of us with our packs on our backs. Some smartass stopped and, noting our beards and backpacks, inquired as to how far we had come. Alan replied, "We came all the way from Whitney." The guy shot right back with, "Oh yes, I was there yesterday and didn't catch a thing."

We spent the rest of the day on the valley floor, meeting old friends who were aware of our possible arrival: Pete Jordan, Bob Maynard, Nancy Taylor and Smith Anderson. Smith had driven with me down to Lone Pine three weeks prior and had brought Alan's jeep back to the valley. Milkshakes at the Camp Curry Grill, dinner in the dining room and off to Alameda at 2230, arriving 0300 the next day at 1236 St. Charles Street.

It was one great trip—one glorious adventure. And for me there was the comfort that I was less the little brother, Donnie, and more an equal in their eyes.

The Weeden brothers –Jack (21), Don (18) and Alan (24) – hiking John Muir Trail, along crest of Sierra Nevada range , south to north, covering 220 miles in 21 days, as related in Jack's trail journal.

Overlooking Owen Valley to east from Whitney Portal, southern end of trail.

Jack looking toward Forester Pass, elevation 13,200 feet.

Alan and Jack at
Bubbs Creek.

South from Pinchot Pass
toward Sawmill Range.

Approaching hut
at summit of
Muir Pass,
elevation 11,955
feet; close to
halfway point of
John Muir Trail.

Alan and Jack make camp, preparing dinner
at cabin by South Fork Kings River ...

... while Don cleans up ...

... after catching dinner.

Chapter 5
After Alameda

I spent the next four years at Stanford University, with summers working in Weeden's New York City office. I then spent one semester at Yale Law School before entering the United States Air Force. After four years of flying, my marriage to Vera and my discharge in Germany, Vera and I traveled through parts of the Middle East and Europe before settling down in New York City. I eventually visited California regularly as a member of the National Semiconductor board of directors, with short visits to Alameda. My parents continued to live at 1236 St. Charles Street until Mother's death in 1988.

My memories of Alameda remain strong and positive. It was ideal for growing up: stable, secure, relatively untouched by the Depression and the war. Despite the enormous growth being experienced in California, Alameda's population remained virtually the same during my upbringing: 64,403 in 1930, 64,430 in 1950. During this time, Alameda was predominantly white, with a good number of Asians, a few Hispanics and almost no African Americans.

The only access to Alameda was by ferry, or by car through an underwater tube or over two bridges. We were a back-eddy, off-the-beaten-track suburban community built on a large sandbar resting next to Oakland across the bay from San Francisco. It wasn't hard to get to Alameda, but there was no reason to unless you lived there.

Our population maintained an atmosphere of a single community. We had one high school, one police station and a police chief who knew all of us youngsters and what kind of mischief we were likely to get into.

The sense of family extended beyond parents and siblings to our neighbors, teachers and local authorities. The entire community was there to help us grow up properly and become good citizens. We grew up uncluttered by too many outside and distracting influences.

After high school, I felt I had absorbed all that Alameda offered. I was grateful for what it had provided me, but I was ready to move on. Stanford was a first big step, followed by working on a Norwegian freighter and my service in the Air Force. Alameda had given me the basic building blocks of life—learning how to tie my shoes, the alphabet and multiplication tables, and how to get along with others—but there was a lot more I had to learn.

My first venture out of California came when Warren Musser, Smith Anderson and I drove cross-country to New York City. We took a southern route, via Los Angeles, Texas, New Orleans and then north through Atlanta. Smith adjusted quickly to driving a '41 Ford convertible rather than the hearse used in his family's undertaking business. We felt like Mr. Toad; top down, clear warm days, wind in our hair, and adventures ahead.

In New Orleans, at our first real-live strip joint, three not-so-good-looking older women sat down at our table and started ordering champagne. Before we knew what to do, they had run up a bill beyond our budget. When we started to complain, three big bouncer types joined the discussion and encouraged us not to make a scene. Our limited budget forced us to seek out a homeless shelter for the night, where a sheet, pillowcase, towel and army cot cost only a dollar.

Warren learned about a place with authentic New Orleans jazz. Upon arrival, we found that it wasn't open to white folk. Farther east, we encountered many examples of the more traditional discrimination when we stopped for gas and bladder relief. This was more troubling to us, but it didn't rise to the level of moral outrage. That would come much later, and more slowly than I want to admit.

Race was never something I thought much about. I remember and liked Wes Pease, one of the few African Americans at Alameda High. He was first string on our basketball team, attractive and unassuming. His color attracted no special attention. I had no thoughts of discriminating against him or any other person because of color. On the other hand, no one suggested we ask him to join our fraternity. How he felt I don't know, because we never had an occasion to be together socially or even on the athletic field where the issue might have come up for discussion. If there was any discrimination in Alameda, it was toward the Chinese, who had a greater presence, but even with them mixing socially was limited.

After Pearl Harbor, attitudes changed dramatically toward the Japanese, who had been long-term residents in Alameda and until then highly regarded. They were a sizable part of the community, owned important businesses and were active church-goers. They also farmed many acres of very rich soil in the low-lying areas adjacent to the bay. This placed them close to several naval installations with considerable activity after Pearl Harbor. Many people along the West Coast had a genuine fear of invasion and now viewed the local Japanese as enemies and potential spies.

In February 1942, by Executive Order of the President, all Japanese along the Pacific Coast were ordered to move out of the region to internment camps inland. This seemed unfair and unnecessary to my parents, but to most it was the only thing to do under the circumstances. To a few it was an opportunity to acquire valuable properties at fire-sale prices. This discrimination applied only to Japanese living in the states along the Pacific Coast and was aggravated by stories of atrocities done to American soldiers at the hands of the Japanese and body bags containing local boys arriving from overseas.

I remember Mom's sad goodbye to Grace, who came twice a week to do the laundry and ironed our shirts and sheets. There was the Japanese gardener, and Mr. and Mrs. Towata, who owned a florist shop and garden center. They had to leave everything behind when they were sent to Utah. It was unfortunate but showed an underlying antagonism toward the Japanese not shown toward Germans and Italians.

Chapter 6
Stanford University

I registered at Stanford in September of 1947, graduating in the Class of '51. For the first year I lived in Encina Hall, the freshman dorm, in room 451. My roommates were Larry MacMillan from Southern California and Jim Stevenson from Arizona. I signed up for the freshman water polo team, which my brother Alan helped coach.

The academics at Stanford proved to be difficult for me. Most in my class were there because of high marks on their report cards. I had never felt it that important to get "A level" grades, nor had I developed good study habits. Sports and extracurricular activities had been an important part of high school, and I expected life would be the same at Stanford. I was good at water polo but was behind the curve in class. My classmates from the Eastern prep schools were constantly raising their hands with the answer while I was still trying to understand the question. The women were also smart and driven to do well. I tried to do everything and ended up with a case of mononucleosis just in time for the Christmas break. Looking back at my four years at Stanford, my first quarter was pretty bad.

The attitude of those setting Stanford policy was to accept students with demonstrated talent and then let them find their own way. Jim Stevenson couldn't handle the sudden freedom and flunked out after two quarters. He had arrived in a brand-new maroon Plymouth sedan and began partying nonstop. Larry and I tried to slow him down, but to no avail.

After a poor first quarter, I figured out what I had to do and made the necessary adjustments. My health improved as well as my grades, and I regained a self-confidence that had waned for a while. During spring quarter, I was the number-one backstroke swimmer on the freshman team. No big deal: Jack was number one on the varsity team and placed fifth at the NCAA meet that year. (The year before, Alan and Jack had placed second and fourth, respectively, in the 100-yard backstroke at the NCAA meet in Seattle.)

Chuck Kelly, a freestyler on the freshman team, became my best friend. This friendship lasted throughout four years at Stanford and our time as roommates at Yale Law School, and it continued when we both lived in New York City.

Chuck came from Wayzata, Minnesota, outside Minneapolis. He was the only son of a highly successful insurance executive and a domineering mother. Chuck was handsome, stylish and intelligent to the point of appearing arrogant to others. To me, he represented a worldliness that was stimulating and enjoyable to be around. Chuck had trouble adjusting to our Western informality, which was one of the reasons I liked him.

Over the years, Chuck got to know the whole Weeden family, mainly through our mutual interest in swimming. He admired my father greatly, having lost his own, and wrote a beautiful obituary about him when he died in 1984. In 1985, Chuck helped me with the financing of the new Weeden and became a founding partner. After our mutual conclusion that a trading firm was not his cup of tea, Chuck returned to law and deal-making in the banking industry. Our friendship, which had cooled when he left Weeden, was renewed and active well before he succumbed to Alzheimer's disease.

After Kathy Moore and I went our separate ways, I stayed in touch with Zoe Ann and dated girls living at Roble Hall, the residence for freshmen women.

Marshall Pearlman was goalie on our freshman water polo team. He lived just across the narrow side hall that separated his room from mine. One day, early on, one of the guys in our class took me aside and asked me whether I knew that Marshall was Jewish. I said that I didn't, but so what? I thought it was a strange question. I knew what a Jewish person was, but no big deal. But apparently it was if you came from Southern California.

Not being religious, I figured that what happened way back in biblical times wasn't very important in how we look at people today. In Alameda, whether someone was Italian, German, English or Jewish made little difference. The same held true with Christians, as to which church someone attended or whether they attended any church at all. There must have been synagogues, even mosques, in Alameda, but I was neither aware of them nor cared.

I still remember a conversation I had with my Uncle Norman. The publisher Avon had recently copied a new book format by Pocket Books: It was smaller in size, had a paper cover and sold for 25 cents. I casually observed that "they must be Jewish." Why I said that and who had put the idea in my head, I didn't know. I had no answer when my uncle questioned me about my remark, and I still don't know. It was one of the few times my uncle got angry and raised his voice (ever so slightly). He told me it was a not a Christian thing to say or think about any group in that context and with the disparaging tone in which I said it. He felt so strongly that I have never forgotten his admonishment and have tried to act accordingly

Uncle Norman was the only one in the family who made any effort to attend church and to give religion its rightful place in one's life. His social friends included the Reverend Shires at the Episcopal Church on Grand

Street and a number of the faculty at the Episcopal Theological Seminary in Berkeley.

Every Sunday morning, he would drive a few of us in his black Buick coupe up to the Episcopal Church on Grand Street, where he hoped we would absorb something from the sermon and the music. I'm afraid the effort fell on deaf ears when it came to me, but two of those in the car, Fritz Maurer and Bill Davis, became born-again Christians after they married. Maybe Uncle Norman's taxi service had some effect.

One Sunday, when I was seven or eight, Uncle Norman took me to San Francisco to Grace Cathedral atop Nob Hill. It was a special event at which the bishop of the Episcopal Church was giving the sermon. Uncle Norman knew him and, I guess, felt that my meeting him might help in improving my interest in the church. At the time I was beginning to learn the game of chess. When the bishop got up and walked over to the lectern, I turned to Uncle Norman and said, in a not-so-quiet voice, "I thought bishops could only move diagonally." I say not so quiet, because several rows of people around us turned to look and then began to chuckle in a quiet way. It was quite embarrassing, to say the least.

It is strange how two brothers—my father and uncle—who spent several years growing up on a three-masted sailing ship captained by their father, would have views on religion that were so diametrically opposed. Uncle Norman was a devoted churchgoer and believer in Jesus as the Son of God; he could quote extensively from the Bible. His involvement was not merely intellectual or social, or a matter of faith. It was everything about him, how he thought about himself and how he treated others. There was no ego about him, despite the fact that he was very smart with an extraordinary memory.

An article in the *Honolulu Times* mentioned the three-year-old son of Captain Weeden who could spell the word "hippopotamus." When urged on by his nephews, he would entertain us by reciting from memory whole sections from Gilbert and Sullivan operettas.

The other brother, my father, had nothing to do with religion or the church. He often told the story of the time his father's ship was anchored in the Mexican port of Veracruz and visiting the town, where the level of poverty was unimaginable: mud hovels lining the main street with naked children playing in the dust, which was mixed with horse and donkey manure, while down at the end of the street sat the Catholic cathedral, lavishly painted and covered with gold leaf. He couldn't understand this disparity or why it was tolerated by those who lived in those conditions. Ever since then, he was critical of the Catholic Church, its pageantry and hypocrisy.

Uncle Norman's effort to encourage my attendance at church proved unsuccessful, yet his Christian thoughts and deeds have been a lasting influence on how I have tried to live my own life.

One of the more influential courses I took at Stanford was Comparative Religions, taught by a Professor Spiegelberg. My interest sprang from curiosity rather than spirituality. I was surprised by the variety of forms that religion took, the similarity in values, its central role in civilizations and, unfortunately, its role as a major cause of wars.

The History of Western Civilization was the only course at Stanford required of all freshmen. The year-long course followed a rather thick tome by a Professor Burns and included lots of outside reading. The classes were small, seminar-style. This encouraged lively discussion and demanded participation. I consider it the best part of my Stanford education, but I was far behind those who went to prep schools in the East who already knew the difference between Plato and Aristotle. During my four years at Alameda High School I had received only one semester of history, and that barely covered the United States.

Initially, it was hard for me to appreciate the significance of ancient civilizations in some faraway place that no longer existed. I thought of my father, with only a high school education, and my mother, who went to work after her sophomore year. Both had done pretty well without such fancy learning. My father even commented that while he was willing to send me to Stanford, he thought the four years would be better spent learning the family business. It wasn't long before I realized that it was Western Civ. that justified those "wasted" years.

In my father's case, he did a lot of self-educating through his reading. The demands of the market required him to be up-to-date on what was happening in the world. He was very proud of the fact that he was on the Pacific Coast regional committee of the Foreign Policy Association. This attention to current affairs did not take him far back into history. There was no curiosity about where the Greeks, the Romans, the Egyptians fit into the scheme of things today. He was a practical man, focused on what was important to his business and to our country.

Out of that one course came a lifetime of further reading. I was surprised to hear that in 1963, Stanford was the first of several universities to drop Western Civ as a requirement. The argument for doing so was its domination of male leaders, writers and philosophers with hardly a word from or about women, the peasant or underclasses, representatives of countries defeated in war, or victims of colonization and enslavement. Even the area of arts and culture were represented almost solely by men. The argument has merit, but the problem should not have required radical surgery to correct.

I would venture that half of my later reading had its roots in Western Civ. I read each of the 11 volumes of Will and Ariel Durant's The Story of Civilization as they were published. I also credit that Western Civ. class for my road trip through the Eastern Mediterranean countries with my wife, Vera, who had flown for Swissair into the capitals of those same countries. She was as eager as I to visit the sites of the ancient civilizations.

My other courses were the usual smattering of subjects in a liberal arts curriculum. They exposed me to subjects I was not familiar with, such as music, the arts, psychology, geology, religion, geography and politics. They became the introductory chapter leading to further reading. Those interests may well have developed without Stanford, but the campus environment provided the time and space to recognize their value and continue my reading.

Spring quarter my freshman year was memorable because of fraternity rushing. The majority of freshmen, including most returning veterans, viewed joining a fraternity, with its comradeship and presumed prestige, as unimportant. They came to Stanford for an education. For me, fraternity life seemed the natural thing to do. It had been a positive experience in high school. All three brothers had joined fraternities. Jack and Alan were still on campus and were members of the Zeta Psi fraternity. Just as I followed them in sports and choice of university, I was destined to become a Zete.

I was asked to help form the Zeta Psi Class of '51, along with Dick Abraham and Don Lucas, both of whom were first string on Stanford's undefeated freshman football team. They already thought of themselves as BMOC (Big Men on Campus), and I admit to having been a bit intimidated by them.

The Zete house was already filled with football players, four of which achieved All-American status while I was there: Bill McColl, Sam Morley, Bobby Garrett and Gary Kerkorian. It also included outstanding athletes in tennis, golf, crew and swimming. One-third of Stanford's rugby team were Zetes. While being an athlete was emphasized, they were also smart and hardworking, and each had a career in mind upon graduation. Most went on to graduate school and became successful lawyers, doctors and businessmen. It was a very challenging and competitive atmosphere. Due to my size, I had to rely on my quick reactions and a sharp tongue to avoid physical and psychic harm.

Dick and Don developed into good friends, and we remained in touch throughout our business and marital lives. Dick got his master's degree in electrical engineering and held high-level positions in various semiconductor companies. Eventually, we formed a venture-capital partnership and achieved one notable success, Cymer Laser, due to his efforts.

Lucas graduated from the Stanford Business School. After a year or two on Wall Street, Don joined a Palo Alto–based venture-capital firm in 1960. He did extremely well and became a large donor to Stanford, Santa Clara University and the Catholic Church. It was Don who encouraged me to invest in National Semiconductor Corporation in its initial private financing. His venture activities eventually took him to China during the early stages of that country's economic growth. His advice on proper business and ethical practices was sought by the rising capitalist managers and entrepreneurs there.

I and 10 others became the Zete Class of '51 and moved into the house in the beginning of our sophomore year. I played water polo that fall and ended up as one of the starting guards. I still struggled academically, barely meeting my language requirements with a D-minus in French. Spring quarter, I was still swimming backstroke in the backwash of my brother Jack. Throughout the year I "hashed" tables at a residence for women. This work, along with savings from the summer, reduced my financial dependence on the parents to the tuition payments of $225 per quarter.

The most remembered part of winter quarter was the Zeta Psi initiation. I have described my high school experience, which started with some paddling at 6 a.m. and lasting throughout the day. The Zete initiation was a three-day event confined to the Zete house: one swat with a humongous paddle wielded by Ming Wang (alias the tallest, strongest Zete) and then hours upon hours of sitting with a paddle held tightly between your knees. As a finale, we were led blindfolded down to the basement and branded with the letter Z on our left forearms.

Looking back, the initiation seems a bit ridiculous except for the result of binding our class of '51 closer together.

Campus life consisted of classes, studying for tests, training for water polo, and swimming and partying on the weekends. Our Zete class stuck pretty close together; we did a lot of double-dating, driving to the snow country and the beaches below Santa Cruz. My major was economics, which allowed plenty of room for my liberal arts courses. I dated a number of different women I thought attractive and interesting, but these relationships were neither serious nor lasting.

That summer, I traveled east again to work at Weeden's New York office and lived in the firm's apartment on West Ninth Street. In the apartment next door was a slightly older woman of French background named Eleanor de la Bouliere. She was the spitting image of Audrey Hepburn but was noticeably cross-eyed. This condition did not impede her dancing skills nor my infatuation with her. Many an evening we would have some wine and dance to the tunes from the latest musicals on 72-rpm records.

At the end of my summer in New York, I flew to Minneapolis and stayed with Chuck Kelly at his home on the shore of Lake Minnetonka. I learned to water-ski behind his father's Chris-Craft and helped Chuck drive his brand-new forest-green Pontiac convertible back to Stanford. On the way, I surprised Chuck with an unusual maneuver while passing on a hill in Wyoming. A truck suddenly loomed up in front of us coming the other way. There was no way of getting ahead of the truck I was passing, nor slipping in behind, so I swerved over to the left onto a narrow shoulder overlooking a rather steep descent. The oncoming truck crawled past us and I resumed passing. It happened so fast that neither of us had time to get scared, but I still get a little twinge thinking about it. Chuck never stopped telling about it.

Stanford offered a relaxed and informal lifestyle away from the classroom. Quad attire was T-shirt and Levis, weather permitting most of the time. For me, the memories revolve around football games, water polo matches, afternoons playing two-man volleyball; nights cruising the bars along El Camino Real and having chugalug contests at Rossotti's Beer Garden on Alpine Road.

Another summer passed in New York and another drive back to school, this time without incident in Chuck's Buick convertible. I had been accepted by the university as a sponsor at Encina Hall, and I roomed with Dick Hughes, another Zete and a premed student, who was head sponsor. This saving in room costs further reduced my out-of-pocket expenses. I also found that babysitting for incoming freshmen was less challenging than the constant interaction with a bunch of high-energy, egocentric brothers at the Zete house.

This raises an interesting aspect of life at the Zete house. There was a strong comradeship and interaction that yet allowed each individual to pursue his own agenda. In my senior year, while making up credits not earned while sailing around the world, I roomed with Rod Hills, Class of '52. He was a highly rated quarterback from Southern California who lost out to Gary Kerkorian, another Zete. Rod and I were concentrating on our studies, with our paths seldom crossing except for dinner. He went on to law school and eventually served as chairman of the U.S. Securities and Exchange Commission. I saw more of Rod then than when we roomed together.

Incidentally, Gary Kerkorian left the NFL after four seasons, studied law and ended up a superior court judge in Fresno, California. Bill McColl did much the same, going to medical school at Northwestern while playing end for the Chicago Bears. It was a highly competitive atmosphere.

In addition to my duties as truant officer and babysitter at Encina, I was working hard to earn a free trip to Europe for the coming summer. A travel agency in Palo Alto was putting together a tour of Europe and was offering anyone a free berth if he could round up 10 others who would pay full fare. I busted my ass and failed miserably. It surprised me when my charming personality and hard sell failed to garner a single sale.

I was now one of two breaking guards starting on Stanford's varsity water polo team. "Breaking" guards meant that we positioned ourselves in front of the opposing team's forwards, rather than behind and between them and the goal. It presumed that we could intercept any toss of the ball to the forwards and then outsprint them down the pool to the opposite goal.

Bob Frojen, the other breaking guard, was an excellent breaststroker with a powerful kick that could raise him well out of the water to intercept almost any pass. I was good enough to make the two of us quite effective. Stanford did well in the conference standings. Bob joined the U.S. Olympic Team in 1952.

Don on Stanford University varsity water polo team (front row, far right).

As Luck Would Have It

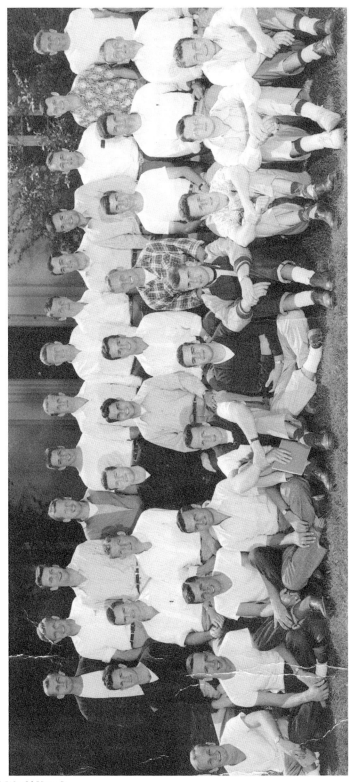

Zeta Psi fraternity in Don's sophomore year with Jack (back row, far left); Don (Front, far left).

Bill, Don, Frank, Jack, Alan at Stanford, 1947.

Don with Tom Wood, friend and classmate, who was
killed in action in Korea soon after graduation in 1951.

As Luck Would Have It

Chapter 7

Life on a Norwegian Freighter

A combination of factors combined with a winter of continuous cold fronts sweeping over the campus to put me into a deep funk lasting into quarter-end exams. I had sold no trips to Europe, had no interest in swimming in the wake of my brother, and my semi-serious dating partner had lost interest in me.

It was in this depressed state of mind that a crazy last-minute, unplanned idea occurred. As Dick Hughes and I were driving up to San Francisco for drinks and dinner, we spoke casually about skipping spring quarter when the thought occurred to pass by the Scandinavian Shipping Office, which was on the way. They must have a freighter going out in a week or so, maybe even to Europe, and could use a couple of eager kids to help out. Dick was all for it for, untold to me, reasons of his own.

To our pleasant surprise, they had two openings available that fit our lack of experience: deck boys on a ship bound for Bombay, India. "Come back Monday morning at 6:30 and if there are no union members looking to sign on, you can have the job. Bring your passport and be ready to board the same afternoon."

It was 4:00 Friday afternoon and our telephone call to the passport office told us that there was no possibility for Dick to get one in time. I already had a passport in anticipation of my free trip to Europe. Our grand idea lost some of its appeal, as I would be shipping out solo. Dick and I had drinks and dinner and I took him to the airport. The idea was still hanging in the air when I got home to Alameda.

Saturday was a lazy day, with a wedding reception that evening in San Francisco. Dick Abraham was there along with Terry Watters, another football player in our class. I told them about shipping out, and they thought it a great idea. Dick said he'd take care of whatever paperwork was needed. The party was a big splash at the Palace Hotel, with lots of champagne.

When I finally came down to breakfast the next morning, Frank was still there, hidden behind the San Francisco Chronicle's "green sheets," containing the sports and business news. I brought up the idea of my taking off spring quarter and maybe shipping out on a freighter going to Bombay. I told him I didn't think the university would mind, inasmuch as my grades were OK. He had no real objections and thought it would be good experience; he was probably thinking about his own time on his father's ship when he was growing up. That was about it. When I chatted with Mom, I put it in terms of it only being a possibility, as union members would have priority.

Monday morning at 7:00 a.m., I signed on as deck boy on the S/S Janna, bound for Bombay that afternoon, with the only restriction that I could only sign off in a European or North American port. I called home with the news and then called Dick to alert Stanford. I got my first cholera shot and transferred my entire bank account, totaling $220, into American Express traveler's checks.

Mom and Dad drove me over to the Port of Oakland where the Janna was berthed. The Janna was an early World War II Liberty ship, probably built in the Kaiser shipyards at Richmond, just a few miles north. It was owned by the Pehrson & Wessel Shipping Company and registered in Drammen, Norway. They had told me at the Union Hall the Janna was considered a tramp freighter; that is, one that has no regularly scheduled route, and is subject to the availability of cargos as to where it will go after Bombay. It was the intention of the owners to have it return to Europe as soon as it could be arranged. That fit perfectly. I was already daydreaming about hiking through the Swiss Alps.

I insisted that the parents let me out of the car before we got to the ship. Mom was anxious to see my accommodations, but Frank understood. It was a good thing they didn't come aboard, because the fellow who greeted me at the top of the gangplank had a gash running from his forehead upward past his hairline to the top of his skull that must have contained two dozen stitches. He was a surly fellow, with whom I would be sharing a small cabin with two bunk beds. I understood later that the gash was caused when the bosun's mate threw him against a bulkhead for having done something he didn't like.

We were soon on our way, and I watched the sun set as we passed under the Golden Gate Bridge. The next morning I met the day crew, with whom I would be working. As we sat drinking coffee, I noticed some things moving in the bowl of dry cereal. They had a name for them in Norwegian, but I call them maggots. All my future breakfasts were of food cooked and dead.

Our first duty after my hearty breakfast was to take the tarps out of the fo'c's'le (forecastle) in preparation for battening down the hatches. Our next task was chipping the rust off the hatch combs and repainting them before securing the tarps. We were now well into the Pacific Ocean, where long swells gently moved us and down as they rolled beneath the ship. The cramped quarters, heavy exertion, gentle motion and too much coffee accelerated any seasickness that I probably would have gotten under normal conditions. Everyone seemed to expect it and left me alone while I fought off the urge to vomit over the next few days.

After a week, two events dramatically changed my situation. I was taken off the day crew and assigned as one of two crewmen who stood watch on the bridge from 4 to 8, morning and evening. This entailed two hourly rotations of standing watch on the port side of the bridge and handling the steering wheel. The first mate also stood the same watch on the starboard side.

The other change came when the union representative moved my roommate to another cabin. I had intended to put up with his messy personal hygiene, including masturbating every night in the upper bunk, but others reported the filthy conditions and told the union representative.

The crew was mostly Norwegian and included all those in the engine room, the bosun's mate, carpenter and a majority of the deck hands. The remaining deck hands included a Dane, a Swede and me. The kitchen crew was composed of a Canadian, an Australian and a Brazilian. All the officers were Norwegian.

I kept pretty much to myself. The only person with whom I had any real rapport was the Swede, Leif Svedner. He was two years older and had some education beyond high school. He did not intend to be a sailor all his life, as did the others, and was going back to school when the ship returned to Europe. The other deck hands had been aboard the Janna for better than two years and were a close-knit group; they were friendly and helpful, but not eager to interact. I saw almost nothing of the engine crew, who spent most of their time in the bowels of the ship or on their bunks. The kitchen crew all spoke English, but they were a motley bunch and were treated as outcasts by the rest of us. My other friendship, if it could be called that, was with the first mate, with whom I shared the 4-to-8 watches. He was a gruff old veteran of the seas with many stories to tell, and I was an attentive listener.

An early lesson learned was not to do anything that wasn't in the job description. Standing watch was rather boring. Looking for something to do, I decided to polish the bronze bell attached to the wall behind the bridge. It required a ladder to reach it. No sooner had I obtained one and began to climb it when the union representative came rushing onto the bridge, yelling something in Norwegian. I couldn't understand him but I knew what he meant.

Life on board was routine, subdued and uninspiring. The job consisted of two hours during each watch standing alone on the port side of the bridge looking for other ships and two hours at the wheel maintaining an assigned heading. The rest of the day was made up of meals, reading and exercise. At a maximum speed of 11 knots, it was 20 days before we saw land or even another ship. We skirted just north of the island of Luzon in the Philippine Archipelago and headed southwest toward Singapore.

So far there had been little to interfere with the endless sea and a cloudless sky. With the warmer air and higher humidity, we began to see isolated rain squalls developing out of nowhere, replete with thunder and lightning. Standing the 4-to-8 watches, I enjoyed in solitude the rising and the setting of the sun. On some days the cloud formations combined to create a dazzling show of color: yellow, orange and red spread across the horizon.

By this time, I had long given up trying to speak or understand Norwegian language and was on my second reading of Creasy's The Fifteen Decisive Battles of the World.

Upon arriving at Singapore, there was a small island in the bay used solely to refuel freighters passing through. It was the closest we got to the exotic pleasures of Singapore. At this point we were only two degrees north of the Equator. It was very hot and very muggy. There was a small shack in which one could buy snacks and drinks. The only beer available was a local brand called Tiger Beer, aptly named, which we drank anyway.

The trip through the Indian Ocean was uneventful except for my confrontation with the bosun's mate. As it turned out it, was not a big deal but it was important to me at the time. I have mentioned the fact of the bosun's mate slamming my early roommate against a bulkhead. It was something I hadn't forgotten, even though I had found him to be a mild-mannered, quiet man, well respected by the crew.

His cabin was situated under the poop deck in the aft part of the ship. The deck was available for anyone wanting to sleep in the open air. Any wind we had enjoyed until now totally disappeared as we slowly churned through the Indian Ocean. The beginning of the monsoon season was imminent, and several of us sought to escape our stultifying cabins by weaving hammocks out of rope and hanging them above the poop deck.

This normally caused no problem with the bosun's mate, until I was awakened at 3:50 a.m. by the man on the prior watch. "The Hyena," as I had come to think of him, made no effort to be quiet when waking me. The bosun's mate arrived topside and tried to take my swing down. I took the position that I wasn't the problem and resisted. The bosun's mate had a V-shaped body and stood well over six feet. Any physical confrontation would have been rather one-sided.

After some verbal back-and-forth while both of were pulling at the net, the bosun's mate retired after grumbling his displeasure. After that, the Hyena treaded very softly when he came to wake me. The bosun's mate and I had nothing to say to each other until we were together drinking rum and Coca-Colas in Port of Spain, Trinidad.

As we swung around the island of Ceylon (now called Sri Lanka) and the southern tip of India, the sea became eerily calm. Schools of flying fish would suddenly appear, skimming over the water and disappearing into the wake of our prow as we made the final few hundred miles north to Bombay.

As soon as we dropped anchor, there appeared half a dozen fat-looking, flat-bottomed dhows swarming with local natives. They were dressed in a curious arrangement of white linens and ready to unload our bales of long-staple cotton. All five hatches were opened and the ship's cranes began hoisting the cargo up, out and down into the waiting dhows.

They worked through the night and into the morning, guided by many floodlights. These cast shadows every which way, magnifying the motion of the cranes, cargo and outstretched hands guiding each bale into the dhows alongside. They worked mainly at night and rested during the heat of the day.

Overseeing this confusion was a Parsi by birth and religion. His English was impeccable and his joy unbounded in talking with a young man from the great United States. I had taken a course in Comparative Religions at Stanford, some of which was still fresh in my mind. I knew about Ahura Mazda, the God of Fire, and the forced migration of its believers out of Persia around the 10th century. Most arrived by ship settling in the area around Bombay. He was happy to have someone listen while he described his people and their ways and the miseries of being a small minority in such a large country. He talked quickly and passionately while not missing a thing going on below him. He was a slight man of middle age, bald with intellectual fire in his eyes. For two nights we talked, and then the unloading was over and my new-found friend disappeared.

It was uncertain how long we would stay in Bombay. The ship's agent had not found a suitable cargo, meaning one that would take us to Europe. While we waited, the ship remained anchored offshore.

India had gained its independence from Great Britain three years earlier. This was followed almost immediately by a very bloody war in which Pakistan emerged as another new nation where Moslems were in the majority.

Both countries were still in a state of high emotion, and the Indian government had outlawed the sale of alcohol. The Seaman's Mission was an exception and became the focal point for sailors of all nationalities to meet, drink and exchange news from abroad. In this social atmosphere, I came to know some of my co-workers better and they included me in their soirées into Bombay's nightlife.

One trip was to a Danish ship, docked along the quay. We heard they were selling ice-cold Carlsberg beer. It was the carpenter who was doing the selling. He stuffed eight of us into a small room and shut the door so we wouldn't be discovered. We all stripped to the waist and guzzled the beers, one after another. The temperature must have been 110 degrees. It was so humid that the beer seemed to ooze out of our arms and shoulders, never reaching our stomach. This mad debauchery ended when the second mate discovered us and sent us packing.

A visit to a brothel was rather genteel in comparison. Everyone spoke softly and spent some time observing and talking with the parade of women who presented themselves (some young and rather attractive). The drawing room was decorated in purple, pink and lavender, as were the ladies. Some of my shipmates struck a deal with the matron sitting at a table and were escorted through a door leading to the bedrooms. I was tempted but scared of contracting some terrible disease. Besides, on a deck boy's wages, I could not afford the experience.

Most of my time on shore was spent wandering alone along the main thoroughfares and into neighborhoods crowded with humanity. With a map and most natives speaking English, I was able to enjoy the little time I was able to spend ashore. Most memorable was a huge park overlooking the bay, which had a swimming pool, a bandstand and lovely gardens. I watched a dance between a cobra and mongoose flare up along a path on which I was walking. When a crowd collected to watch, it ended in a draw, with the two protagonists disappearing. Earlier, I had gone to the Queen Victoria Hospital to receive my second cholera shot and then pay a visit to the American consulate. There I met a young woman vice-consul who must have felt sorry for me, as she invited me to dinner later in the week.

In the meantime, a rumor developed that we would not be sailing on to Europe. This had a demoralizing effect on most of the crew, including me. I decided to leave the ship, even though my contract prohibited it. I decided to claim a pain where my appendix was located. I went to the first mate, who reluctantly agreed that I visit a doctor suggested by the ship's agent. I arranged to go on the day of my dinner invitation. If the doctor would not cooperate, I had my friend, Leif Svedner, carry my suitcase ashore with my few belongings and leave it at the Seaman's Mission.

Once ashore, I bought a pack of local cigarettes and smoked half of them on the way to the doctor. When I arrived, I was visibly sick: dizzy and on the verge of vomiting. After his examination, he was not convinced. He sent me off to the Queen Victoria Hospital for a second opinion. As luck would have it, I was shown to the same doctor who had administered my cholera shot. He did not believe my story either and refused to give me the necessary approval to remain in Bombay.

I hung around the Seaman's Mission, recovering from the cigarettes. Dinner was at nine. The other guests were two American correspondents for the Associated Press and the Herald Tribune. They had been stationed in Bombay since before the war. I had plenty of questions, and they were quite talkative. When I told them about my plans, they told me in no uncertain terms that it was a really stupid idea to try to travel to Europe by land. They pointed out with graphic examples the various dangers I would encounter along the way.

Reluctantly accepting their advice, I now had to get back on board the ship without being discovered. It was late when I headed to the docks. It seemed like the whole city was stretched out on mats placed in the middle of the sidewalks. They had finished cooking their scanty meals on small charcoal stoves and were already asleep. At the pier where the water taxies were located, I found a crew with a small dhow willing to make the trip for what was less than a dollar's worth of annas.

The air was sultry, with a thin fog resting close to the water. It was difficult to tell one ship from another. There was no wind, and the two men had to use their paddles. It was not what they anticipated. After I made two bad guesses on which of the lighted ships was the Janna, the men became agitated. I sensed the possibility that I could be sacrificed to the water gods, so I persuaded them with a few more annas to make one more try.

When they finally pulled up to the Janna, it was past midnight. I crept up the gangplank and, fortunately, no one was there to greet me. Luckily, I unpacked my suitcase before dropping off to sleep. At seven o'clock the first mate knocked, entered and, without a word, opened the closet where my clothes were kept. I learned later that the union man had told him about seeing my suitcase at the Seaman's Mission.

Finally, the word came down that we would be sailing to Lourenço Marques, the main port of Portuguese East Africa (now Maputo, Mozambique). There we would take on a cargo of manganese ore bound for Baltimore. During my final shore leave, I spent all my traveler's checks on a Persian rug, an ivory chess set and a tea set made of brass.

Arriving at Lourenço Marques, we docked alongside a pier with tall cranes that could lift and dump the heavy manganese ore into our holds. They started loading immediately. Time was provided, and some of us spent a day crossing over to South Africa to visit a national animal preserve. I also visited a swimming club where I might meet some of the locals. The language difference was a barrier, and I never went back. I frequented the bars close to the docks and mingled with the men off the American ships that were also taking on manganese ore.

On my 20th birthday, June 7, I went to the restaurant/bar most frequented by our crew and set up a table in the corner, inviting any and all to join me. After two or three hours of comradeship, I paid the bill, got up and left. I threw up all the way back to the ship and then some, but considered it a successful birthday celebration.

Loading of the manganese ore was completed in a week, and we were again on the high seas. We rounded Cape of Good Hope in perfect weather and headed for Trinidad, where we would bunker additional fuel oil for the final leg up to Baltimore.

The ship was moving along at 6 knots, with one engine down, when we heard the news that the North Koreans had invaded South Korea. The crew was naturally concerned how this would affect the Cold War between the Soviet Union and the United States. They worried that it would involve Europe. They were all tired of war, most having suffered under German occupation. South Korea was a long way off, and most of them were indifferent to the outcome.

I had no knowledge about what triggered the invasion and no strong commitment to the interests of the South Korean people. In one sense, the fact that the country had been divided after World War II seemed artificial and set the stage for this to happen. I accepted the logic of the domino theory and the need to stand one's ground against the spread of Communism.

The decision of the United Nations, led by the United States, to get involved turned my thoughts to my eventual involvement. I had never thought of myself as a doughboy, slogging through the mud with a rifle on my shoulder. On the other hand, I had three older brothers, a father and an uncle all having served in the preceding two wars, and I intended to do the same.

My immediate decision was to abandon the idea of Europe. By summer's end, I would return to Stanford, sign up for the ROTC program and apply to become a pilot. Flying was something I thought I could do well. My eyesight was better than most (20/10), I had quick reactions and good hand-to-eye coordination, and I was very competitive. I was also a romantic who viewed fighter vs. fighter combat as it was portrayed during World War I.

The mood of the whole ship had become "get to Baltimore and sign off." Soon we were back on two engines and a max speed of 11 knots. Our stop at Port of Spain, Trinidad, turned out to be a circus. We bunkered in the bay and had no shore leave. The crew was restless and semi-mutinous, if disregarding the Captain's insistence of no liquor on board came under that definition. We were the only ship at anchor and immediately attracted every size and shape of dinghies, rowboats, canoes—you name it. They surrounded the ship, offering all sorts of native handicrafts, fruit, monkeys, parakeets and rum.

The captain was cloistered in his cabin; the mates, who should have been policing matters, were discreetly out of sight. I was having a good time taking in the scene when one of the day crew told me there was a little party going on in cabin 10. When I got there, it was in full force, fueled by large quantities of rum and Coca-Cola. By evening we had finished refueling and the native boats had departed. Engines were restarted, the anchor run in.

The Janna gathered speed on a heading 015 bound for Baltimore. How it was accomplished safely, I have no idea. Everyone was still partying in cabin 10. I was sitting on a couch next to the bosun's mate when he put his arm around me and told me, "You are OK!"

The next thing I remember was being wakened by the Hyena. It was just past 4 a.m. (eight bells) and he was in a scruffy mood. I had failed to relieve him on the previous watch. Someone had found me passed out in the outer passageway and got me onto my bunk.

We had sailed into a large storm system and heavy seas since leaving Port of Spain. It was forecast to last another 24 hours. They dressed me with suitable outdoor gear and guided me up to the wheelhouse. I remained on the bridge, embracing the full force of the storm and trying to clear my head. When my time came to handle the wheel, the high winds, the ocean swells and my condition made keeping on course a challenge. I did my best. We didn't hit anything, and no one complained.

Once the storm abated, our passage through the Caribbean was hot and uneventful. Upon arrival in the port of Baltimore, two-thirds of the crew and half of the mates signed off. There were a few "Goodbyes" and "Good lucks." Leif Svedner and I exchanged addresses and promised to keep in touch. I took the train up to New York, where I found Alan and Jack working in the New York office of Weeden.

Chapter 8
Back on Dry Land

W hen I had arrived back in New York, Alan told me that the New York Athletic Club water polo team would be going to the nationals in St. Louis the end of August. I was in good shape, but needed to catch up on my swimming. Warren Musser invited me out to his stepfather's blueberry and mink ranch in East Setauket, Long Island, where I paddled around Port Jefferson Bay all day long pushing a water polo ball.

In St. Louis, our coach, Paul Wacker, played me for a few minutes on their senior team. I started as a guard for the junior team, and we won the division. There was a player on the team from the south side of Chicago who kept beating me up above and below water whenever the referee wasn't looking. I finally got him pinned on the edge of the pool and grabbed his balls as tight as I could until he said he'd lay off with the elbows.

Stacy Sullivan and I got dates after the meet and went partying outside St. Louis. At the end of the evening, we were in a bar about to close. We went slow in finishing our beers. The waitress complained to some of the boys at the bar. They turned out to include off-duty cops also enjoying their beers. I claimed discrimination, tore a badge off a shirt and ended up at the local police station. When they got in touch with my brother Alan, asleep at the Missouri Athletic Club, his reply to their question of what they should do with me was, "If he's OK, just keep him there 'til morning."

Stanford reconvened for their fall quarter and I took added courses to graduate with my class. I was elected co-captain of our water polo team and Bob Frojen and I were elected All-Coast, even though we lost the league championship to Southern California.

In October, I had applied to the Air Force to enter their pilot training program. The next month, I drove up to Hamilton Air Force Base, just north of San Francisco, along with Dick Abraham, for an interview and a physical. I passed muster, signed up for three years and was told to wait for further orders. They turned Dick down because of a previous knee operation. The war in Korea was in full swing and our troops were encountering severe reverses. It appeared we would be fighting there for a long time.

I was boarding again at the Zete house and rooming with Rod Hills. My course load was heavy and I decided not to hash. I trained for swimming during spring quarter. Without any brothers to compete against, I was number one in backstroke, but nowhere near their accomplishments. Where I did excel was a real surprise.

As Luck Would Have It

The Zete house wanted to enter someone in every event in the annual intramural track and field competition, but they ran out of likely candidates when it came to the two-mile run. The meet took place the week after the end of swimming, and I volunteered. What the hell!

I spurted out of the starting blocks and just kept running. After a few laps I was right behind Otis Chandler, an Olympic shot-putter running for the Dekes (DKE: Delta Kappa Epsilon). I tried my damnedest to catch him. As soon as I crossed the finish line, in second place, my swimmer's muscles tightened badly. They had to carry me back to the house.

I had moved with my newly acquired dog, Caesar, to join Duvall (Dewey) Hecht, another Zete, who lived off campus with his dog, Melonie. Dewey was on the Stanford varsity eight-man crew training for the two-man with coxswain. Dewey and I got along very well, but his dog was an irritating dachshund with a small-dog complex, very possessive and jealous of my lovable, good-natured Australian shepherd. One afternoon they disappeared for several hours and only Melonie returned. I believe to this day that Melonie deliberately lost him.

As graduation day loomed, I realized that my draft status would change from Class 1-D to Class 1-A when I received my diploma. Chuck Kelly had been accepted to Yale Law School and encouraged me to apply. I never had any interest in the law, but I decided to give it a try. My results on the LSAT (Law School Aptitude Test) put me in the 93rd percentile. This, combined with Yale's desire to admit more students from the "Wild West," meant I was accepted.

I chose not to stay around for the graduation ceremonies. Instead, I drove Dewey's Ford sedan across country to New York City (in four days) while he finished up his season with the crew. When Dewey arrived by air, we both did a stint at an Auto Wash on Queens Boulevard. Chuck Kelly's uncle managed to get me a job as lifeguard at his club, the Piping Rock Club in Locust Valley, Long Island. It turned out to be very cushy, with lots of very nice, well-to-do members to watch over.

Dick Abraham, with degree in engineering, had gotten a job at Sperry Rand nearby. During our evenings, spent mainly at a clam joint in Bayville Center, we dreamed up an idea for using recently graduated students in useful projects overseas.

We wrote the Whitney Foundation to see whether they would sponsor a group of recently graduated men and women with varying interests—engineering, business, education, agriculture—who would travel as a team to a prearranged village, say in India (or anywhere). They would remain for a year or more and provide training and information on how the villagers could improve their economy, sanitation, infrastructure, etc. We felt that there were many graduating students who were not in a rush to start their careers and wanted to contribute something to those less fortunate.

A lot of details had to be flushed out, but, if the program were successful, it could be a way for many of us to do some useful public service, see some of the world and serve as goodwill ambassadors from the United States. (It was similar to what became President Kennedy's Peace Corps 10 years later.) We never got a reply.

At Yale Law School, Chuck Kelly and I shared a two-bedroom suite on the first floor of Yale's Sterling law school. We could eat, sleep, study and attend class without leaving the Law Quadrangle. And during many damp and dreary days, that is exactly what we did. The weather was not the only difference between Stanford and Yale. There was a focused intensity among the students that eliminated the many wasted hours we enjoyed at Stanford. I don't mean to say that they didn't party or weren't social, but the high level of competition for grades and recognition kept them at the books as much as did the weather. If it hadn't been for Chuck and a couple of Yale swimmers who had moved on to the law school, I would be looking back on a rather lonely period.

Our class of '54 came largely from the East, with a large contingent from New York City and surrounding suburbs. The talent and focus those students exhibited, while not giving me an inferiority complex, made me realize I was not in the same league. Anyway, I was there as a draft dodger, so to speak, who didn't expect to remain too long.

As it turned out, my temporary status, the absence of pressure to excel, and the comfort in knowing a family firm was beckoning caused me to make the most of those five months at Yale Law. I loved going to class, reading the cases, organizing my own arguments and rendering my own opinions. It was an exhilarating experience. I can recall all my professors: James, Shulman, MacDougal, Mueller and Emerson. Except for one or two professors at Stanford, I have no lasting memory good or bad.

Outside of class, I met almost no one. An exception was Bob Beshar, who lived upstairs. He asked me to be a witness in a mock jury trial in which he was counsel for the defense. We became good friends and I kept in touch with him, and his family, until his death in 2015.

During Christmas break, I received notification to report to Rome Air Force Base in upstate New York for further processing. I was staying in New York City with my brother Alan and his wife, Barbara. They were nice enough to put me up for two weeks, and I reciprocated by helping to paint their living room. At Rome AFB, I went through another physical examination, some more written tests and a final interview. I sensed they were determining whether I would be best as a navigator, radar observer or pilot. I made it absolutely clear I only wanted to be a pilot. Period!

Late in January, I received orders to report to Whitehall Street in Lower Manhattan for formal induction into the United States Air Force. My orders were to proceed immediately to Spence Field, Moultrie, Georgia. for pilot training.

Meanwhile, I had met Evelyn Grey at a party on the Upper East Side. We started a whirlwind romance that culminated in our becoming engaged in June of 1953.

Chapter 9

With the United States Air Force

There are similarities between my time in the U.S. Air Force and at Stanford University; more specifically, the time at the Zete house and my three years with the 496th Fighter-Interceptor Squadron (FIS). Both were challenging, lively and male-dominated.

An important difference: the pilots in the 496th shared a serious mission that carried a heightened level of risk. This bound us tightly as a team and subordinated our individual interests to those of the group. The admiration and friendships forged flying together have found reinforcement through a number of reunions where many of the stories that follow are told again and again.

Learning How to Fly

The four years began on the first day of February, 1952. I had traveled by train from New York City to Atlanta, and then by Greyhound to Moultrie, Georgia, where a local bus took me to Spence Field. The previous day I had been sworn into the United States Air Force Reserve at 1 Whitehall Street in downtown Manhattan, not far from the Weeden & Co. office at 14 Wall Street. It had been over a year from the time I signed up for the Air Force's Pilot Training Program. I was eager to begin flying.

The first person I met at Spence Field was Tom Wilson. He already wore an Air Force uniform and appeared to know his way around. I stuck close to him while we were processed onto the base. By coincidence, our base assignments turned out to be the same over the next four years and we ended up being discharged together in May 1956 at Landstuhl Air Base in West Germany.

For the next six weeks, we newly inducted cadets were introduced to military life: lots of physical exercise, emphasis on personal hygiene, and a reshaping of our civilian ways into a respect for authority. This last requirement was exacted through constant and sometimes humiliating "chicken shit" from our upperclassmen. I guess it served a purpose, as some of the class barely knew how to use a knife and fork properly. I had a problem myself at the mess table when I was forced to reply to an upperclassman after only three bites and a swallow.

The typical cadet was quite different from my classmates at Yale and Stanford. Most had only finished high school, were mainly from the South, and came from a rural environment. They were physically able but not athletic; intelligent but not intellectual. Some spoke with accents that I had difficulty understanding. The one thing we all had in common was the desire to fly.

Quite a few had already soloed in small planes. One fellow named Uhalt from Jackson, Mississippi, had over 500 hours under his belt—in his log book, I should say. In our section, he was the first to solo, disappointing my instructor, Mr. Smith, who singled me out to be first. In personality and looks, Mr. Smith reminded one of Pete Rose, who played baseball with the Cincinnati Reds. He played quarterback for Florida State in the 1930s and began his flying career with the Canadian Air Force at the start of World War II.

Mr. Smith was very competitive. He put me up for solo after barely 10 hours of instruction, but I didn't pass the pre-solo check ride. I ended up soloing second.

I had never been in a small plane before Mr. Smith gave me my orientation flight. I was placed in the back seat of an AT-6 and told to buckle up and not to touch the stick. It was a single-engine, low-wing trainer with tandem cockpits where the instructor normally sat behind the student.

The AT-6 was the last trainer with a tail wheel. The newer planes had a nose wheel instead. This difference greatly reduced the difficulties encountered when landing, especially when the winds were gusty or blowing at an angle to the runway.

Mr. Smith thought I had a natural gift for flying. On my next flight, instead of demonstrating how to anticipate a stall or how to recover from one, he showed me all the acrobatic tricks he had learned: loops, Immelmanns, snap rolls and nameless configurations of his own. I avoided getting sick during the flight, but after landing, I remained outside our flight shack for a long period of deep breathing to settle my stomach.

Learning the essentials of flying came quickly. Instruments were also easy and ground school a no-brainer (except for learning the Morse code). As a result, I had plenty of free hours at the end of basic training. George Stegman was another cadet who soloed early. We would take off together and, when no longer visible from the base, we would join up and fly formation (a no-no). On occasion, we would head down to the Gulf of Mexico, looking for fishing boats to buzz (also a no-no) before returning to Spence.

One day, I flew at treetop level over the Okefenokee Swamp in southeastern Georgia, reported to be filled with alligators and cottonmouth snakes, keeping my fingers crossed that the engine wouldn't quit.

When flying alone, I loved cavorting in and around the small cumulus clouds that formed as the air heated up.

A few of the cadets flunked ground school, and others found that they just didn't have the right stuff for flying. Then there was Charlie Wallace, who washed out for being too short. The engine on the AT-6 generated so much torque, one had to use a lot of left rudder when applying full throttle during a touch-and-go landing. If you didn't, the AT-6 would tend to cartwheel off to the right. Charlie, at 5 feet, 6 inches, would touch down and then disappear completely as he applied the full weight of his body onto the left rudder. It was hilarious to watch, but also disturbing to the instructor responsible for his safety.

Most of the guys in my class were there because they had a long-standing passion for flying. The war in Korea was a factor, but mainly they just wanted to fly. I soon came to share that passion, but it was not what initially brought me to Moultrie. The United States was at war again, and I felt a duty to serve.

(As an aside: My draft number was finally drawn in 1959, three years after my discharge and during the time I was flying with the New York Air National Guard. I wrote to my draft board, still located in Oakland, California, that I had already served more than four years, was married and had a child and was now flying with the New York Air National Guard—"but, If you really need me ....")

Flying suited my talents as well as my temperament. Being a romantic, I could visualize images from World War I: flying over France in little bi-planes, man-to-man combat, something akin to jousting in the days of King Arthur. It seemed an okay way of killing, if it came to that. When I signed up in November 1950, I assumed I would end up flying F-86s in Korea. As it turned out, no one in the Class of 53-Baker went on to Korea, but in January of 1952 that was where I determined to be headed.

Spence Field was located about a mile out of Moultrie, a pleasant hike if it wasn't in the middle of the day. About Moultrie itself, all I remember is the pool hall, the VFW headquarters, the American Legion Hall and the drugstore that sold milkshakes called Frostees. I met a girl there one weekend; she would sometimes come to the perimeter fence of the base and we would talk about nothing in particular. It was an environment that kept one focused on his flying.

On the occasional weekend off, a group of us would rent a car and drive to an exotic place like Albany, Georgia. One long weekend we went to Daytona Beach, Florida. It was memorable in that none of us were apprehended or put in jail. We had no money for formal accommodations, so we made the beach our temporary home. The sand was warm and our brains sufficiently distilled by the time we got around to a little shut-eye. I have

As Luck Would Have It

a photo somewhere of our group taken early in the morning, lying on the beach, covered with a thin film of sand that is especially noticeable on the face, around the ears and in the hair.

The Daytona Beach Hotel was the center of activity. Our appearance was not welcomed by the management, so we started playing hide-and-seek with the security guards. This was after the girls at the bar discovered we were all schmooze and no money. By scrambling across the hotel's red-tiled roof, we were able to elude them—the guards, that is. We ended up at a nearby bar, where we listened to great jazz until it closed. On Sunday, we had barely enough money for a breakfast of Brandy Alexanders and gas for the return drive.

The rest of our time at Spence seemed to "fly" by without incident, and graduation was upon us. There was a day full of formal ceremony followed by a boisterous evening at the cadet club, where the end of six months of "chicken shit" was loudly toasted,although we did realize that instilling military discipline was necessary for transforming us into good soldiers, and maybe even making us better pilots. Some even saw humor in the process.

I was privileged to witness what I will call the "Bressi" incident.
The next morning began with the base loudspeaker calling the cadets to assemble for their daily march to the breakfast hall. Slowly, single cadets and then larger groups emerged from their barracks and casually began sauntering down the Squadron Street toward the mess hall, all formalities now behind them.

To Captain Hoffman, the base military training officer, this "informality" was not acceptable. He ordered Cadet Captain Roger Bressi, the only cadet close at hand, to assemble anyone still in their barracks. Bressi saluted the captain, and, after Captain Hoffman returned the salute, executed an about-face. Using the public-address system, he called for the company to form. No one appeared. Bressi turned back to Captain Hoffman, saluted and made his report.

Captain Hoffman returned Bressi's salute, acknowledged the report and ordered Bressi to try again. Bressi again called the company to form. Nothing happened. Bressi again reported. Salutes were again exchanged. Time hung in the air. It was as though the whole world had momentarily ceased rotating.

And then, slowly, there appeared at the door of Barracks B a figure, sleep clouding its puzzled face, shirttail out, c--t cap in hand. It was cadet Bob Wistrand. Immediately, Bressi bellowed out, "Company-y-y, fall in."

Let's stop for a moment and savor the dynamics of this classic confrontation: the individual vs. the state. Captain Hoffman was convinced that he was acting in the best interests of the military and the United States of

America by insisting that individuals subordinate their desire for freedom and independent action to a higher responsibility to the State.

Cadet Captain Bressi, on the other hand, had been accepted into the air cadet program not just because he was smart, healthy and willing, but because he was cocky, fearless and capable of making the most of a situation.

With a wink to Wistrand, Bressi bellowed out "Company-y-y, Attention!" followed by a sharp about-face. He added, "The company is formed," along with the prescribed salute, held until returned by Captain Hoffman.

Captain Hoffman now began to suspect that he was being drawn into a situation that was not in his best interest—that he was in danger of losing the respect he had nurtured over the past six months of being the base's chief "hard ass"—and so he tried to end the farce by saying, "Carry on."

This command of course required an immediate "Yes, Sir!" and with it the usual salute, held until acknowledged. Bressi, with the instincts of a pit bull, grabbed onto to this important military formality and ran with it. Executing another smart about-face, Bressi ordered the company to report.

Wistrand was mumbling something to the effect of "What is this bullshit, Bressi?" Bressi again about-faced and reported that the "company is present or accounted for." This was followed by the customary salute. Captain Hoffman now looked at Bressi for a long time before acknowledging, and then, with the wisdom of someone who knows he's been bested and who now thought that Bressi might just make it as a fighter pilot, released the company to march down to the mess hall. The last thing he heard from the safety of his office was "Hut two, three, four; Hut two, three, four," fading off into the distance.

Tom Wilson and I had orders to report to Webb Air Force Base in Big Spring, Texas. The three-day drive was uneventful except for an overnight stay in Dallas, where the ladies at the hotel bar felt we needed companionship. Normally we might have been amenable, but somehow the age difference and the hardness around their eyes put us off. Temptation followed me to my room, but price and indifference scotched the transaction. My halfhearted mention that I was on my way to Korea cut no mustard.

A final half-day of driving due west, and Big Spring loomed up ahead as a lonely seven-story building in the middle of the desert. Several miles farther west, oil derricks could be seen burning off useless gas. As it had been at Spence, the interaction between the cadets and the townsfolk was minimal. The presence of the air base had considerable economic value to the community, while the pent-up energies of a gang of off-duty cadets wandering around town on the weekend with nothing to do had little value to the locals.

At Webb, we flew every day the weather permitted. Ground school focused mainly on insuring that we got the airplanes up and down safely. For three months we flew the T-28 Trojan jet trainer, which had greater power and was more stable than the AT-6. It also had a nose wheel instead of a tail wheel, which made landing far easier and safer.

Most of our flying time was solo; sometimes we flew with another student while we practiced instrument flying under a hood. On one occasion, I was in the front cockpit and another cadet was under the hood in the rear seat. I put him into the "unusual position" of a steep diving turn. Instead of leveling the wings first and pulling back on the stick second, he did just the opposite, exaggerating the speed of the descent and creating significant G-force. I had relaxed in the front seat only to find my arms pinned down by the G-forces. He soon figured out his mistake and corrected it.

The weather was perfect for flying, except for occasional sandstorms. When this happened, it happened fast, and you would have 30 or so little silver moths trying to land at the same time. The few cadets from France never seemed to understand what the tower was saying; sometimes this led to their landing from the opposite direction.

Time passed quickly. The transition into jets was seamless. The T-33 Shooting Star jet trainer was easy and fun, less complicated than a propeller-driven aircraft. The rudder was almost never used, there were fewer instruments displaying the condition of the engine, the cockpit was more ample, and takeoffs and landings were much smoother. The main difference was its speed. It was like turning in your Model A for a Mustang. Its sleek lines, reduced instrumentation and much greater speed made one feel that he had finally arrived. I still flew instrument flights under the hood, practiced formation flying, and completed a number of cross-country flights solo. Those were the most enjoyable; for two hours it was just I, the sky and the desert below.

As it had been at Spence, the flight line was the center of activity, although there was still plenty of ground school and military chicken shit. Saturday nights were free to spend on or off the base. Tom Wilson and I usually went to Carlos' Bar and Restaurant, a partially enclosed structure on the edge of town that served tolerable Mexican food and lots of beer. We would relax from the rigors of the week and exchange flying stories while our eyes followed Carlos' wife as she moved from table to table. Carlos cooked and his wife served. I never knew her name. She was always Carlos' wife. She would bring us mugs of cold beer and we would watch as she bent over our table, savoring a momentary glimpse beneath the white blouse that hung loosely from her shoulders. We would ask her silly questions to encourage her to stop and talk. We reveled in her laughter when she did not understand. She made lovers of us all and gave us things to dream about.

Tom Wilson's Air Force career almost ended at Carlos'. Carlos' wife had an especially strong effect on Wilson. One evening, he became increasingly romantic and possessive. She was busy serving beer to others and paying no attention to him. Tom was morose. Suddenly, his attention was drawn to the goats bleating in the field next to the restaurant. Grabbing one of the restaurant's bright-red napkins, Tom staggered outside, climbed over the fence and, in toreador fashion, challenged the goats. The noise woke their owner, angry shouts were heard, shots rang out, and an eerie silence descended over Carlos' Bar. The moment hung in the air like a plane on the edge of a stall. Then the front door slowly opened. Tom, with dust and grass stains covering his uniform, sheepishly entered, to a round of "Olés" from the crowd.

Tom's survival maintained our foursome, which was planning a four-day pass to Fort Worth. The other two came from Wayzata, Minnesota, a fancy suburb of Minneapolis. One, Eben Dobsen, was already an officer and entitled to have a car on base. His canary-yellow Buick convertible became our transportation. Eben's mother had arranged an invitation to attend the big debutante ball being held in Fort Worth that weekend.

Fort Worth was 250 miles due east of Big Spring on U.S. Highway 80. Along the way, we stopped for gas, beer and a load of fireworks. We took turns driving. My turn came last, when everyone was dozing. Then I nodded off as well. The change in the feel of the road instantly woke me. I regained the asphalt only to run into an old jalopy plugging along in the right-hand lane. The driver was a musician going home from a gig at a local barn dance. We chastised him for driving too slow and resumed our trip. Unfortunately, our radiator had been smashed and it soon ran out of fluid. By then we were close to Fort Worth and made it to a motel just outside the city.

By good luck there was one vacancy left. It was a spacious suite, separate from the main building, with bedrooms straddling an enormous sunken living area. The next morning Terry Watters joined us from Vance Air Force Base in Enid, Oklahoma, where he was training to be a bomber pilot. Terry was a fraternity brother of mine, was 6-foot-5 and had played varsity football at Stanford.

The invitation to the debutante ball offered by Eben's mother neglected to include the other three of us. Using the refrain of our imminent departure to Korea, our names were added and, yes, uniform plus black tie would be acceptable. (The owner of the auto repair shop replacing our radiator also demonstrated his patriotic spirit by providing us "Korea-bound" flyboys a car for the weekend.)

The event was held in the largest ballroom between the Mississippi River and California. The room was overflowing with Fort Worth's rich and elegant—and nice-to-look-at—young ladies. We were well treated but seated far away from the action. Ned Phelps, our social director from Wayzata, created our own little action center by insuring that the champagne would keep flowing. As the evening wound down, our table became very popular and we were let in on where the late-evening parties would be held.

Our first stop was at Fort Worth's reproduction of an enormous French villa, complete with towers, circular driveway, massive entryway—and a receptionist checking names. Neither our names nor future mission were on his list. Rejection was soon replaced by activity. We went back to the car and unloaded our stash of roman candles, established ourselves behind a hedge across the entrance road, and began lobbing broadsides at those leaving for other parties. Boredom eventually ensued, and we returned to our motel. We used up the remainder of our Roman candle supply lobbing them at each other over the hotel's swimming pool.

As I write, I find myself somewhat chagrined in retelling the events that followed. We had heard that there was another party, at the home of a family named Young. Without an address, we began the tedious task of giving the hotel operator the number of various "Youngs" listed in the telephone directory. Her suspicions were aroused, and she refused to make any more calls. She then had the audacity to send the security guard out to our villa. Meanwhile, in frustration, we began lighting our remaining arsenal of fireworks and throwing them out the front door.

At this point, my memory fails as to what happened next and who was to blame. I am told that a cherry bomb was tossed out the door just as the security guard was approaching. The reactions inside were varied. Tom Wilson dashed into the bathroom and climbed into the shower stall; I believe I slipped into the hall closet; and Eben escaped through a rear window. Making the most absurd effort to hide was Terry Watters, who squeezed his 6-foot-5-inch frame under the bed, where he became stuck with his feet showing out the lower end. The only one who remained calm and clear-headed was Ned Phelps, who, after slamming the door shut, asked in his best clipped, nasal squadron-leader accent, "Who is it?" Thank God the cherry bomb hadn't gone off.

Everything worked out just fine. We invited the security guard in for a beer and explained our unusual behavior. The old boy turned out to be a veteran of World War I and was sympathetic to the antics of a bunch of young kids on their way overseas. We broke out another round of beers and listened to war stories from a real soldier.

After six months at Spence and another six at Webb, we had learned how to fly and were considered "safe." We looked forward to our second graduation, getting our wings and becoming officers. We were asked what kind of assignment we preferred after graduation: overseas or stateside, fighter-bombers, day-fighters, reconnaissance or training command. For me, the only reason for being in the program was to fly day-fighters in Korea. That must have come across during my interview, as I was one of eight in our class of 130 to be assigned to Nellis Air Force Base. Nellis was the only training base for the F-86 Sabre jet and was located just north of Las Vegas. I was ecstatic.

Another hairy experience in an automobile should be recorded here for the record. I was driving alone after a night of carousing in Midland, an oil and cow town 40 miles west of the base. I had had way too much to drink and was weaving erratically along the highway. Fortunately, it was very late at night and almost no other cars were on the road. That experience should have taught me then and there not to drive while drinking. It took me more than 50 years before that "penny" dropped.

Nellis AFB, Las Vegas, Nevada

Upon arrival at Nellis, I presented my orders at the front gate and received my first salute as an officer with the modesty and indifference of an old veteran.

Nellis was exactly what I wanted. The entire base program was geared toward teaching us to fly in combat: to dogfight, to survive and maybe become heroes. Training missions started at 6:30 a.m. to avoid the intense heat of midday, followed by ground school through the morning and early afternoon. There were classes on Korean topography and weather, learning the silhouettes of enemy aircraft and memorizing survival procedures. But mostly, it was listening to our instructor, recently returned from Korea, telling us about flying in combat. He would recount his missions as far north as the Yalu River (which formed the border between China and North Korea), spotting MiGs (usually high and into the sun), the art of engagement, the Lufbery spiral from altitude to treetop and then making it back to base.

These tales would become our Bible. They would be retold in the evenings at the officer's club with more and more color as the evening wore on. They would become the nexus of our dreams of becoming aces. And then the next day we would practice what we had learned over the green spot.

The green spot was a square of alfalfa on a one-building ranch some 100 miles northwest of Las Vegas, situated adjacent to the Nellis gunnery range. From 25,000 feet, it was the size of a postage stamp surrounded by a moonscape of rugged lifeless terrain. It was over the green spot where we would meet our sister squadrons and engage. Sometimes we flew as a flight of four, sometimes only two. An instructor would lead and show us how the game was played.

Soon we were doing it on our own and being debriefed on the results. There were three training squadrons, the 96th (Blue tails), the 97th (Red tails) and the 325th (Yellow and Black Checker tails) making up the 325th Training Group. Major Blesse (the returning ace) was commander of my squadron, the 325th. My instructor was Lieutenant Etheridge.

My memory of these training missions is a blur of hassles and rat races. The air space was often overloaded with aircraft diving and turning for advantage. On some days, weather conditions left a crisscross of contrails lingering in the air that heightened the confusion. Red, Blue and Checker tails chased one another until the fuel tanks showed almost empty and we broke off and went home. The instructors were engaged as much as the students and played the game to the last drop of fuel. Sometimes a wingman ran out of fuel before he reached home base and had to dead-stick the last few miles. To us, this was almost as good as the real thing. We loved every moment.

On one mission, I was lead aircraft with a wingman named Pewitt. We arrived at the green spot at the normal starting altitude of 25,000 feet. Already there was a lot going on between flights with Red and Blue tails. Among the melee, I saw two Red tails at 9 o'clock low, going left to right under my nose, in loose formation and apparently unengaged. I radioed Pewitt while pointing out their position. With a "Let's get 'em," I nosed down and banked to my right. Pewitt slid behind me and followed. They must have just finished a dogfight, as they were a good 10,000 feet below us and traveling pretty fast. I continued to turn with my throttle full open.

The next thing I remember was waking up with my aircraft upside-down, flamed out, over inhospitable terrain and little altitude to spare. Fortunately, I was straight and level. After first rolling over right side up, I began the emergency restart procedure while scanning the terrain for a possible landing spot. Bailing out didn't occur to me. The engine fired up almost immediately and seemed to be working fine. I tried the radio and contacted Pewitt. He said he was somewhere at altitude, having been unable to hang on during my dive. We agreed to return to the base separately.

My first reaction after turning toward the base was chagrin over having somehow screwed up. To compensate, the least I could do was make a tighter-than-normal 360 overhead approach for landing and demonstrate to myself that I still knew how to fly. Considering the condition of the aircraft, it was the dumbest thing I could have done.

After parking the aircraft and shutting down the engine, I noticed that the crew chief kept looking at the aircraft. Then he slowly walked around it, pointing out various things to a quickly gathering crowd of ground personnel. I also began noticing things out of place, like the left aileron twisted and the wing itself not quite in line. Those on the ground were pointing out that several access panels had popped out and the elevator on the right side of the rudder was hanging by a single bolt. Eventually they found the fuselage to be twisted beyond repair. The aircraft was designated "Class 26," meaning it couldn't be flown again.

It became clear, after inspection, that I had overextended the capability of the aircraft and caused it to suddenly flip (the nose snapping up with the tail ending up in front). It happened occasionally with the A model of the F-86 when the elevator cables became overstretched during high-speed, high-G-force maneuvers. Lieutenant Etheridge had experienced the same thing not long before and spent three months in a neck brace.

As for me, there was a lot of debriefing and three days of no flying. They concluded that there was nothing physically wrong with me and, I guess, determined that the incident hadn't changed my attitude about flying. I must have done well in the psychological interviews, as I was in the group of graduating students receiving orders to Korea.

Among this group, Tom Wilson and I were more similar than most in background. Our hometowns, Westfield, New Jersey and Alameda, California, were typical white-collar, middle-income suburbs where our parents were wealthier than most and considered leaders in the social life of the community. We both had had live-in servants throughout the Twenties and Thirties and were insulated from the economic trauma of the Depression years. Both of us attended university and, when the Korean War started, we understood our responsibility to serve.

In addition, our siblings were all boys (Tom had two brothers to my three), which, along with a shared Protestant morality, compounded our awkwardness toward women, especially when it came to establishing a strong sexual relationship. I mention this because Las Vegas, for newly commissioned hot-shot fighter pilots on their way to Korea, should have been a gold mine when it came to seducing women. With our open-necked khaki uniform, 2nd Lieutenant shoulder bars, cocky gait and fresh-looking faces, we were just what the young ladies of that crazy town in the desert were looking to snare—if not forever, at least for an evening. Soon on our way to save the world, we would be satisfying and safe.

One of my classmates, Mel from Richmond, California, became entangled in a situation that almost cost him his commission. He met a young lady who he described as having the kind of body that ends up on the walls of auto-repair shops. He proudly showed us pictures that confirmed his description. She took a liking to him and dominated his off-duty time, including most of his nights. This round-the-clock schedule was not sustainable. The first indication was a gunnery mission when Mel flew into the rag rather than just shooting at it. Then, after parking his aircraft one morning and filling out the Form 2, he returned to Operations while leaving the engine running. They say the girl was heartbroken when Mel chose flying over, well, her.

On the other hand, Jim Blake, another classmate, met up with a gal in one of the casino swimming pools and ended up marrying her. Joy and her sister were a nationally ranked duet in water ballet, and the four of us spent the afternoon playing keep-away with a water-polo ball. Jim, a college-level swimmer, had never met a girl who was that athletic. After a few midnight horseback rides through the desert together, they got married and remained happily together for 61 years, until Joy's death in 2015.

My own encounters along the Las Vegas Strip were constrained by my having become smitten with a terrific girl while visiting New York City the previous December. Evelyn Grey was a Barnard undergraduate whom I had met at a party the summer before. Evelyn was beautiful, blonde and living with her aunt on Park Avenue. While not attending class or doing part-time modeling, she would show me the best of New York's nightlife. We dated almost every evening during the Christmas week. We had drinks at the Plaza, dinner and/or dancing at the Stork Club, a late-night stop at Eddie Condon's jazz club. There was even a horse-drawn carriage ride in the snow from 59th Street and Fifth Avenue to her aunt's apartment near 82nd Street. Evelyn was a fantastic dancer, fun-loving and smart. She was that "sophisticated" woman from New York City; I was that "Western" man on his way to war. We did a lot of hand-holding and kissing and promised to stay in touch.

Las Vegas in the Fifties was quite different from what it is now. There was the same focus on gambling with lots of nightlife, lonely people and opportunity, but the scale was modest in comparison with today. Las Vegas was still a Western town, glitzy but friendly, with the smell of horse manure hovering along the Strip. As newly appointed second lieutenants on flying status, our pay had jumped from $90 a month to $425. For most of the afternoons and evenings we were free to do as we pleased. Most of us would wander down to the Strip, hang out around one of the casino swimming pools, flirt with the chorus girls and waitresses, and wait for the evening to bring us some excitement. I spent a lot of time at the Desert Inn, where an old swimming buddy from the Athens Athletic Club in Oakland was the head lifeguard. His wife handled reservations for dinner and the nightly entertainment.

At the time, there was no minimum, no cover charge. She would arrange a stage-side table for us to watch Frank Sinatra or Lena Horne or Danny Kaye perform. The bill might be as little as $3 to cover one round of beers.

The gambling was just outside the dining room. It was difficult not to stop for a roll or two, or maybe a hand of blackjack. There were evenings when I would cash several checks for $20 each as I tried to get back to even. There were evenings when a number of us would exhaust our ready cash but were not ready to quit the tables. The Desert Inn had cabanas attached and golf carts available for attendants to pick up and return guests after they finished gambling. They usually closed up around midnight, leaving the golf carts unattended with the keys hidden on the cart. The obvious quickly came to mind. The tips we earned let us extend our gambling until the wee, wee hours. Then, with no more than $1.50 left, we would drive to the newly opened Sahara Club and gorge on their "everything you can imagine" buffet for the late, late gamblers. This was only on those days when we didn't have a 6:30 a.m. takeoff the next morning.

The four months of training passed quickly, and soon we were ready for the real thing. The news about Korea suggested that those in charge were trying to wind down the war. Just before graduation, the orders were cut, and most in the class were disappointed in being assigned to stateside duty. I was one of those assigned to some forgotten wing at Osan Air Base(K-55) in Korea. On the day of graduation, we were told that these orders were being reviewed. We were told to report each day to Group Headquarters for further information about our status. I had been counting on 10 days in the San Francisco area, and Evelyn was arriving at Oakland Airport the next day. Tom Wilson agreed to cover for me, so I hurried off to Alameda.

Evelyn arrived and stayed at our home in Alameda. Mom and Dad put on a typical "swimming group" welcoming party for their "almost hero" and his beautiful blonde creature from the Big City. I was nervous, knowing how particular Mom was about "girls brought home by her sons," but Evelyn quickly passed muster. This helped move us through the courtship phase more rapidly than is normal. After a few days showing Evelyn around my early life (which of course she was fascinated with), Wilson called me to say they had become suspicious when all the sign-in signatures looked the same. They told him there would be a formal roll call the next morning.

My brother Jack had told me that Ken Wentz, the treasurer of Weeden, would let me fly his Bonanza to Las Vegas if I had to get there quickly. The day I returned, Ken and I drove down to a small local airstrip on the Peninsula so he could check me out in his plane. It was a Bonanza, single-engine, two-seater distinguished by its V-shaped tail. After one "touch and go" landing, Ken said, "Use it anytime you need it."

After Tom's call, bingo! I'm on the phone to Ken. He said, "The gas tanks are full. Go for it." In less than two hours, Evelyn and I were buckled in and taxiing down the runway.

It was one of those beautiful California days with not a cloud in the sky: VFR all the way to Las Vegas. There were maps in the cockpit, but I had a good idea where I was going and set a course east-southeast.

It was great to be in a small plane, feeling the wind flowing past the windshield, bouncing around as the updrafts and offshore winds played with each other. Evelyn was not so happy, never having been in a small plane before. I explained that I had never been in a plane this small either, which was probably not the best thing to say. Soon we were leveled off at 10,000 feet, which, I found out later, was not far from the Bonanza's ceiling. The air turned calm and we had time to look around and enjoy the view. And what a view! Looking due east, we had the full range of the Sierra Nevada before us—not way down below, as one sees them from 35,000 feet on cross-continental flights, but right there at eye level.

As we continued east and south, the land below became drier and the mountains closer. Soon we had the Central Valley behind us and the foothills of the Sierra Nevada began. We were suddenly right over Florence Lake and heading toward the peaks ahead. Not over them—at them. It came back to me that Muir Pass was at 11,900 feet, nestled under 13,000-foot peaks named after various 18th-century evolutionists (Darwin, Huxley and Spencer).

That was more than 2,000 feet above our present altitude. No sweat! A little more throttle would do the trick. Slowly, ever so slowly, we crawled up those last 1,500 feet, waving to the hikers gathered around the hut at the top of the pass. I could picture seeing the whites of their eyes, we were so close. Not a word from Evelyn. As I guided the little Bonanza through Muir Pass, I described the time Alan, Jack and I had made our way on foot to this very same hut back in 1947. The rest of the flight was literally downhill, reaching Las Vegas in time for cocktails and dinner with Wilson.

The next morning, I made roll call and signed in, and we were off again heading back to the Bay Area. This time, at Evelyn's insistence, I flew south and then west, skirting the Sierra and refueling at San Luis Obispo. At one point, I let go of the controls and told Evelyn to try her hand at flying. "It's easy," I assured her, insisting that she try. At the time I dismissed the panic and tears that resulted as being something feminine. Long after, I realized this was one of those negatives that were being collected by her as she was getting to know me.

The rest of the time was a whirlwind of meeting people, overnights in Carmel, the wine country, bars along El Camino Real, culminating with our announcement that we were engaged. This caught Mom and Dad off guard, but they seemed pleased, especially Dad. Then another trip to Las Vegas, where I received my new orders to report to Hamilton Air Force Base, just north of San Francisco. I was no longer on my way to war, and Evelyn had to get back to New York City to do some explaining and planning.

After Nellis, stateside duty was a letdown. Four months hugging the wings of aces, near-aces and survivors had stirred my desire for action. They not only trained me well to be a lethal fighter, but brainwashed me into thinking I had the makings of a hero. I remember standing toe-to-toe at the bar of the officer's club drinking with my instructor (in flight suit, high-top boots and c--t cap) and listening reverently while he recounted his stories of combat.

After saying goodbye to Evelyn at the Oakland Airport, I took the long way home and considered the next three years. We had said all those lovey things to each other that you would expect, but there was no discussion about when and where we would get married. I also thought about my classmates from Stanford who were into their careers or only had short tours of duty remaining.

As a condition of receiving further training at Nellis, I had to sign up for an additional three years of active duty. This was OK with me, when it implied that my next stop would be Korea. When my orders were changed to stateside, I wondered whether I would have been better off completing the remaining two years of my original commitment and getting on with my career.

It was a momentary thought, but too late to do anything about. Thank God! I would not have gone to Nellis, flown F-86s and spent over two years in Europe. No other experience would have made me the person I am today. As for duty at Hamilton, now that the war was over, being based in Marin County, not far from Alameda and my Stanford buddies, should not be bad duty at all.

As Luck Would Have It

I have no recollection how my parents felt about the war ending and my not going to Korea. They must have been relieved. As for the wedding that supposedly was in the offing, nothing was said, and it soon became a non-issue.

My assignment to Hamilton was more of a letdown to Evelyn than it had been to me. Maybe it had nothing to do with the way she had begun to think about me and merely accelerated a decision already in the making. Once the glamour of my going to Korea was gone, she compared me against others without patriotic glasses and found me lacking in those things she really wanted. Or maybe it was getting back to reality, the Big City, a mother who was skeptical about this "hotshot" from way out West, or a desire for security that was not part of being married to an Air Force pilot. Who knows?

For a while, we wrote back and forth. Then her letters became less and less passionate, which I didn't notice, until I reread them later on. And then a short note saying that it wasn't going to work out. That was that. "Please don't call." "No, I don't want to see you. There is nothing to talk about."

My father, Frank, was in New York on business later in the year and ran across a small announcement in the *New York Times* that an Evelyn Grey and some guy named John Muller had announced their engagement. In December, I traveled back to New York City on my leave and went to her apartment. I was full of love and pleadings, but to no avail. That was 1953.

And then, sometime in the late '70s, I got a call from an "Evelyn Muller," who wondered if I would meet with her. And so we began again the love affair I had put out of my mind long before, but which, it turned out, she had never forgotten.

Dog Days at Hamilton

When Evelyn flew home to New York, I cut my leave short and reported for duty. At Hamilton, the 496th Fighter-Interceptor Squadron had just been reactivated and no one knew where it was located. I was finally directed to a Captain Lamp, located in an eight-by-eight-foot hole in the wall adjacent to a maintenance shack. Lamp was attired in summer khakis and a torn T-shirt. He introduced himself as the Squadron Adjutant for the 496th FIS. He didn't bother to remove his feet from the top of his desk when returning my salute. He explained that I was the first to report in from Nellis. After instructing me where I would bunk and how to get to the officer's club, I was dismissed.

Captain Lamp was not a good first impression; bulky and bald, weigh-

With flight instructor Mr. Smith (right) at Spence Field, Moultrie, GA.

North American's AT-6, Don's first aircraft.

Suited up to fly two-seat version of Lockheed's F-80 Shooting Star, at Webb AFB, Big Springs, TX, 1952.

Lockheed T-33 Shooting Star jet trainer.

As Luck Would Have It

Route Don flew in Bonanza (right) with Evelyn Grey, from small airport south of San Francisco to Las Vegas, NV.

Sierra Nevada Range to north as they flew over Muir Pass.

ing well over 200 pounds, with eyelids that looked like they had been burnt off (they were, I found out later), he seemed more appropriate running an airmen's mess hall. Over time, however, I came to like and admire this West Point graduate who served in three wars, flying combat in two.

Being the first from Nellis to report, I obtained a slight seniority over the others. As such, I was first to attend ground school and then to check out in the soon-to-arrive aircraft.

When I arrived, there was a group of pilots already assigned to the 496th from other squadrons on the base. They were older, veterans of World War II, with considerable flying time in their log books. Most of them had families and enough action under their belt for one lifetime. Yet they had volunteered for duty with the 496th so they could fly a cutting-edge aircraft with a front-line mission.

The "D" was quite different from the "A", "E" and "F" models we had flown at Nellis. Its mission was flying against bombers at night and in weather. It was armed with 24 three-and-a-quarter-inch rockets in a pod located within the underside of the fuselage. They were aimed and actuated by means of an electronic guidance system that located and locked onto the target and directed the aircraft into firing position. A newfangled drag-chute system was introduced to aid in landing.

"Dog" was the usual description when referring to the way this plane handled. Except when using afterburner, it was considered slow, heavy and difficult to maneuver. But all things are relative. The fact was that it had just set a world speed record at sea level. This was impressive, but it still did not satisfy those of us fresh from day-fighter school.

When the first planes arrived from the North American factory in Southern California, I traveled to McCord AFB with our Operations Officer, Captain Jack Rockwell, for ground school. After returning, I was assigned to Flight A, commanded by Captain Batt. I was checked out and took my first flight.

The Dog was the first all-weather interceptor without a radar operator in a rear seat. Instead, there was a screen located in the middle of the pilot's instrument panel. With the initial help of radar stations on the ground (ground-controlled interception or GCI sites), the pilot would be directed into range of an enemy "bogie," whereupon he would use his on-board radar to lock onto the bogie and make a "blind" pass down to "splash," "splash" being that moment when the E-4 fire-control system would release the rockets. This system enabled us to engage the enemy at night or in bad weather.

At the beginning, none of this equipment was yet operational, so we

As Luck Would Have It

flew the aircraft, as we had at Nellis, looking with our "eyes" for bogies to engage with. Occasionally, we would spot some Navy types in straight-wing Panther jets or swept-wing Cougars. They were weekend warriors flying out of Moffett Field near Sunnyvale or regulars off the carriers docked at the Alameda Naval Air Station. With our afterburner, they were hardly competition. We looked for other targets.

The most obvious and attractive challenge was to fly under the Golden Gate Bridge. There it was, handsomely guarding the entrance to the Bay in its dull red coat of paint, perched high over the water and always visible from the air, even when the fog was its thickest. One of our flight leaders, Captain Jan Barmore, had done the deed flying a P-38 during World War II, when doing this stunt was easier to get away with. I must say, I was tempted, but never quite found the right moment. Anyway, I had done my share of low-level flying back at Big Spring. The target was usually a lonely farmhouse. The challenge was to come in low enough to be looking up at the arms of the windmill and hope that no telephone or other lines connected it to the farmhouse.

I don't believe the Golden Gate Bridge or any of the other four bridges around the Bay were violated by our more "spirited" pilots, but there was one incident that might be considered "low flying."

"Stretch" Riddle was the other early arrival from Nellis. He and I flew training missions together. We would climb to altitude over Sacramento and make radar-controlled passes against one another. While one of us acted as the target, the other would establish contact with the GCI site on the top of Mount Tamalpais. The ground controller would guide him into range of his on-board radar. We would have to activate our IFF signal (Identification Friend or Foe) to make our "blips" large enough for the GCI operator to establish positive identification.

One Saturday, Stretch and I were scheduled for just such a mission, after which I would be driving home to Alameda. It was one of those crystal-clear days with the whole of San Francisco Bay spread out below us. Earlier, I had telephoned home, telling them when I thought I would be arriving. When my father mentioned that he would be vacuuming the swimming pool, the thought occurred to me that we could fly over the house and rock our wings.

The idea was fine with Stretch, but we agreed that it ought to be done with some discretion. We would fly up toward Sacramento and make a few passes against one another with our IFF turned on. And then we would turn off the IFF, rapidly descend toward San Francisco Bay, make a 180-degree "teardrop" turn while still over the Bay, and cross Alameda directly above my house on St. Charles Street. We would climb back to altitude, switch our IFF back on, and resume our radar passes. It shouldn't take more than five minutes.

During the descent we slowly picked up speed. As we made our turn, Stretch slipped out into a loose formation while I located St. Charles Street. At the same time we went into afterburner and increased our air speed to .96 Mach (close to 700 mph at sea level). I did not look at our altitude when we made landfall. We were back up over Sacramento in no time at all. Everything had worked perfectly, except for my aft fire warning light (aft of the turbine wheel) lighting up.

Upon reporting the incident, we were told to throttle back and return to base. Maintenance explained that a transducer, which checks for higher-than-normal temperatures, was probably pulled a bit too close to the tailpipe when making a tight turn at altitude. That made sense to everyone, so I took off for home hoping that my father had been able to see me wave as I flew by.

He barely saw the aircraft, much less my waving. But he certainly heard us. In fact, the whole neighborhood heard us. According to the Alameda Times-Star and the Oakland Tribune, in front-page articles the next morning, the entire East Bay had heard us. My father said the noise came without warning, as though someone smacked you without notice on the back of your head. My father assured me he had told no one of my intention to fly by. We agreed to keep it between ourselves. He explained that Tova Peterson, our next-door neighbor and former second in command of the WAVES during World War II, had emerged from her house in a fit and told him that she had called the commandant of the Alameda Naval Air Station, demanding the "name, rank and serial number" of the pilot that conducted what she described as a totally irresponsible treetop "strafing mission."

This, of course, was not what we intended, and the potential ramifications of being caught were readily apparent. I agreed that "mum's the word" and put in a call to Stretch back at Hamilton. He said that our squadron's Executive Officer, Major Jack Rockwell (he had been promoted from captain in the interim), had asked where we had been flying. The major corroborated Stretch's story from the radar operators on Mount Tamalpais. I said, "Mum's the word—to everyone," and then told him about the reaction back home.

Fortunately, it was one of those perfect flying days and the sky was filled with aircraft. There was an aircraft carrier docked at the Alameda Naval Air Station, plus local Air National Guard weekend pilots from Moffett Field were filling the sky with all sorts of undirected fun and games. I am told the investigation went on for days. For some reason, our squadron was overlooked—possibly because the only two planes flying that morning were fully accounted for.

Stretch and I agreed we were clever to have thought of the IFF cover, but not being able to tell even our buddies from Nellis took away much of the pleasure.

Stretch and I shared other adventures during those early days. Another mission, this time involving a simulated enemy air attack exercise, had us both ending up on the active runway at Travis Air Force Base in Northern California with broken aircraft.

To test our squadron's intercept capability, the Air Force High Command directed a flight of B-36s in toward the Northern California coastline from somewhere over the Pacific Ocean, timing unspecified. The GCI site atop Mount Tamalpais was to pick up the incoming "enemy" on their radar and notify the alert shack at Hamilton, which in turn would scramble the two F-86D Sabre jets waiting at the end of the runway.

Our Operations Officer, Captain Mitchell, and I were on standby alert when Tamalpais spotted "unidentified aircraft" entering the ADIZ (Air Defense Identification Zone). We were scrambled and directed toward the "enemy." We were given a course of 280 degrees: "bogie 120 miles flying east, altitude unknown." As we flew toward the target and farther away from the GCI site, static increased and radio contact was temporarily lost. When contact was reestablished, the communications improved. The voice on the radio continued to direct us due west, indicating that the target was getting closer but still out of range of our "on-board" radar.

The weather was scattered to broken clouds, from the tail end of a cold front that was lingering in the area. I had been flying in loose formation and thinking, This is what it's all about. My daydreams ended when Captain Mitchell began arguing with the radar operator, explaining that if we went any farther on this heading we would soon be short of fuel for our return to base. At that point, we both concluded that we were communicating with someone other than our radar operator on Mount Tamalpais.

As we learned later, a radio operator in one of the B-36s had taken over from the operator on Mount Tamalpais. In playing the game with his sophisticated equipment, he forgot that he was close to sacrificing two million-dollar aircraft, not to mention the pilots, who might not be able to swim. Captain Mitchell broke off the intercept mission and turned back to Hamilton.

As we were approaching Hamilton, Murphy's Law kicked in. We were notified by the tower that the air base was closed temporarily due to an emergency landing request and we should proceed to our alternative, Travis Air Force Base. The weak cold front had stalled just over Travis and we were faced with IFR conditions down to 1,200 feet. I was approaching minimum fuel and decided to remain on Captain Mitchell's wing rather than use up another 10 minutes of fuel in a holding pattern.

In thinking about it afterwards, it was probably the wrong decision to stay on Captain Mitchell's wing while he tooled around at 2,000 feet in bumpy overcast conditions. Mitchell, being a World War II bomber pilot, had not done a lot of IFR flying, and certainly not with someone on his wing. It was a bit hairy hanging on, but we both landed safe and sound. The debriefing was spent trying to figure out what had happened with our communications with Mount. Tamalpais.

Meanwhile, the second flight scrambled, consisting of Captain Batt and Stretch, was also diverted to Travis, landing shortly before we were scrambled again.

Scrambles being what the name implies, Captain Mitchell decided to take off on the nearest runway, even though it would be "taking off downwind." The runways at Travis were very long and posed no problem. We took off in loose formation, using afterburner until airborne. As I came out of afterburner, I did not feel the expected drop in power, and I quickly accelerated past Captain Mitchell. At the same time, my Aft Fire warning light came on. I further reduced power to idle. The warning light remained on, so I immediately stop-cocked the throttle.

What to do next? SOP (Standard Operating Procedure) called for landing straight ahead, but that was not very inviting. The alternative was to attempt a "teardrop" return to the runway. I decided on the latter, feeling that the added power gained from the malfunctioning afterburner just might give me enough airspeed to make the turn and reach the runway. With flaps full down and gear up until the last moment, I was able to float just far enough to reach the extreme right-hand corner of the runway before touching down.

Shortly after, Captain Batt and Stretch were scrambled, but this time into the wind. The long trip down the hot runway caused Stretch's aircraft to have a blowout as he was gaining speed for takeoff. He skidded off the runway and came to rest not far from my aircraft. The base commander at Travis had had enough of the 496th for one day.

It turned out that my afterburner fuel nozzle had stuck in the open position. This caused an overheating, which melted parts of the tailpipe. My decision to return to the runway turned out to be the right one. It also increased my self-confidence in my ability to handle an emergency.

As Luck Would Have It

Mechanical malfunctions aside, there were also times when I did something really stupid, like forgetting to lock my canopy on takeoff and having to abort with the assistance of the arrestor chain at the end of the runway. This had happened in Germany while I was giving Captain Bob Hale an orientation flight. Insult was added to injury: I had gotten into a fight with him at the officer's club earlier in the week, arguing over the caliber of our pilots vs. those in his old squadron. I would have preferred a real black eye.

I find my memory doing a lot of bobbing back and forth, from exciting adventure to stupid mistake to close call. Life remembered is mostly the peaks and the troughs.

There were the dogfights with the Navy pilots. The Dog's afterburner and our training at Nellis made it clear to all that over San Francisco Bay, the Air Force was king.

There were also those memorable moonlit nights flying solo and watching the fog bank far below creep in through the Golden Gate and over the hills, slowly covering the Bay. Those flights often ended with a GCA-assisted landing through 3,000 feet of dense fog that persisted almost to touchdown.

I also remember the loss of John Blum, from Nellis, whose plane exploded after takeoff, and Ben Short, who had to bail out when his aircraft caught fire for no apparent reason.

We had lots of maintenance problems, in part because the planes were brand new. The manufacturer was constantly changing systems and parts with each new series (nine in the first year). The Friday-evening song at the officer's club soon became, "Did you go boom today? I blew up yesterday." Still, everyone wanted his share of flying time and jockeyed eagerly for his turn to fly the Dog.

I was beginning to forget Evelyn and started dating a gal from Hawaii who was a junior at Stanford. Gaynor was gorgeous in a bathing suit and fun to be with. I had met her at a Zete party and must have impressed her as an older (23), more-serious type. My stories of dog-fighting and accident-prone aircraft, exaggerated of course, kept her interested, and we had something serious going when I left for Europe.

A rumor began circulating that our squadron would be the first all-weather squadron assigned to the European Theater, with a May departure. More aircraft began arriving from the factory along with additional pilots from the F-86D training schools at Moody Air Force Base in Georgia and Tyndall Air Force Base in Panama City, Florida. Our commander, Major Bradley, was replaced by a colonel from the Pentagon. Colonel Fischel had been one of the youngest commanders of a fighter squadron flying in

England during World War II. It didn't cut bread with most of us, who had developed a strong loyalty to Major Bradley.

Part of our preparation was a month of rocketry at the Yuma Air Force Base gunnery range, located on the Colorado River where it flowed into Mexico (it doesn't anymore). Our squadron would be the first to actually fire the three-and-a-quarter-inch Mighty Mouse rockets. Use of rockets was a new concept, but a sound one, if you were firing at an enemy you couldn't see.

Flying the entire squadron with new planes to Yuma became an adventure. Twenty aircraft took off in pair formation, climbing into broken cloud conditions almost immediately. They never joined up as a squadron and remained scattered in weather for the major part of the leg to George Air Force Base northwest of Victorville. It was a flight that put hair on the chest of every pilot who participated. It was amazing that there was no midair collision. After arriving at Yuma safely, the risk of flying into our target ship (a B-45) in full daylight seemed minimal, even though the pilot had to keep his head in the cockpit through "splash" on his radar screen.

Sometimes after target practice, our flight leader would put us into trail formation and fly low-level through and around the mesa-like formations in that part of Arizona. It was exhilarating and macho and dangerous as hell if you were number four in the formation. As number four, you hung in and hoped you didn't black out as you pulled the G's needed to avoid being splattered all over the side of the mesa. I guess it was part of what we had been trained for and wanted, but, looking back, it appears as though it was pushing the envelope a bit too far.

A successful month of gunnery was spoiled on the trip home when another of my classmates from Nellis, Joe Young, lost his life during takeoff. It occurred when he lost control of his aircraft and cartwheeled into a fire truck next to the runway. This fatality was attributed to pilot error, although some felt the leadership had been at fault in taking off in formation with a strong crosswind. The accident reminded us that flying was not all fun and games. I was assigned the duty of taking Joe Young's personal effects (nothing was left of him) back to his family in Oklahoma City. I remember the meeting with them as being subdued and unemotional.

In May, the squadron was ready to embark for Europe.

As a final sendoff, my parents and neighbors invited the squadron officers and their wives to a party around the swimming pool. Frank was the host. He was at his best and made everyone feel right at home. He mixed up a large bowl of what he called "the seducer," a punch made mostly of rum, freshly squeezed lime juice and just enough grenadine syrup so the ladies thought they were drinking Shirley Temples. This helped to relax the wives, as well as the husbands, who were not sure when they would be seeing each other again. The men quickly loosened their ties, their tongues and their inhibitions.

At one point, the squadron commander and the operations officer ended up in the pool, along with several others. Beds were made available for those who couldn't make it back to the base.

To this day, that party in May of 1954 is remembered by all who attended. It was memorable because of the instant camaraderie and mutual respect that emerged between the civilian hosts and their military guests, a throwback to the spirit that had prevailed during World War II. The host families were honored to show their appreciation to these fine men soon to go overseas, while all of these fine men were pleased to be honored with a good, rollicking party. One surprise came when Major Bradley casually asked Stretch what he thought of Alameda from ground level.

I had now been with the 496th FIS for almost a year. A lot of time had been spent on the flight line or at the officer's club with my fellow pilots. Our conversations usually were about flying: problems with the aircraft, weather conditions, how the "D" was different from the "F," "incidents" we encountered while flying the Dog. Little was discussed about where anyone came from or what they had done previously. This was especially the case with the older pilots. As for those like me, there was little else to talk about.

The older pilots, on the other hand, had flown during World War II or Korea, or both, but for the most part, they were modest about their experiences, even reluctant to discuss them. It was only many years later that I fully understood the extent of their flying. It came about when I put together a book about the 496 FIS titled Dog Days for our 2003 reunion, in which I assembled the entire military history of each of the pilot/officers. Here are some highlights:

Captain Jan Barmore: Entered the Cadet Program in 1943 at age 18. Flew the P-38, 39 and 51 over Germany; had two midair collisions; flew 101 missions over Korea in an F-84. He flew a total of 37 different aircraft in his 30 years of service.

Captain Rick Lamp: West Point graduate, began his flying in the Far East and China after World War II and later flew P-51s and P-80s, completing 100 missions in Korea; had a collision with one of his students at Luke Air Force Base west of Phoenix and was hospitalized for six months recovering from broken bones and severe burns; retired in 1974 after another tour of combat missions in Vietnam.

Our new Squadron Commander, Lt. Colonel Robert Fishel, flew P-47s out of England and became the youngest squadron commander ever when all the pilots with seniority were lost in battle over France and Germany in World War II.

Captain William Murphy, our Maintenance Officer, flew over 100 missions in B-24s out of Africa, including the famous, but disastrous, raid on the Ploiesti Oil Refineries in Romania. Sadly, little more is known about him because he never talked about himself.

Other names deserve to be mentioned. A number of our first and second lieutenants—Rouse, Pattison, Michaud and Leitch—went on to serve in the Vietnam War, where each of them flew in excess of 100 combat missions.

Their résumés mainly reflected the cold facts about their tours of duty, airplanes flown, missions completed, and name of wife, number of children and grandchildren. Only slowly did we younger pilots begin to appreciate who these men were and what they had accomplished during their flying careers.

With the 496th at Landstuhl, West Germany

Spending two years in Europe was not what I had in mind when I applied for the Air Cadet Program in 1950 when I returned to Stanford in the fall. If I were successful in becoming a pilot and went to Korea, my time in the service would be a minimum of four years, with some risk of not coming back. It would delay my joining the family firm, where my brothers Jack and Alan had already started their careers.

I was assured by my father, my Uncle Norman and my two brothers that there would be a job waiting when I got back. "Sow whatever wild oats you need to sow," said Frank, "and get them out of your system." I hadn't thought about it in quite that way, but I appreciated his support and commitment. I knew that he was anxious to retire, he thought my talents and interest would be valuable to the company, and he felt strongly that having three sons who had already served in some capacity was enough for one father. The fact that I would be going to Europe rather than Korea was comforting to him, but he still was bitter that it would be another three years before I settled down.

The party at my parents' home marked the end of the squadron's informal activities at Hamilton. We were soon broken up into three groups heading for Germany. I was assigned to be "Supply Officer" for the advance party, and I left immediately for New York and then to Germany. Goodbyes were brief. Mom said she would try to visit next spring. Gaynor and I agreed to write often.

As Luck Would Have It

In New York, I had lunch with Bob Beshar, a friend from Yale Law School, and his new bride, Christine von Wedemeyer. After looking me over closely, Christine provided me with addresses of her family still living in West Germany. I thought about contacting Evelyn but never tried.

Europe had not been on my radar screen since my failed effort to get there in 1950. Its role in the conflict with Communism had became secondary to the war in Korea. Even after our deployment to Germany, my focus was on the day-to-day and not the bigger picture. It was only when I was putting together the Dog Days book about the 496th that I began to study the larger picture—the why and when and how we came to be sent to Germany. The following "purple prose" is the way I described it in *Dog Days*:

"The story begins in 1945. While our men came home from the war, received their discharges, went to college on the GI Bill, and began to enjoy the peace they had fought for, the United States found itself in Europe with a large occupation force and a growing uncertainty over the anti-Western tactics of the Russians.

"Added to this was the fact of Mao taking over mainland China, growing tensions between Communism and the West throughout the world, and Russia's rapid development of a nuclear capability. Then there was the invasion of South Korea and the reality that Russia and the United States were in serious confrontation. World War II pilots, who had earlier been riffed, eagerly volunteered for duty in Korea. Many more were recalled and pilot training programs were reactivated to teach young and eager kids still in school how to fly the latest fighter planes.

"The F-86F was the 'latest and hottest' and soon came to rule the skies over Korea. The 'Sabre Jet,' as this swept-wing fighter was called, ended its tour of Korea with a 4.5-to-1 kill ratio against the Russian MiG-15. While the MiG climbed faster and higher, it couldn't match the 86's tighter turn capability, heavier armor and more stable gun platform. Nor were its pilots, mostly North Korean and Chinese, and to some extent Russians, as well trained as were our veterans from World War II.

"Then in early 1953, the Korean War was beginning to wind down. This challenge to the West was being mastered among the hills along the 38th Parallel and in the skies above the Yalu River. The generals now turned their attention toward Europe and the ominous rumblings from behind the Iron Curtain. Here they found a front 2,000 miles long with a million Communist soldiers stationed along its length. Even more threatening were the squadrons of modern aircraft, fighters and bombers, capable of raining destruction on all of Western Europe.

"Our defenses in the air were strong and alert: Canadian, British, French and American day-fighter planes standing ready to repel whatever on-slaught came through the air. But those who knew the terrain, the weather and the distances realized all too well the inadequacies of those defenses. For early in 1953, at night or in weather, there was no defense against invasion through the air. According to official Pentagon documents, the Russian military would make an advance on Western Europe sometime between 1954 and 1956. As a result, the 496th FIS was reactivated. Its mission was to meet this challenge and fill the void."

I arrived at Landstuhl Air Base and found little to do. "Supplies" were on an aircraft carrier making its way toward the Panama Canal and wouldn't be arriving at Saint-Nazaire, France, for five weeks. The nearest village was Landstuhl, which housed a large American military hospital, and just across the road was Ramstein Air Base, the headquarters of the 12th Air Force. The western end of Hitler's Autobahn, and one pointed directly at the heart of France's Saarland, ended nearby. Occasionally, it was mistaken for runway 9/27.

Not one to sit around, I put on civilian clothes and hopped a ride into Kaiserslautern, 10 miles east of the base. It was the largest town between the Rhine River and the French border and had been the target of several daylight air strikes and intense softening up by the advancing Allied troops.

Kaiserslautern was my first introduction to the destruction caused by war. Ten years after World War II, whole sections of the city were still nothing but rubble. Broken blocks of the locally quarried red sandstone were heaped up in piles side-by-side with small shops that had managed to survive the barrage. I wandered down street after street of massive destruction, passing the occasional pedestrian wearing shabby and ill-fitting clothes, some carrying a beat-up briefcase or paper lunch bag.

Suddenly, in the midst of all this devastation, I came across a Volkswagen dealership carved out of the rubble. Nestled behind a large showroom window was a single silver-blue Volkswagen convertible (cabriolet) looking as cute as a newborn kitten. The owner of the dealership spoke some English and quoted a price of 1,500 American dollars, and "Yes," he would take my personal check from the American Trust Company in Oakland, California. The deal was made on the spot, and I drove my kitten out of the showroom and back to the base—without military license plates, without a military driver's license and without insurance.

The next day, I went to the Air Police headquarters to take care of the above. I told them that the auto in question was parked outside, and yes, I had driven the 10 miles from Kaiserlautern to the base without any of the required papers. This caused quite an uproar and required several levels of superior officers to resolve. I was attentive and subdued while they debated my future in the Air Force. Eventually, I obtained insurance, a driver's license and plates, but not without further remarks concerning pilots with no sense of responsibility. Finally, like Mr. Toad, I was "ready to explore the countryside."

The very next weekend, I was speeding along the Autobahn north of Frankfurt, top down, enjoying the scenery and oblivious to giant cumulus clouds forming in the distance. Suddenly, I found myself driving into a patch of heavy rain. A quick decision was needed: Stop the car, unsnap the canvas protecting the top, haul the heavy and ungainly top up and forward into place, and then snap it shut; or accelerate my 30-horsepower engine to its maximum speed of 60 mph and plow through to the other side of the rain squall. My hope was that, at that speed, the windshield would divert the rain over the seating area, keeping me dry.

Not interested in turning into a drenched Mr. Toad, I opted for the latter. The rain became intense, making it more difficult to see. The other autos on the road began to slow down. To maintain the necessary speed, I began flashing my headlights and honking my horn to move everyone out of the passing lane. Fortunately, these obedient Germans dutifully moved over and let me pass. The look on their faces said, as I waved thanks, "And these are the people to whom we lost the war?"

Our advance party soon visited Phalsbourg, west of Landstuhl, on the other side of the border with France, where a new airfield was being constructed, presumably for us. Our trip included checking on the availability of living quarters off-base. Nothing sounded attractive until the real-estate agent described a castle located on the edge of a small village by the name of Sherrach-Bergheim. Major Bradley, Captain Murphy, Lieutenant Short and I went off to see for ourselves.

The castle was straight out of medieval times: On a slight hill above a cluster of tiny farmhouses was a castle-like structure, four stories high, encircled by a moat (complete with water). Access was over a wooden drawbridge that still operated.

We were greeted by the Countess de Sherrach-Bergheim, an elderly matron, tall, bosomed, with a formidable air of authority. In halting English, she welcomed us with a friendly but regal air. She became a widow when her husband heroically, but unsuccessfully, defended the castle and the inhabitants of the village from the German Panzers. She spent the next five years hiding members of the underground movement in the bowels and hidden passageways of her castle. She would be honored to make it available to the Americans who had helped to win the war.

The castle contained small garret-like rooms accessible from the outside via narrow openings and circular stairways. There were larger interior rooms that brought the visitor to two enormous rooms, one on top of the other, with ceilings reaching two stories high and fireplaces that were 12 feet wide and 10 feet tall. Faded tapestries covered the walls; heavy oak and walnut furniture completed the medieval look. It was the perfect bachelors' quarters.

My reaction was the same as with my silver-blue Beetle. I was ready to do a deal on the spot, and so was the Countess. In anticipation, the Countess insisted on offering us some of her best "Kirchwasser," produced locally. She carefully filled five tumblers to the brim, toasted us and drained hers in one gulp. Sensing tradition, we tried to follow suit.

Kirschwasser does not go down easily. It has an unusually sharp bite that makes swallowing difficult. Our leader was first to notice, his cherubic face reddening noticeably; Captain Murphy hardened his jaw and made no attempt to swallow, while Lieutenant Short had to spit this acid-tasting liquid back into his glass. The Countess' offer of another round was graciously refused. Sadly, the squadron never moved to Phalsbourg.

Landstuhl ended up becoming the permanent headquarters for the 496th and 440th fighter interceptor squadrons. We would be sharing the runway with two day-fighter squadrons which had been operating there for two years. The distain with which these "hotshot Charlies" viewed us "hooded weather rats" was palpable in the officer's club. A few dogfights between their best and our Nellis graduates changed their attitude.

The weather also helped. It was high summer, but unseasonably cold and overcast. Ceilings were low, visibility poor. Flying was mostly on instruments. The old-timers said the weather was worse than any they remembered back in the States.

The aircraft began arriving and were put into flying condition. The bad weather, plus rigid procedures for checking out, slowed our ability to become combat ready. Our sister squadron, the 440th, was determined to be first. They began cutting corners and the accidents began piling up. The comment floating around our flight room was, "One a week and they'll all be gone by Christmas."

Away from the kidding, the weather forced us all to become very serious about our instrument flying and to hone our formation techniques. Ceilings below 1,000 feet were not uncommon. Alternate landing sites were limited or nonexistent. Rapidly deteriorating conditions was another concern. Landstuhl had a radio beacon but no ILS (instrument landing system) or GCA (ground control approach). When one considers that scrambles were being conducted on a 24/7 schedule, the squadron's record of weather-related accidents was pretty phenomenal.

While I was there, the squadron incurred only one fatal accident attributed to weather. It happened at night in heavy weather less than a hundred yards short of the runway. The pilot, J.B. Lang, was part of our group from Nellis and was considered an excellent all-around pilot. He had recently married Major Bradley's daughter, who was pregnant at the time. J.B. was probably the best-liked pilot in the squadron.

Summer slid into fall with little change in the weather. By then, the 496th had established a full-scale 24/7 alert operation at Wiesbaden, located 100 miles north and east of Landstuhl. A full-scale alert shack with cots, hot plate and toilet was constructed just off the west end of the east-west runway. Each flight (four in a squadron) with seven pilots spent one week a month doing round-the-clock alert duty. It was an opportunity to do a lot of flying in an informal, front-line atmosphere; there was also lots of card-playing, bullshitting and reading magazines.

Contrary to movies about World War II and the more hyped films such as Top Gun, there was very little in the way of personality conflicts or confrontations between the lower-ranking pilots and their seniors. There was almost no smoking. Drinking? Yes; lots of it, in the officer's club and off-duty. This was how I had envisioned life in Korea. We all had the feeling we might be doing something similar at any time.

With bad weather continuing and available flights decreasing, four of us—me, Stretch, Bill Leitch and Tom Wilson—took leave time and drove to Zermatt, Switzerland, with the intention of climbing the Matterhorn. I had read The White Tower and an account of the first ascent by the Whymper party with its tragic ending. Since then, the professional guides had determined the safest routes that enabled non-climbers in good condition to reach the summit.

We piled into Stretch's new Mercedes 190 sedan and drove the 270 miles in one day. Leaving the car in Visp, we took the narrow-gauge railway up the side of the Rhone Valley to Zermatt, a wonderfully picturesque village nestled below the most-photographed mountain in the world. Unfortunately, the bad weather had followed us down. For the first several days, we never even saw our Matterhorn.

We engaged two reputable guides who would teach us the art of mountain-climbing and see to our safety. After three days of conditioning, the guides took us to a couple of smaller peaks and taught us the rudiments of rock-climbing, complete with belaying. After two more days, we still hadn't seen our Matterhorn. With a forecast for more of the same, I left the others and headed off to London, where my Uncle Norman was due to arrive from New York.

It was during my Swissair flight from Geneva to London that I first met Vera, who would become my wife of 32 years. That was in mid-September 1954. The details of how that romance developed, prospered and dissolved will have to wait for a later chapter.

Back in Zermatt, Tom found out very quickly that he was not meant to be a mountain climber; he never went back. I have visited Zermatt several times since, but only for skiing. Bill and Stretch returned the next year and had a successful ascent. Bill managed to lose one of his mittens on the way up. He completed the climb, but not without a bad case of frostbite. Pure Leitch.

I had not been asked to join them, probably because I had not shown much enthusiasm for trying again. After our limited practice ascents, I had decided that it was not my cup of tea, even though I savored the challenge and satisfaction of completing two minor climbs. Nevertheless, I would have joined them if asked. My experience heightened my admiration for the one mountain climber in the Weeden family, Bill's oldest son, Norm, who has the passion and natural ability for it.

One would have thought that there would be a close similarity between mountain-climbing and flying fighter planes. In the case of Stretch and Bill, particularly Bill, there was. Bill was the consummate risk-taker; he craved any challenge and constantly sought opportunities to demonstrate to himself his ability to excel, overcome and succeed at whatever task (risk) he took on. He loved to gamble and was very good at it. He craved fast cars and owned the first Ford Thunderbird delivered in Europe. He volunteered for every flight that became available and went on to be a test pilot at Edwards Air Force Base in Southern California (of "The Right Stuff" fame).

On a later tour in Spain, Bill had to bail out of an F-104 and was told they would have to amputate both legs above his knees, which shattered on his exit. Bill refused the offer, recovered and spent a year with the Canadian Air Force. He was then assigned to George Air Force Base, again flying the F-104. From there he went to Vietnam for two tours of duty, returning in 1966 after completing 500 missions over South and North Vietnam. He had flown every conceivable type of aircraft available. Bill was always ready to push the envelope to a point where, as his wingman, it would have been a challenge to keep up with him. That said, I would have jumped at the chance, anytime, anywhere.

My interest in taking physical risks was limited. There were times when I wanted to impress others with my "fearlessness," counter a silly fear, or help with my self-image. As a boy, I declined to join my buddies when they biked over to Berkeley to race down its hills as fast as they could. On the other hand, I was the only one to make the high dive off the rocks into a small pool of water at summer camp. Fast driving never appealed to me, and certainly not the game of "chicken."

I tried riding a motorcycle once at Stanford, just for kicks, but quickly concluded that the risks outweighed the kicks. But 20 years later, I drove a Yamaha 90 through the congested streets of Lower Manhattan and along the East River Drive during my Congressional campaign. Flying in Korea had a genuine purpose involved. Having said that, what remains unknown is how I would have reacted in combat. I presume I would have measured up, but absent actually having done it, that question remains unanswered.

Risk was on all our minds during the long waiting periods while standing alert. We would review our emergency procedures and mentally practice what we would do "just in case." When it was nighttime and snowing a bit, the sphincter might even tighten a bit just thinking about an upcoming scramble. Surprisingly, there was no organized system for this kind of review. I don't remember my flight commander ever sitting down with us and asking what we would do in case of ... It was the continuous bad weather, the accidents and close calls that kept our minds focused on the possibilities.

The weather was not always bad. As autumn rolled into early winter, we saw more of the sun, and the temperature remained reasonably warm. The grapes that were left on the vines going into November filled with sugar and became a once-in-a-lifetime specialty. Meanwhile, Jim Blake and I joined the swim team representing the 12th Air Force and went up to Berlin for the All-European Swimming Competition. It was being held in the same indoor pool where the 1936 Olympics took place. I came in first in the 100-meter backstroke and part of the winning 300-meter medley. Jack Nelson swam the breaststroke leg using the new butterfly, or dolphin, stroke and was the reason for our winning.

A couple of weeks earlier, Jim and I had driven down to Fürsten-feldbruck, in Bavaria near Munich, for the 12th Air Force trials. On the way back to Landstuhl, we detoured down to Garmisch-Partenkirchen, a quaint mountain village in the Bavarian Alps that served as an R&R center for American military personnel. We got rooms at the Hotel von Steuben and woke the next morning with a beautiful view toward the Zugspitze, Bavaria's Matterhorn. Also in our view was the parking lot below with a familiar-looking silver-blue VW convertible in the middle of it. We decided that Tom Wilson was also in the hotel, vacationing with the nurse from Landstuhl Hospital he was dating.

As co-owner of the VW, I had a key with me. Jim and I decided I should move the VW and watch the reaction when Tom came down to claim it. The parking attendant assumed I was the rightful owner who had merely lost the ticket. I drove it around the block and returned to the hotel room. Soon Tom appeared with a suitcase and presented his ticket. A sort of discussion ensued with Tom waving his ticket while the attendant was indicating that someone else had claimed the auto and had driven it away.

The problem, of course, was that Tom knew no German and the parking lot attendant knew no English. Suddenly a police car drove up and the two were taken away, presumably to police headquarters for questioning. The police car returned and another round of explanations ensued. The police paced off the distance from the entrance to the site of the missing VW, took photographs of the empty site and made extensive notes in a small notebook. It was vintage Chaplin, complete with uniforms, arm-waving and people running here and there. Jim and I were alternating between peeking out the window and rolling on the bed with laughter.

Now enters the nurse, wondering why Tom had taken so long to pack the VW. Another round of explanations and arm-waving. Suddenly, a second police car arrives on the scene with the information that there was a silver-blue VW cabriolet parked on the street a few blocks away. Surprise, denial, indignation, irritation and relief appeared on the various faces clustered around the entrance of the parking lot. After the Polizei left, Jim and I appeared and everyone had a good laugh together—after we calmed Tom down.

In late November, I was sent off to the Escape and Evasion School located in a village south of Munich named Bad Tölz. Bad Tölz, long known for its hot springs, was a summer gathering spot for the German aristocracy. During the '30s, it housed an SS Junkerschule (officer candidate school for the SS) in a new complex called the Flint Kaserne, complete with eight underground levels used as prison cells and interrogation rooms.

Our host was the Army's 1st Battalion, 10th Special Forces Group (Airborne). The schooling lasted two weeks. During the first week, we attended classes on how to escape, evade the enemy and what to say when being interrogated. For the second week, we were taken out into the Bavarian forest at night and left to find our way back to safety—safety being on the other side of an imaginary border defended by guards, German shepherds and floodlights. We were given sleeping bags, a day's worth of C-rations, a map of the area and instructions to a rendezvous site where we would obtain further instructions leading us toward the border. The enemy would be the American soldiers stationed in Bad Tölz who would be out searching for us. The game was to evade for six days, reach the border and cross into freedom. The exercise was made as realistic as possible.

John Wurtzel, Tom Wilson and I were dropped off the back of an army lorry at midnight and told that we had a half-hour head start before the men of the 101st began their search. After running and stumbling blindly for an hour through the forest, noisily breaking dead branches and tripping over rocks and roots, we settled into four days and nights of carefully avoiding all contact with human beings. Each day we had to pick up a new set of instructions left at a crossroad or mailbox by our "partisan" friends.

All three of us were having a ball until the third night. We had been carefully making our way around an isolated farmhouse, with Tom leading us along what felt like an elevated pathway. Suddenly, Tom disappeared, followed by an "Oh, shit!" as he broke through ice covering a pond some 15 feet below. There had been an early snow that still covered the ground in the open areas and the temperature had dropped below freezing. Tom was soaking wet but uninjured, except for his ego. We helped him out of the pond and scrambled away from the farm. Making our way up into the denser part of the forest with our shivering buddy, John and I decided to hole up and risk the chance of capture by building a small fire. Slowly, Tom's flight suit dried out and he stopped shivering.

At the next rendezvous, the instructions informed us that the border was close by but there was now an intense search going on for our whereabouts. By early evening a light but steady rain began. We plodded through the woods, reading our map by match light and trying to figure out where we were. The rain became freezing and only let up as dawn began to break. We spied a logging road that offered some relief from the rain-soaked forest. We were as wet as hound dogs when we came to a small logger's shack on the side of the road. Throwing caution to the wind we went inside, opened our C-rations and lit our Sterno cans for a little warmth.

Tom went out to relieve himself and immediately barged back in, whispering, "There is a jeep coming down the road." I ran out the back door past Tom, straight to a quarry about 100 yards away. Momentum got me up the back side, where I threw myself behind a fallen log and covered myself with wet leaves. I heard voices and then a car starting and driving away. I lay there for an hour. No one came looking for me. I presumed that Wilson and Wurtzel had been tagged and taken prisoner. Cautiously, I retrieved my sleeping bag and C-rations and continued to the final rendezvous. (The rules required them to leave your equipment if they didn't tag you, so you could continue the "game.")

As it became dark, I could see across an open space ahead to a group of lights on the hillside, indicating the border and safety beyond. The rain tapered off and the sky cleared. The moon appeared and the temperature dropped again below freezing. As I came to the edge of the meadow, I now saw the silhouettes of sentries patrolling among the trees. The water-soaked grass had become stiff with ice, making every movement sound like firecrackers going off. It took me an endless amount of time to slither through the meadow and reach the trees on the other side.

Finally, that moment came when I left my sleeping bag behind and sprinted toward the tents and freedom.

The entire exercise was as realistic as they could make it. Cold War tensions in Europe were high at the time, and pilots were likely to be the first to end up behind enemy lines.

In 1954, the CIA and the Pentagon were quite familiar with Communist interrogation methods. These methods included isolation in a small cell, constant light, sleep deprivation, alternating cold and heat, heavy exercise, and lack of food and water. At Bad Tölz, the prisoners were subjected to all of the above, and the interrogation was conducted by actors in Russian uniforms brandishing pistols and talking in heavy accents.

The Geneva Convention stated that a prisoner of war was required to give only his name, rank and serial number. But our instructors told us that the experience of World War II demonstrated that those who were willing to answer questions in a creative and careful way were mentally better able to resist "breaking"—that is, telling things that would be helpful to the enemy. Wurtzel was one of the many who "bobbed and weaved" and was considered "fit" to be shot down and captured.

Tom was stubborn, sticking to "name, rank and serial number," and was paraded before the class through a one-way glass partition as an example of how not to act. The opposite example was a captain who actually "broke" and willingly blurted out all the information that was considered secret.

(I think back on that experience and relate it to present times in which the form of conflict has complicated the definition of "prisoner of war." Both sides knew then that the treatment would not be fun, but it would be limited by the Geneva Convention. At least, that was the assumption.)

As we entered the winter season and the weather turned cold with plenty of snow, an incident occurred that brought the sense of our mission to a new level of reality. As Captain Lamp, Commander of "D" Flight, described it later:

"Upon first arriving at Wiesbaden, I was briefed that the Soviets had occasionally sent single flights of fighter planes at night into West German airspace around the border town of Fulda. They would penetrate 50 or 60 miles before returning to their bases in East Germany. The penetrations were becoming deeper and there had been little we could do about it until our squadron's arrival. I had asked the colonel in charge at 12th AF what the rules of engagement were and was told that we were not to fire until we received certain code words. I then asked about weather conditions and what minimums would we have to observe. The reply was, 'You're an all-weather squadron, aren't you?'

"I tucked this comment away until one night during winter when the blowing snow made conditions almost zero/zero (zero ceiling, zero visibility). When the scramble horn sounded, I and my wingman, Lt. Wurtzel, settled into our aircrafts and took off, guided by the newly installed strobe lights glowing faintly at the edge of the runway. When we were airborne, I contacted the forward ground radar station and was told, 'We've got some bandits coming across.' We climbed until we were in the clear and headed due east. Soon, I was told, 'Bandits are going home. You are cleared to return to your base.' That was easier said than done. One can take off under zero/zero conditions, but landing with the instruments we had was close to impossible and certainly not permitted. Finally, the weather at one of our alternates went above minimums and we landed without incident.

"The next night the same thing happened under similar conditions with the same results. The following morning the same colonel called and said, 'OK, Captain, there is no question you all-weather guys can cut it, but we don't want to press our luck. Let's take it easy while this kind of weather lasts.'

"The same weather persisted for several days, but there were no more calls to scramble. A few weeks later, I learned that on the second night a flight of four MiG 17s had augured in while returning to base and no more attempts to penetrate had occurred."

We had fun speculating for a while on what might have happened if the scramble had led to an engagement.

We also speculated about what would have happened had Jim Morrison not shown the good judgment to do a "split-S" into the clouds when confronted with two Soviet MiGs.

The incident occurred when he and Jim Mathews were on a cross-country flight to Copenhagen. They were flying the two-man T-33 when suddenly there appeared three of the Soviets' brand-new MiG 17s at four and eight o'clock high. Because their route from Landstuhl took them reasonably close to the East German border as they approached Denmark, stronger-than-predicted winds at altitude might well have pushed them into unfriendly airspace, setting up the possibility of an unfriendly encounter.

With a broken cloud cover below preventing them from knowing exactly where they were, Morrison decided that by diving immediately into the clouds, he would avoid the possibility that they might open fire. It was a smart move and allowed the incident to end up quietly in some "near incident" file at the Pentagon.

(Jim Morrison is the artist who painted all the watercolors of the F-86D.)

On days that began with scattered clouds, we young bucks would often climb to altitude and look for someone to play with. On one of those days, Bill Leitch and I headed southwest in search of the Canadians based at Zweibrücken or Solingen. They flew a version of the F-86F called a Mark VI with an Orenda engine and were tough competitors in a dogfight.

I was lead with Bill on my wing. Contrails were sighted. We climbed to altitude and engaged, oblivious to the clouds thickening below. We used afterburner in our climb, and after jousting for position and a few passes at one another, we found ourselves low on fuel and had to break off. Upon switching channels, I found that other flights had also been caught unprepared by the change in weather and had already called in for an IFR letdown. By reporting minimum fuel, we could to go to the head of the line. This would not go down well at the officer's club and would require some explaining why so little fuel remained after such a short flight.

I asked Bill if he had enough fuel for a minimum-power descent into Wiesbaden, some 90 miles to the northeast. There should be less traffic ahead of us, if any, and we could refuel at our alert operation there. I figured if we crossed the Rhein-Main radio beacon at 10,000 feet instead of the normal 20,000, I would have enough fuel, but Bill might not. (The wingman normally ends up with less fuel due to moving his throttle back and forth to stay with his leader.) Bill was okay and Frankfurt Approach Control cleared us for approach and landing, there being no other traffic ahead. They also cautioned us that weather at Wiesbaden was reported as 400 feet, 1-mile visibility with occasional snow flurries. Bill elected to stay on my wing, as his fuel level was too low to make a separate approach. The approach and landing were uneventful even though the weather conditions were as reported.

After refueling us for our return to Landstuhl, the sergeant in charge quietly mentioned to Bill that his fuel tanks took in more fuel than its published maximum capacity. Bill's comment: "That's interesting; must be the cold weather."

As Luck Would Have It

Early in 1955, NATO decided to conduct a week-long exercise involving several waves of bombers, up to 40 at a time, penetrating the West German airspace from Great Britain. Its code name was "Carte Blanche." Daytime sorties were accompanied by fighter cover and involved dogfights with cameras substituting for machine guns. Flights at night were flown without lights against the 496th and the other all-weather squadrons. This effort at realism ended when NATO lost a number of aircraft and scores of airmen. The 496th lost one aircraft when it collided with a Wellington bomber. Our pilot was able to eject and parachute to safety, while the entire crew of the Wellington was lost.

As one of the younger pilots, I never learned whether the exercise was considered useful or not. No pilot in our squadron locked onto any of the invading bombers. None of the ground radar sites could keep our blips separate from enemy blips, and thus were unable to help guide us to the targets. To us, it was pretty stupid to put upward of 100 aircraft in the same airspace and not be able to see one another. Even among our own aircraft, there was danger of a midair collision. We knew this and were very, very careful, but we had no idea where the enemy was, and this resulted in the tragic loss of the five crew members in the Wellington.

Sometime later, I heard that our squadron commander's latest report to the Pentagon said the "effectiveness" of the 496th was over 70 percent. My own gut feeling was quite different, if effectiveness meant our ability to "actually shoot down enemy bombers flying in from the east at night or under weather conditions." This led to my organizing a test of "effectiveness" based on actual flights against real aircraft heading our way. The test would also give some purpose to our daily flights out of Landstuhl and Wiesbaden and might even increase our flying time.

After designing the test, I kept records (which I still have) as to what happened each time a flight was completed according to our protocol. We took into consideration the number of planes available for flying each day, the number that supposedly had good radar and the number of nights when the weather was above minimum. But mainly we tested how we performed when scrambled in response to a call that an enemy plane had penetrated our airspace. The enemy plane would be a T-33 or one of our own F-86Ds sent out close to the Iron Curtain and then turned back toward the west.

One of the GCI sites, with the call sign "Logroll" or "Dora," would pick it up and signal our alert shack to scramble an aircraft. We would record whether or not the scrambled aircraft made radar contact, locked on successfully and flew it down to splash. (As you'll recall, "splash" was the moment when the rockets would be fired automatically.)

Over a three-month period, we ran more than 100 missions, involving a minimum of two aircraft to a mission, recording scramble time, time to first radar pickup, time to lock-on and time to splash. We also recorded the number of aborted takeoffs, lost communications, malfunctioning radars and other reasons constituting a failed mission. The bottom line: "effectiveness" was 2, 3 or 4 percent, depending on the generosity of the reviewer. This figure did not even consider that the target was a single aircraft, flying straight and level, taking no evasive action.

Our test had received a reluctant go-ahead by our operations officer and the results were reported to a staff officer at the 12th Air Force Headquarters. Maybe it got to the Pentagon. Who knows? One thing that did come out of it was more flying time for all of us who participated.

Unfortunately, it had its own tragic results, in the loss of two of our aircraft in a midair collision and the loss of John Wurtzel, who was flying the intercepting aircraft. Our instructions, when flying these tests, were to break off just before splash, the reason being that upon completion of splash the intercepting aircraft would pass just below and slightly behind the target, too close for comfort. Wurtzel either had a bad signal at splash or was not quite on target, as his aircraft cut off the tail of the target F-86D. Both pilots were able to bail out, but it turned out John was badly cut up in the process and bled to death. A search had ensued all night and into the morning for him, in which I declined to participate.

Frankly, I was afraid that I might be the one who found him. John had come to the 496th from Nellis the same time I did. We had experienced Escape and Evasion school together, among other activities. He was an excellent pilot and a good friend. A sense of guilt lingers with me to this day.

During these tests, two other incidents occurred, one in which I was involved and the other involving Tom Wilson. Tom had been scrambled to intercept a target coming in from Munich and was somewhere between Ulm and Augsburg when his Aft Fire warning light came on. Upon reducing power, the light did not go out, and Tom turned toward home base about 170 miles distant.

Meanwhile, the GCI site handling his intercept directed the target ship to Tom's aircraft where he could observe its condition. The tailpipe was clearly on fire and the issue became whether Tom should abandon the aircraft or try to make it back to Landstuhl. Over the next 40 minutes, Tom nursed the aircraft down using minimum power and hoping that the fire would not extend further forward.

He finally landed safely, reported the incident, and returned to his barracks, where he woke his roommate to tell him about it. I was his roommate, and I remember telling him that I thought under those conditions, he should have bailed out.

It wasn't more than a week later that I was climbing toward Nuremberg to be the target ship when I experienced several severe jolts coming from the engine, followed by extreme vibrations. When I throttled back to idle, the vibrations ceased. Efforts to increase power brought back the vibrations, so I turned the aircraft toward Frankfurt as the nearest place to land. I was about 100 miles southeast of the Rhein-Main International Airport. It was immediately apparent I would not get there in idle. What to do?

It was a beautiful night, with scattered cumulus clouds and a full moon. Suddenly, at 10 o'clock low, I saw what looked like an abandoned airfield. I asked Logroll, the GCI site that had been tracking me, if they knew of an airfield in that area. They did. In fact, a sister radar site, with the call sign Dora, happened to be located next to the runway. (This was the third fortunate coincidence in a matter of minutes—moonlight, runway, Dora.) When I contacted Dora control, the operator explained that the runway was under repair with heavy equipment on site except for the western end. I made a high 360 over the field and decided it was worth a try.

Keeping the field in sight and still in idle, I made another 360, using my flaps to land at the far end of the runway. With a final adjustment, I landed just beyond a crane and bulldozer. My drag chute operated perfectly, and I was able to stop while still on the runway.

After landing, I learned that the radar operator, Lieutenant Ken Norris, who directed the headlights of his jeep at the equipment on the runway, was a classmate of mine at Stanford. Strange!

After some reminiscing, one of the airmen drove me back to Landstuhl. It was late when I woke Tom Wilson, my roommate. Tom is a very sound sleeper and doesn't like to be awakened. All he said was, "Bullshit, Weeden, you're making it up," and he went back to sleep.

Naturally, I felt pretty good about how I handled the emergency until my debriefing in the morning with Captain Murphy, our maintenance officer. He wanted to know everything that happened. He asked me what the fuel pressure gauge said, and the oil pressure and God knows what other readings he wanted.

I left the briefing thinking I did a pretty lousy job in the eyes of Captain Murphy.

This story has two endings. One occurred about two weeks later, when I ran into Captain Murphy. In the meantime, maintenance had gone over to Giebelstadt, the name of the abandoned airfield (and one of the few from which the German "Düsenjägers" flew). They replaced the engine, smoothed out the damaged fuselage and had some of the equipment moved, after which Captain Murphy flew the plane back to Landstuhl. When I next saw "Murphy of few words," as he was called, he looked me over and said, finally, "Weeden, I don't know how you landed without busting your ass."

The real significance of bringing the aircrafts home and not bailing out was the opportunity for maintenance and safety to analyze what had gone wrong. Both aircraft, complete with the new J-47 engine, had flown about 500 hours, quite a bit more than other aircraft to date. The analysis pointed out several weaknesses that were developing, called metal fatigue, and was critical to correcting the problem.

The other ending occurred six months later, when Wilson and I received the Air Medal in front of the entire Wing, standing at attention in subzero weather. Both of us were surprised, and pleased, with the award, but we saw nothing about what we did as being brave or courageous. We had no other choice except to bail out or take our chances landing at night onto unknown terrain.

Two other Air Medals were awarded to Lieutenant William Chambers and Airman Munoz, both from the 496th. They were operating a mobile control unit at the end of the active runway when an aircraft from our sister squadron crashed just short of the runway and ended up upside-down. The two of them, without hesitation, rushed to the aircraft and, using the Bowie knife Bill always carried, dug the pilot out and dragged him to safety just before the aircraft caught fire and exploded. Quite a difference between what they did and what Tom and I had done.

During this period, the squadron made its first trip to Wheelus Air Base, located just outside Tripoli, the capital of Libya, on the southern shore of the Mediterranean Sea. We spent four weeks in gunnery practice, testing the capability of the on-board E4 fire-control radar and our ability as pilots to respond correctly to its instructions from lock-on to splash. Splash included the actual firing of the rockets at a target sleeve towed by a B-43 jet bomber. This created its little adventures when the radar was not calibrated correctly or the rockets flew in unpredictable directions after being fired.

It was one of those blissful months. We lived out of Quonset huts on desert soil right next to a beach with nothing to do but fly, play volleyball and swim. Some went to see the old Roman ruins along the coast. My only trip was by bike to the end of the active runway when a Wing of B-47s landed in the space of an hour. I counted over 40 aircraft swooping down in precision-timed landings, four powerful engines purring, flaps full down and a gaggle of wheels reaching out for the ground. I learned that they had come from a dozen different locations around the world and were part of a globe-spanning exercise that demonstrated the awesome reach of our Strategic Air Command (SAC). This was 1955. I was impressed, and I'm sure most of the Arabs watching the scene were impressed as well.

My friend Stretch and I were given the job of obtaining the liquor for the officer's party to be held on the last Saturday of our month at Wheelus. The city of Tripoli, being in a Muslim country, had no liquor stores, and the officer's club on the base pleaded short supply. The alternative was flying to the island of Malta, where we were told liquor was available at discount prices.

We left early in the morning in two T-33s and planned to spend the day sightseeing while we ordered the liquor and had it placed in the rear cockpit, five cases per aircraft. It was a beautiful day and Malta was absorbing. The picturesque harbor was filled with all types of ships of the British Navy, and the stone houses were crowded on top of one another reaching from the low hills surrounding the bay to the very edge of the water. The streets were lined with quaint little shops offering tax-free goods from all over the world.

Mom had always talked about the lacework from Malta, so I spent much of the day going from one shop to another trying to get a handle on price vs. quality. I finally made a purchase that was well received at home. It was close to sundown before we returned to the airbase for our flight back to Wheelus.

The operations officer at the Malta base was a talkative chap who enjoyed the occasional visit by a couple of U.S. fighter pilots. He casually mentioned that the last visit involved two F-84 fighter-bomber pilots who neglected to consider the high noonday temperature when calculating how much runway they needed. They were unaware of the radar shack just off the end of the active runway, with the result that the wingman sheared off his gear on takeoff. "Ruddy bad luck." It was a casual sort of reaction you would expect from a Brit, and so we casually absorbed the information. We finished our flight plan, taking into account it was evening and the cool offshore breeze was rapidly dropping the runway temperature.

We took off separately and intended to join up and fly back together. To my surprise, I never saw nor heard from Stretch until we met again in the operations room at Wheelus. He straggled in about 10 minutes after me, looking very white and a bit shaken. As Stretch told it: "After gaining speed, I was unable to lift my nose gear, as the stick would not go back beyond neutral position.

Meanwhile, the concrete radar shack was looming ever closer. Finally, the nose gear hit a bump in the runway and bounced up on its own accord, which allowed me to miss that shack by no more than a cat's whisker." The culprit, of course, was the five cases of liquor stacked up on the rear seat, preventing the "tandem" stick from moving further to the rear. Insult was added to this almost-disaster when we discovered that several of the bottles were empty.

In early fall of 1955, the squadron was notified that it had won the Hughes Trophy as the outstanding fighter interceptor squadron of the U.S. Air Force worldwide for the year. The award was determined by such things as percentage of aircraft "operational ready," level of radar systems "functioning" and number of sorties flown. I like to think that our effectiveness tests contributed to our being considered.

After my trip to Zermatt, I returned to Switzerland several times to visit Vera Knauer, the Swissair stewardess I met flying from Geneva to London. Initially refusing to see me, she accepted my invitation to go skiing over New Year's. That began a relationship where we went skiing at various resorts in Switzerland and France whenever our respective flying schedules allowed.

Mom came over in May to visit. She hoped we could drive through Italy during the height of the spring, as far south as Naples. Mom met Vera in Lucerne, Switzerland, arranged by me, to keep her entertained until I could pick her up on our way to Italy. By coincidence when we were in Rome, Vera's schedule brought all three of us together for an evening.

We had dinner at a small outdoor café, just off the Via Nazionale, when, due to an innocent misunderstanding by the waiter, Vera and I agreed to marry. The waiter had assumed we were celebrating our engagement and had brought us an after-dinner drink as his contribution. Vera and I had talked about marriage but hadn't quite gotten around to making a decision. On Mom's insistence, Vera translated what he had said to her in Italian. As a result, Vera and I exchanged looks which said "Why not?" and with that we explained "Yes, we have decided to get married."

Mom proceeded to drop her glass onto the stone floor, which provided a shattering exclamation point to her complete surprise (and probably some anxiety in "losing her baby"). Mother recouped sufficiently to write a nice "welcoming letter" while we were driving home through Florence. The wedding was set for September 30 in Basel, Switzerland, where Vera's mother lived, along with four of her siblings.

Tom Wilson agreed to be my best man and organized a bachelor party with my classmates from Nellis before we left for Basel. It was held at the Ramstein Officer's Club. It was the usual toasting and roasting. I was soon feeling no pain. The next thing I remember was waking up cuddled around a pine tree somewhere on the Ramstein Air Base. It was early morning. The sun had barely risen and there was an autumn chill in the air. I found the entrance gate, crossed the road to Landstuhl and sought the privacy of my base officers' quarters.

Some of the others did not fare so well. Bill Leitch gunned his Thunderbird while in reverse when leaving the parking lot and smashed into a lamppost. Four others continued to party outside the protection of the officer's club and were taken into custody by the Air Police. This required the squadron's operations officer to obtain their release. Tom Lowery almost made it back to his apartment in the married officers housing complex, where he was found the next morning sleeping quietly on the fire escape one floor down from his destination.

I found out later that when I passed out they planned to have me immobilized by means of a hip cast courtesy of a doctor "friend" of mine. They had the "passing out" right, but lost track of their patient.

(Note: These were the same men, minus Tom and me, who later on the evening of November 4, 1956, interrupted their partying at the officer's club to help fly, in foul weather conditions and without incident, the entire squadron of F-86Ds to Hahn Air Base as a precaution against a possible escalation of the Soviet Army entering Hungary.)

The wedding went off smoothly. Mom was the only one from my family attending, but there were many Rheinbergers and Notzes to make it a lively celebration. Mom had arrived two days before and stayed at the 250-year-old Three Kings Hotel (Les Trois Rois), where she enjoyed a spacious suite overlooking the Rhine River as it made the turn north running through Germany to the North Sea. There was one little hiccup. The weather was unusually cold and Mom asked whether they would mind turning up the heat a bit. The answer was so Swiss: "We are sorry, but we have never turned on the heat until the first of October."

After a short honeymoon, Vera and I returned to our newly rented apartment in Dansenberg, a 15-minute drive from the base. With her marriage, Vera could no longer fly for Swissair. Her efforts to obtain a marriage visa to the United States were complicated by her birth in Athens where, due to the war, her original birth certificate was lost. She quickly settled into the life of this small village tucked away in the upper end of a hidden valley off the beaten track.

Dansenberg was surrounded by cultivated fields and soft meadows that ended abruptly at the edge of a crowded but neatly groomed forest. Her main language being German, Vera quickly came to know the local shopkeepers who provided their individual specialties: meat, dairy or fresh vegetables. Also, in the apartment below, there was a couple from Frankfurt, whose background and education were more suitable to Vera's, and they became good friends. This was fortunate, as the squadron was soon to leave for another month in Tripoli.

I had told my squadron commander, Colonel Habeck, that I had decided not to extend my military service beyond May of 1956. It wasn't a hard decision, as I was anxious to go home and start my career with Weeden & Co. Nevertheless, I was tempted to consider staying when a Captain White from 12th Air Force, Adjutant to Major General Lee, suggested there might be a role for me as the General's aide if I would extend for another four years. I had first met Captain White after winning the 12th Air Force Handball Championship with Sergeant Estrada, also from the 496th. He told me the general had played handball at West Point and wanted to take up the game again. He had had the squash court at Ramstein modified with a tin stretched across the front row and was looking for someone to work out with. This I did, and it led to many of my fellow pilots taking up the game. As for the offer, or maybe offer, I ended up turning it down.

My decision not to extend affected my flight time against the rag, although I got more than enough time flying chase while the others had their head in the cockpit practicing for an Air Force–wide competition to be held the following year. My only excitement was flying down as wingman to our new Commander, Colonel Habeck. His landing pattern at Pisa was so wide that he lost sight of the airfield on downwind. I was focused on staying close to him as he bounced up and down and changed throttle settings. Luckily, we spotted the leaning tower with its head above the smog and got ourselves reoriented.

Over the next few months, I still got my share of flying, although a good bit of it was in a T-33 flying cross country. The one with Hank Zinke in the rear seat was the most fun and rather exciting to boot. We took off from Landstuhl on a beautiful spring day bound for Naples' Capodichino Airport with a full tank of fuel and the whole weekend to do whatever we wished. I had my Bolex camera with me and took a whole roll of film as we flew over the Alps.

When we arrived, we had plenty of fuel remaining, so I flew south to Capri and the Amalfi Drive and pointed out the places I had visited with Mom. Then we flew to Mount Vesuvius and circled several times before heading back up to the airport. Plenty of fuel left for an easy landing. After reporting in to the tower and being cleared for landing, I made a neat 360 overhead pattern, lowering my gear while turning onto final approach. Only two of the three landing gear lights showed green; the nose gear light remained red. No sweat! We notified tower that we were going around to make another approach. Communications were not the best, but they seemed to understand.

This time, I used a normal approach pattern, giving us more time to lower the gear while straight and level. Same thing occurred. We notified tower that we were declaring an emergency and would they please put some foam on the runway. This was not easily understood by the tower, and it took several minutes to get across to them what our problem was. Meanwhile, the remaining fuel was being used up rapidly as we tooled around at sea level. Hank and I concluded that foam or not, we had only one more pass available. As we set up our pattern, we could see a lot of trucks racing down the runway. We stretched out the final approach to allow the trucks to do their spraying and put the gear handle into the down position. Glory be! They all showed green. We landed without incident.

Toward the end of my flying days in the F-86D, I finally had that experience one never wants to have. It involved a friendly dogfight with a pilot flying an F-86F out of Hahn Air Base. We had spotted each other somewhere between our respective bases at an altitude of around 25,000 feet. We identified ourselves by radio and then switched to a little-used channel to communicate in private. We agreed to fly in opposite directions for a minute and then turn toward each other.

As we closed, I began to climb, as he did, while initiating a circling maneuver to seek an advantage. By advantage, I mean the ability to slip in behind him and claim a "kill." But just being behind was not enough. As long as he maintained a tight turn, I could not point my nose (and rockets) far enough ahead of his aircraft to make the claim. This is similar to what one does when shooting birds or skeet. The maneuver is called a "Lufbery." Normally, the two aircraft descend while maintaining airspeed just above stall. In our case, having begun the engagement while climbing, our airspeeds decreased and the angle of the aircraft became more vertical.

I had the heavier plane and was gaining less altitude while benefiting from my afterburner's added thrust, which kept me from stalling while going slightly slower. This allowed me to slip neatly behind and below my adversary, who was now squarely in my gun sights. Suddenly, his aircraft stalled out and began to fall off on one wing—10 tons of metal falling straight toward me. I had no ability to maneuver out of his way, being an inch from stalling myself. I can still see it all in slow motion, the aircraft above me gently rolling and dropping directly toward me. Not a word was said by either of us. He passed close enough for me to see a face as white as mine.

While I'm at it, I will recount another flying adventure (sort of) where wiser heads finally prevailed to head off an informal reprimand—or worse.

When I arrived in Germany, I discovered that dollars had more purchasing power there, especially German-made products in the government-run PXs. When I saw a Bolex 16 mm movie camera, manufactured in East Germany, selling for $600, it was too good to pass up. At the time it was the premier movie camera selling below $10,000. It had three separate lenses, wide angle, telescopic and normal, all situated on a swivel that allowed for easy rotation.

With the arrival of all-weather and night capability, the U.S. and NATO began upgrading the landing lights of their more active bases. The first bases included Landstuhl and Soesterberg, a NATO airfield near Utrecht in the Netherlands.

Somehow, the higher-ups learned of my purchase and inquired whether it could be used to test the relative effectiveness of the two newly installed systems under actual nighttime and weather conditions. I thought it could, if we mounted the camera on a piece of iron stretched across the forward cockpit of a T-33. It would have to be high enough to clear the instrument panel and be able to swivel right and left. The idea was to take a series of motion pictures from all possible approach angles: high-low, left-right, night and weather, to determine the relative merits (brightness/clarity) of the two systems.

Floyd Woody and I were assigned a T-33 and all the Kodak film we could use. I would fly front seat and be in charge of the camera while "Woody" would handle the approaches from the back seat. No one, including me, considered the possibility of having to bail out. The bar for the camera mount would have made it difficult to impossible if it came to that.

We started with the tests at Landstuhl and found that our contraption worked perfectly. The weather was accommodating, and we completed our runs in short order. Then it was off to Soesterberg. We had plenty of film at our disposal, so we decided to film the countryside on the flight up, some at low level and some, as you would suspect, at very low level. Then the idea came to us that we could make up a little travel film to show the ladies what Germany looked like from the air.

After finishing the project at Soesterberg, we started back to Landstuhl. By this time the idea had blossomed a bit to include a section where we would fly along one of the autobahns and make it appear that we flew under one or two of the overpasses along the way. So the next week, Woody and I took my Volkswagen down the same Autobahn with top down and filmed as we drove under the same overpasses.

The airmen in the photography section of the 12th Air Force were very cooperative. They even created and spliced into the reel little headings that explained what was being shown and conversations that Woody and I were having as we were making our runs. One I remember was, "How about the overpass ahead? And Woody replying, "Let's go for it."

We had most of it put together when we decided to test it on some of our peer group to see where we could make improvements before the grand showing. The reaction was instant and unanimous: "Fantastic! Hilarious! But don't show it to any of the higher-ups—or the women. So much for a good idea.

The daily commute from our apartment in Dansenberg would vary depending on traffic. I would brag to Vera each time I reduced the trip by a minute or two. One afternoon, after picking me up at the alert hangar, she proudly told me that she had beaten my best time by a minute. "Amazing," I thought. Later, Tom Stafford, who traveled much the same route to the base, described an incident that had occurred a few days earlier. "As I began to cross the bridge at Vogelweh (a narrow bridge that had a fairly sharp incline at both ends), a silver-blue VW convertible began passing me. Ahead of us there was a large Army truck bearing down rapidly. That little bug finally passed me and squiggled back to its side of the road with barely inches to spare. Amazing how close it was." Tom, a very precise person, was not want to exaggerating. I thought "lucky" was more appropriate than "amazing."

And so, an exciting four years of flying came to an end. They allowed me to fly when planes were available right to the end. There were engagements with the Canucks and the day-fighter jocks based at Hahn and Bitberg. There was also the final split-S from 45,000 feet, forcing the Dog through the sound barrier. And, finally, that last flight when the sky was all mine; lazy turns at altitude, gazing down through scattered clouds for a final glimpse of Germany. Returning to base alone as the sun was setting, I throttled back to idle and drifted slowly down through layers of stratus as the sky turned from blue to grey. The sun would disappear and then reappear and disappear again, bathing the clouds in unforgettable hues of yellow and red. The silence, the beauty, the freedom; it was a wonderful ending to my four years in the United States Air Force.

Note: As of this writing, many of those mentioned in this chapter have died: Stretch Riddle, Bill Leitch, Tom Wilson, Rick Lamp. Other close friends—Jim Blake, Jim Morrison, Larry Rouse—are still hanging around, but the gang is thinning out.

Back in 2005, we had our reunion in Seattle. Jan and Marilyn Barmore were host and hostess. Jim Morrison, the artist who painted the watercolors, and I decided it was time to make up a history of the 496th FIS during its first four years, starting at Hamilton and going through the time it was located at Landstuhl. With 50 years having gone by, we wanted to record everyone's remembrances and stories before they drifted away. We called the book *Dog Days* in honor of the plane we flew.

The effort was imperfect in many ways, but it served its purpose of documenting the lives and full military experience of most every officer and pilot in the squadron at that time. I find it helpful to keep my memory current on those years and those men, for whom I have the highest respect.

2nd Lieutenant Don, leaving
Weeden & Co.'s Manhattan apartment
(14 W. Ninth Street) to play squash
before taking off for Landstuhl Air Base,
West Germany, 1954.

F-86D with colors of
496th Fighter Interceptor
Squadron and
squadron insignia.

F-86Ds
parked at
Landstuhl
Air Base
near
Kaister-
slautern,
West
Germany.

12th Air Force medley swim team (right): Jack Nelson, butterfly; Don, backstroke; unidentified, freestyle.

Members of C Flight, 496th Fighter Interceptor Squadron, Landstuhl Air Base (clockwise from upper left): Tom Wilson, Stanley Batt (flight leader), John Wurtzel, Don, Jeb Blount.

Don's Air Medal, August 1955.

FIRST LT. DONALD E. WEEDEN ON A PRACTICE NIGHT INTERCEPT MISSION FELT A SUDDEN JOLT FOLLOWED BY SEVERE VIBRATIONS IN HIS F-86D, HE IMMEDIATELY RETARDED HIS THROTTLE AND SWITCHED TO THE EMERGENCY FUEL SYSTEM.

REALIZING THAT HE COULD NOT MAKE IT HOME HE ASKED GCI THE STATUS OF A NEARBY AIR FIELD. GCI ADVISED THAT ONLY TWO THIRDS OF THE RUNWAY WAS USABLE... THE OTHER THIRD WAS TORN UP AND HAD HEAVY EQUIPMENT ON IT. CONTINUING HIS GLIDE HE CAUGHT A GLIMPSE OF THE RUNWAY AND DECIDED TO ATTEMPT A LANDING.

HE ASKED GCI TO CONTACT SOMEONE TO MARK, WITH THE LIGHTS OF A MOTOR VEHICLE, WHERE THE USABLE PART OF THE RUNWAY BEGAN. COMING OVER THE FIELD IN A FLAME OUT PATTERN HE COULD SEE THE LIGHTS OF TWO VEHICLES ABOUT ONE THIRD DOWN THE RUNWAY.

RAISING THE GEAR IN ORDER TO ADJUST HIS PATTERN FOR TOUCHDOWN BEYOND THE VEHICLES HE MANEUVERED OVER THE EQUIPMENT ON THE APPROACH. THEN LOWERED GEAR AND FLAPS AND LANDED ON THE 3,000 FEET OF THE USABLE RUNWAY — WITH THE DRAG CHUTE HE STOPPED THE AIRCRAFT ON THE RUNWAY!!

JANUARY, 1956

As Luck Would Have It

Montage of the F-86D in paintings by Jim Morrison, a pilot in the 496th FIS (clockwise from top left): "In formation"; "Looking for Canucks"; "Touching down"; "Keeping it close"; "Scramble toward the East Zone"; "Night weather letdown"; (center) on final at Wheelus AFB, Tripoli, Libya.

Chapter 10
Five Months in a Volkswagen

The title is accurate. Vera was in agreement that we should move to the U.S. and live in New York. She had looked forward to flying to New York as a Swissair stewardess, but that opportunity ended with marriage. Instead, after my discharge from the Air Force at Landstuhl Air Base, we decided to take a trip by car to cities she had flown to with Swissair. They included Rome, Cairo, Beirut, Athens and Istanbul.

That itinerary fit with my interest in visiting some of the centers of antiquity I had studied in my Western Civilization course at Stanford. We decided to take enough time and see as much as possible before settling into a life of business and family.

Those plans expanded to a five-month Grand Tour, covering most of Italy, Egypt, Lebanon, Jordan, Syria, Turkey, Greece and Yugoslavia; then through Switzerland and France, over to England and Scotland, and back to Germany. Five months on $1,500, or $10 a day—all the money we had in my bank account.

In early May of 1956, Vera and I began our five-month adventure, using my Volkswagen convertible as our primary sleeping quarters. There were some exceptions: three nights in a cave outside Damascus and four nights as guest of the director of Egypt's Antiquities Service. In Istanbul, I stayed at the American Hospital and Vera at the Istanbul Hilton. Our budget of $10 a day kept us in the VW most of the time.

With the help of the German mechanics at the Landstuhl Motor Pool, I had the front seats modified to move farther forward and the back rest altered to lie horizontal. By removing all baggage from the rear seat area, the space provided just enough room to extend our air mattresses full length.

The first test of this arrangement came after leaving Bologna and driving up the steep mountain grades toward Florence. Night descended and the clouds hung ominously. We found a level spot next to the highway. We unloaded our baggage outside under a tarp and had the air mattresses blown up tight when the downpour began.

The German mechanics also created a small compartment behind the dashboard. This became our safe deposit box for my newly acquired Italian Beretta .32-caliber pistol and our American Express traveler's checks. (Passports and wallet were always with us.) I purchased the official maintenance manual for the VW cabriolet and some basic tools and obtained a set of World Aeronautical Charts covering the entire route of our trip. We took my 16mm Bolex movie camera, a dozen rolls of film left over from filming the landing lights, and a Kodak still camera.

We took minimum clothing; one outfit for traveling and another for formal events. Vera's consisted of a colorful peasant skirt and blouse and a simple black shift. For cooking we took a small two-burner propane stove plus the obvious accessories.

Visas were a problem. You could not get them from any of the Arab countries (Egypt, Lebanon, Jordan and Syria) if you already had one from Israel. And if you obtained a visa from Israel afterwards, the Arabs would not allow you to enter their country. Fortunately, the ancient sites of interest to us were in Arab countries, which, at the time, included the old section of Jerusalem.

We took travel brochures, auto maps, a book on how to read and converse in Arabic, and a beautiful book on Egyptian Art by the Swiss publisher Skira. Last but not least was a pump for the air mattresses. Our budget of $1,500 included the cost of visas, air mattresses, pistol, boat tickets, travel books, etc. Our itinerary was not fixed in stone. This flexibility allowed for several unusual adventures. We were young and adventurous—naive, but confident.

In the preceding year and a half, I had learned something about Vera's past. She was 25, a month and a half younger than I, and was born in Athens, Greece. Her father, Kurt Knauer, was a German engineer working under contract for a German construction firm. Her mother, Hildegard Rheinberger, a German Fräulein, had left her family to seek adventure and a job in Athens. Little is known of Herr Knauer except that he was originally from Leipzig, Germany, and had been previously married. Soon after Vera's birth, he was killed in an automobile accident. Hildegard and her newborn daughter returned to Basel, Switzerland. With little in the way of resources, Hildegard took up the work of a seamstress.

Hildegard was the second-youngest of seven children born to Herr and Frau Rheinberger, who came from Leipzig. Herr Rheinberger managed a series of industrial-type companies; the family moved almost as often as a new child was born.

This lifestyle finally proved impossible for Frau Rheinberger, who separated from her husband and moved with three of the children to Freiburg, north of Basel. The political situation in Germany (1937) grew more difficult for them due to their outspoken attitude toward the Nazi party. Frau Rheinberger then moved to Basel, Switzerland, where two of her children were living: Hildegard with daughter Vera in the center of Basel, and Lillie, who was married to Herr Doktor Emil Notz, director of Swiss Radio

International in Basel. Frau Rheinberger, with her children Ilse and Richard, moved into Dr. Notz's spacious home, situated on the Bruderholz, a farming neighborhood bordering the city.

At the age of six, Vera had been diagnosed with tuberculosis and was taken to Davos, known the world over for its work in curing TB. She stayed in a sanitarium similar to the one described by Thomas Mann in his epic 1924 novel The Magic Mountain. It offered a quiet environment and the pure, infection-free air of the Swiss Alps.

After a long period with no improvement, Vera's mother brought her to a sanitarium in the Black Forest, where the infection finally came to a head and was operated on successfully. At this point, Vera was old enough to enter high school. Vera moved in with her two aunts, Ilse and Lillie, who had convinced Hildegard that it was better for Vera's health if she stayed with them in their spacious house on "Der Bruderholz."

Upon graduation, Vera entered a school for languages in Neuchâtel. After two years, despite the family's opposition (or to spite their opposition), Vera applied and was accepted by Swissair as a stewardess. She moved to Kloten bei Zurich, where the international airport was located. She had been flying for almost two years when I met her in October 1954 on a night flight from Geneva to London. Our marriage in September 1955 ended her career with Swissair. Our move to Dansenberg prevented her from continuing her study of law at the university in Zurich.

In early May, we began our journey by driving south into Switzerland and then through a tunnel below Altdorf that took us from the cold northern edge of the Alps into the sun-drenched land of Italy. We passed by Lake Como, skirted Milan and were soon driving on the main road running along the Po Valley toward the walled city of Bologna. The top was down, the sun poured in and we felt as free as the birds flying above us. The highway was only two lanes, but we were in no hurry.

Suddenly, a small Fiat sped past us. It was filled with men who took a lot of pleasure in passing our little VW. A little later, I was right behind them and a large, slow-moving truck. The road ahead was clear, and I shot ahead of both Fiat and truck, waving pleasantly as I passed. This was enough to stimulate the race-driver mentality of all Italians. For the next 10 miles, we alternated the lead position several times. The game was to gauge the distance of the oncoming traffic to pass at the moment when the other would not have enough space to get back in time—a variation of "chicken." Each time one passed the other, there was lots of waving and laughter.

Vera was not happy at all. It was an early indication of what she had married.

Florence turned out to be a one-day stopover filled with art museums. I pointed out the modest pensione near the bridge spanning the Arno River where Mom wrote Vera the note apologizing for dropping her glass and welcoming her into the family.

We spent more time visiting Rome, with which Vera was quite familiar from her overnight trips with Swissair. Then, a nonstop drive to Naples and a shorter drive to the tiny village of Paestum on the coast south of Salerno. We found a field in which to set up for the night in anticipation of visiting the little-known and seldom-visited Doric temple built by a colony of Greeks in the early 6th century B.C. Our plan was to visit it in the morning.

We awakened to a gentle nudge from a man who introduced himself as Francesco, the owner of the field. Vera used her limited Italian to introduce us in return. Americans were well thought of in these parts, being remembered for their heroic effort while landing at Salerno. The conversation ended with the man inviting us to attend his daughter's wedding (two days away) and to join his family for dinner. That evening began four days of celebration in which we became the special guests of the bride-to-be and were welcomed as celebrities by the wedding party.

That evening we were introduced to the informality of Italian family life in a small rural community. The dinner was held in a small room with a large table that managed to accommodate everyone. The family's first married daughter breastfed her latest child while enjoying spaghetti and the excitement of having two guests visiting from far away. We slept in the same field and were awakened again by our host, who brought us breakfast and a gift: a small vase he had found near the temple. It was worth every mile getting there.

We visited the temple, after which we searched for a shop that carried items suitable for a wedding present. The only store we found specialized in glassware, and we were able to buy a nice set of dinner glasses that fit our budget.

The next day, the day of the wedding. started by visiting the family and sitting around the wall of a large meeting room sipping a sweet greenish liquor (not crème de menthe) with Vera testing her Italian. From there we began a 2-mile march past the temple to the main church in Paestum. The church was overflowing, as was the courtyard outside. Inside were the women; outside were the men, chatting.

Before we joined the festivities, we deposited our present in a room already filled with other presents. There were at least a dozen sets of glasses unwrapped and on display. Now the penny dropped why the saleslady in the store had apologized for the lack of selection.

The traditional four days of celebration began immediately in a beautiful courtyard filled with old olive trees and tables laden with bread, cheese, fruits and wine. We ate, and drank, and danced, and wondered how they could continue for three more days. When I think about it now, the film Mamma Mia! comes to mind. Later that evening, we returned to our field for an early start back to Naples to catch the boat to Alexandria, Egypt.

The boat from Naples arrived in Alexandria harbor mid-morning. We declared our VW "personal and not for resale." Its unloading took time and involved much quibbling over fees and tips. All was complicated by our not having local currency. There was no Thomas Cook or American Express office to change our traveler's checks. Somehow everything was resolved, but the day was shot for any sightseeing. The fees and tips blew our carefully planned budget.

Our map showed that there was only one road to Cairo that one could call a "highway." We began driving with our now-established plan of camping along the way and outside the built-up areas. The highway ran beside one of the many channels of the Nile, which north of Cairo spreads out into a broad delta as it approaches the Mediterranean. After an hour or so, we found an area off the road that seemed quiet and suitable for camping.

As we began emptying the car, people began to gather around us; first they came in ones and twos, and then it seemed as if whole families were showing up. They were quiet, obviously curious. They squatted down in a circle at some distance. We couldn't see where they lived—the only building in sight was a small power transformer station with a little mud hut beside it.

It became impossible to ignore our visitors, and we tried to engage in some friendly exchanges. This resulted in the children becoming more talkative, edging closer and finally putting their hands out for anything we might be willing to give them. It became rather uncomfortable, with a growing concern that it would get out of control. We had decided to pack up and leave when there appeared a gentleman who, with great authority and clapping of hands, managed to disperse the crowd.

The man appeared friendly and lived in the mud hut beside the transformer station. He only spoke Arabic but seemed intelligent and of a class above the others. He gestured for us to spend the night, and we moved our baggage and auto next to his modest dwelling. We set up our Coleman stove, which intrigued him immensely. Vera cooked some spaghetti, which we shared, and we ate something or other which he prepared. When it grew dark, we brought out our flashlight, also something intriguing, and began reading from our English/Arabic phrase book.

Finally, we all retired, he to his room with his dogs and we to the other room, which we learned the next morning normally housed his dogs.

Vera and I combined our two sleeping bags and crawled in for the night. I was comfortable throughout, but Vera seemed agitated and troubled by a growing itchiness in her private parts. At daybreak, whatever was bothering her became too much, so we got up and decided to depart immediately after making the normal pleasantries. A fearsome rash had developed and was quite painful. Of course, what had happened was that the dog's colony of fleas had been left behind in the room to torture Vera, leaving me unbitten.

Reaching Cairo, we found a hospital and had Vera attended to while I found an inexpensive hotel where we stayed until she recovered. Our youth, nationalities and mode of travel were unusual to those we met. We were given a lot of help in planning our sightseeing around Cairo and the drive south to Luxor.

The pyramids appear on the horizon as soon as one leaves Cairo going south. After a guided tour, we camped in an area with an unobstructed view of the three pyramids and the Sphinx, complete with sun slowly setting behind them. Our destination was now Luxor, and we were in no hurry. We stopped along the way and visited a couple of schools. We were welcomed by those in charge and were shown their modern facilities with pride. The teachers knew either English or French and enjoyed meeting us. The children were in uniform and orderly. The teachers had lots of questions, as we did.

The main subject was Israel. We were surprised at the level of hatred expressed. It was reflected in the paintings by the children displayed along the corridors. Colonel Gamel Abdul Nasser ran the country at the time and was constantly using incendiary language toward Israel. (It was less than five months when war between Egypt and Israel broke out over who controlled the Suez Canal: the Suez Crisis of 1956.)

We were the only tourists on the road to Luxor (400 miles). It was the beginning of the hot season, war was in the air, and traveling by auto along a partially dirt highway was not the method of choice for travelers. The redeeming factors in doing it "our way" were cost and the absence of traffic.

In Asyut, we visited a missionary school run by the British. We were invited to stay overnight by the director and his wife. The dinner conversation was dominated by our host's desire to hear from the outside world and our interest in the local culture and attitudes. Asyut had a large Coptic Christian community. The hysteria over Israel was diminished here, while concern for the non-Muslim population in general was openly discussed.

We arrived at the outskirts of Luxor in mid-afternoon and located a picturesque place to camp at the edge of the Nile. It overlooked one of the typical wells seen all along the Nile: a bullock tethered to a long pole connected to a vertical shaft that draws the water as the animal stoically circles the well.

Not far away was the vast complex of temples, pylons, statuary and assorted buildings known as Karnak. Our guidebook explained that the structures were built over a period of 1000 years, beginning in about 2000 BC and spanning the eras known as the Middle and New Kingdoms. On our map it looked enormous. Exploring it even cursorily would take more than a day, and we were eager to get started.

The main entrance was reached along an avenue bordered by ram-headed sphinxes. We had no sooner purchased our tickets, reached the Great Hypostyle Hall, opened our guidebook and craned our necks to take in the height of the pillars when an attendant came and told us it was closing time. It was not yet 4 o'clock, with plenty of daylight remaining. We complained that they shouldn't have sold us the tickets if they were about to close. Everyone was sorry, but it was impossible to return the entry fee. The language barrier prevented any extended discussion over fairness and other solutions, like letting us in free the next day. There was nothing we could do about it except return to our campsite.

I drove into Luxor to find a gas station that could repair the tube on our spare tire. I found a gas pump beside the road and a number of locals hanging around. One of them agreed to fix the tube and would have it ready in an hour. Back at our campsite, Vera was cooking dinner. Over dinner we watched the Nile sweeping by and a large yellow sun disappear behind the hills to the west. When I returned to the gas station, I found my Good Samaritan sitting cross-legged on the ground with needle and thread, stitching the tear in the tube back together again.

We returned early the next morning to Karnak to resume our visit. We had decided that in fairness we did not have to pay for another ticket. We left the car in their parking area and circled the outside wall by foot until we found a break in the wall. Then we made ourselves as inconspicuous as possible while visiting one extraordinary architectural wonder after another. It was the most impressive collection of ancient architecture on our whole trip.

By midday, we were hot, exhausted and ready to cross the river to the Valley of the Kings. Our auto was parked just beyond the Karnak entry gate. If they hadn't noticed our illegal presence already, they would surely see us exiting and want us to buy another ticket. We sauntered pass the ticket office without stopping. Halfway down the Avenue of the Sphinxes, we heard shouting behind us. We accelerated our pace to the car and were quickly out of there.

The Valley of the Kings lies directly west of Luxor on the other side of the Nile. To get there, we had to drive 70 miles south to a town called Edfu, cross a bridge, and then drive back 70 miles north again to the road leading into the sacred valley.

Before starting south, we visited the Temple of Luxor, another extraordinary site situated close to the Nile. A shop nearby was selling artifacts. Among many beautifully carved alabaster vases and other modern pieces of art, the owner cautiously showed us some carvings and pieces of wall paintings that he said came from tombs of the Middle Kingdom. They were broken and imperfect, yet enough remained to give the appearance of age and authenticity. We decided to splurge and spend £7 ($20) for a selection of figures carved from basalt and red granite. The owner wrapped them tightly and told us not to mention their origin, as it was prohibited to take antiques out of the country. Twenty dollars poorer but happy with our purchases, we spent the last four hours of daylight driving 140 miles to end up just across the Nile from where we started.

It was dark when we pulled off the road and prepared our little VW for bed. We were right on the edge of the Nile and could hear its purring as it slowly moved north. There was not a person, building, or tree in sight on our side of the river. It was an eerie feeling, and a bit uncomfortable. To feel safer, I decided to take my Beretta out of its secret compartment—just in case.

Daybreak found us safe and sound, and hungry. Vera went through the morning routine of boiling water for coffee and making breakfast while I surveyed our aerial map. It showed a dramatic division between the cultivated greensward along the edge of the Nile and the stark waterless terrain beyond.

Our destination today was the Valley of the Kings, the burial site of the Pharaohs who reigned during the Middle Kingdom (2000 to 1500 B.C.). From our sumptuous riverside accommodations, we drove through a narrow section of green farmland and then began a long, twisting climb into a narrow valley littered with outcroppings of brown sandstone. Suddenly, the road ended at a one-story Arrival Center, where we waited to purchase tickets into the sacred valley beyond. We were the first visitors of the day, and the ticket window had not yet opened. We took out our book of Egyptian paintings and looked again at what we came to see "in the flesh."

After a time, we were approached by a diminutive gentleman in Western attire but clearly Egyptian in looks. He was immediately curious about

As Luck Would Have It

our book. After glancing at the photos, he apologized for not introducing himself. He said, "I am Ibrahim Kemal, the Director of Antiquities for the Egyptian Government." After further perusal, added, "This is one of the finest collections of Egyptian tomb art I have seen." He then turned his attention to the two of us.

Brushing away our willingness to buy an entrance ticket, Mr. Kemal insisted on being our personal guide through the Valley of the Kings. He spent the next few hours telling about each of these ancient kings, the high-light being the tomb of Tutankhamen.

Hearing about our sleeping beside the Nile, Mr. Kemal invited us to stay with him. His house originally had been built for the Metropolitan Museum of Art staff during their archaeological excavations here in the early part of the century. When we arrived at his residence, we were greeted by his chief bodyguard, Sheikh Abdel Margoud, a tall, swarthy, ferocious-looking man who said he already knew of us. We were the couple who didn't pay to visit the Karnak complex the day before. When I explained the situation and our reaction, he understood and broke out in a great big smile.

Over dinner, we showed them our artifacts. Both were outraged over the owner's suggestion that they had some value as antiques. Mr. Kemal explained that they were recently made to be sold to naive tourists. They insisted we return them. Mr. Margoud said he would go with us and do the talking. Next morning, the three of us drove back to the river, took the ferry over to Luxor, and reentered the antique shop. After much back and forth, none of which Vera and I understood, the owner agreed to take back the "antiques" and exchange them for two tall and beautifully carved luminescent alabaster vases.

The next three days were a whirlwind of tomb visits, a moonlight eve-ning with Queen Hatshepsut, and lunch with a descendant of the most famous tomb robbers in Egypt. Each morning, when the sun was high enough, Mr. Kemal would have us drive into the desert to an inconspicu-ous mound that housed a tomb not yet shown to the public. An aluminum sheet would be placed to guide the sunlight into the chamber room of some palace nobleman who, presumably, was entombed beyond the farther wall.

We sat cross-legged on the floor and Mr. Kemal read to us the story of this man, his family, his work and his relationship to his Pharaoh, as described in the hieroglyphics on the walls surrounding us. It was mesmer-izing: We were sitting in the midst of this man's life, pictured on his living room walls and painted more than 3,500 years ago—and with him still resting in the next room.

The visit with the queen was a different experience altogether. Queen

Hatshepsut played an important role and had a big ego. She reigned for 20 years, during which the land and people prospered, trade expanded and peace prevailed. She was strong and popular, but she eventually anointed herself King, and was portrayed on later statues with a beard.

One evening, Mr. Kemal escorted us to her temple. The moon was at its fullness; not a cloud, not another visitor, not even the stirring of a breeze disturbed the serenity of the moment. Mr. Kemal told us many stories about her and those times of peace and majesty of the Middle Kingdom. What an experience!

The next day, we had lunch with Sheikh Ali Abdel-Rassoul, the last living descendant of the Abdel-Rassoul family, known as the most infamous tomb robbers in Egypt. He was a large man with a huge mustache. We were accompanied by Mr. Margoud, thankfully, as it was clear from the moment we met Mr. Abdel-Rassoul that he had an eye for Vera—and for me as well. (Later, I read that at age 70, he married a girl of 18.) The four of us had a lunch of pigeon eggs and other delicacies along with wine, while two of Mr. Abdel-Rassoul's armed henchmen stood behind him.

It was an unforgettable four days. We would have spent further time with Mr. Kemal to absorb more of his knowledge, but we had many other places to visit. We decided against driving back to the bridge at Edfu and headed north along the west bank of the Nile with the intention of crossing over at Nagaa Hamadi, 40 miles north. Our World Aeronautical Chart did not show a road along the Nile, but it did indicate a trail going through the desert. The drive began along a dirt road on the edge of woods that ran along the river. A few miles on the road crossed a dry creek bed. The bridge was a raised slab of concrete, on which the VW got stuck trying to go over it. My insistence on trying upset Vera, who then stomped off, totally fed up with me. It took some time to get unstuck and catch up with her. Women from a nearby convent directed us to a seldom-used desert road that we had overlooked.

With the picture of Bedouin tribesmen lurking over the horizon, we started off onto the desert, presumably a shortcut to Nagaa Hamadi. Everything was going smoothly on the hard-packed sand until we became stuck in a small dip that had collected soft sand. The dip was no more than 20 feet wide. I emptied the VW, used our carjack to raise the back wheels, and stuffed every piece of clothing and towel underneath for traction. Over the next hour, with Vera in the driver's seat and me pushing, we managed to walk the auto the 20 feet to hard ground. My lasting image of this is Vera scanning the horizon for Bedouins, switchblade in one hand and the Beretta in the other. The rest of this "venture" was without incident. We arrived back to normal countryside, where we set up camp in a little glade of greenery.

Our first chore upon arriving in Cairo was to service the VW. When they opened the rear hood, the engine had accumulated so much dust that you could barely see it—yet no harm had come to the engine, thanks to good German craftsmanship. Then we visited the National Museum, where the Tutankhamen treasures were housed. The individual items were spectacular in their brilliance and composition, but poorly displayed, being scattered about the floor and in old-fashioned glass cases without descriptive material or story. When they were later shown by the Metropolitan Museum of Art in New York, the art of presentation had reached a level equal to the quality of this extraordinary discovery.

From Cairo, we had planned to return to Alexandria and take a short boat ride to Beirut. Instead, we became entranced with the idea of seeing the Suez Canal. At the time it was the focus of an international dispute over the right of the Nasser government to prevent its use by vessels deemed unfriendly. We then toyed with the idea of driving through the southern part of the Sinai Peninsula into Jordan. Mad as that sounds, we drove toward the canal and the city of Suez, located at its southern end.

Shortly before reaching Suez, we were stopped at a military checkpoint. There was a long line of people waiting to go through inspection. We soon began a conversation with the group ahead of us. One of them spoke excellent English and told us they were going to camp out on the Gulf of Suez for a long weekend of sunbathing and snorkeling. When we told him our plans to visit the Suez Canal, he said it was dangerous even to think of trying. We would certainly be caught if they didn't arrest us on the spot as foreign spies if they even suspected our intentions. The whole area was a high-risk military zone and heavily patrolled. As an alternative, the one doing the talking offered to include us in their party. We immediately accepted.

It was an unusual group of three married couples. Magdi Banoub and his wife were Coptic Christians. He worked in the government-owned insurance company. Another was Jewish and they owned a small hotel in Cairo. The third couple was Muslim, he being a professor in the university.

They immediately embraced us as the fourth couple in their weekend sojourn. We followed them down the coast to a suitable campsite. They were very friendly and open in discussing the situation in Egypt, their concern over President Nasser's provocative statements, the fear of another war, and the high level of corruption in government and discrimination against all but a favored few. As an American, I had little to offer except sympathy and no opinion on how our government would react if war broke out.

We came to know all three couples. After the hatred toward Israel seen earlier, it was encouraging to observe their level of compatibility. We saw them again in Cairo before we retraced our steps to Alexandria to catch the boat that would take us to Beirut, the capital of Lebanon.

Our time in Lebanon was a series of sprints from one ancient site to another. We visited all the old Phoenician ports—Tyre, Sidon, Byblos and Tripoli—each having its unique history. Then we drove into the hinterlands. We climbed up to Les Cedres, the highest spot in Lebanon (2,000 meters), and took pictures of the 50 remaining cedar trees of a forest which had once blanketed the entire country. The main culprit for this spoliation had been the Egyptians, who greatly valued this hard, long-lasting, scented wood.

South of Les Cedres, we carefully navigated our way high up into the mountains along a tortuous single-lane dirt road to where the Adonis River sprang from the side of the mountain. The Romans had erected a temple in honor of Adonis' lover, the goddess Venus. It was hard to imagine how they transported the gigantic pieces of red granite up that same tortuous path, all of which must have come from the quarry at Aswan, Egypt.

We also wandered through southern Lebanon and discovered the Druze, a special people with their own variation of the Muslim religion. They were friendly and generous to us while making it clear that they were very different and independent of everyone else we might meet in Lebanon.

In our wanderings around Beirut, we came to know the owner of a store that specialized in Persian rugs. He was impressed with the fact that we were traveling by ourselves by auto at a time when tensions were high and tourism was minimal. George was Greek and owned stores in Beirut and Damascus. We wasted a lot of his time and drank lots of Orange Crush while poring over his inventory. We met him again in Damascus, where he took us to dinner and sold us a beautiful Persian rug. We maintained a short correspondence with him after returning to New York and then lost contact.

George put us in contact with someone who would take us into one of the Palestinian refugee camps. The one we had in mind was located in the Baalbek Valley between Beirut and Damascus, not far from a famous Roman temple complex. We had heard about the crowded conditions and indifferent attitude of the host countries with respect to all the refugee camps surrounding Israel. We wanted to see for ourselves. (When I say "we," I am not sure that Vera's "wanted to" was as strong as mine.)

The beginning of the visit went well, with a camp administrator giving us a tour and some background. He invited a few of the elders to meet us and answer whatever questions we might have.

We were doing this out in the open, and soon there formed a sizable crowd. Upon hearing that we were Americans, they began to grumble and then speak out about their animosity toward the United States and President Truman. Soon it became apparent that they were not interested in our questions. They wanted to express their own feelings to an extent that our guides and the elders felt it best that we leave before it became violent. These people had been kept confined for eight years and had reason to be agitated. "But to whom?" was the unanswered question as we left. It was the first time during our trip that saying we were Americans did not receive a friendly response.

The Roman ruins at Baalbek were just as spectacular as those at Karnak, although younger by almost 2,000 years. The columns of the Temple of Jupiter are 90 feet tall. Some blocks of cut stone were transported up 500 feet from their quarry and weighed 1,200 tons (2.4 million lbs). I had a field day, using my movie camera to take single-frame photos of everything of possible interest. I would bracket what the light meter said to insure that one frame would be perfect.

The next stop on our tour of antiquity was the Greco-Roman city of Gerasa in northern Jordan, now called Jerash. We were the only visitors.

Jerash was the first time that I succumbed to a diarrhea that had been troubling me since our last days in Egypt. It would come on for a day or two and then subside. It could have been from fresh vegetables or the beer. We even wondered whether it was a bug caught the time I went swimming in the Nile. While at Jerash, I was wiped out and spent the day resting by our car while Vera absorbed the remains of a once-thriving metropolis.

Jerusalem was our next overnight destination, with the "Walls of Jericho" as a midday stop. Not much to see except for a large hole in the ground with what were supposed to be the very same walls that Jacob had destroyed. While we were there, a little puff of wind blew some dust into Vera's left eye and caused an irritation that persisted during the remainder of our drive to Jerusalem.

In 1956, the old city of Jerusalem was part of the Hashemite Kingdom of Jordan. It contains many of the ancient sites important to the Jews, the Christians and the Moslems. It was an important stop on our trip. Our map had us arriving by way of the Mount of Olives that lay just to the east of the city. With evening upon us, we decided to camp there, if possible. There was a grove of olive trees just behind one of the churches with a wonderful view of the city and no one around to ask permission of or to prevent our driving into its midst.

Vera had no time to cook before darkness fell, so we removed the baggage and set up the car for sleeping. No sooner had we settled into our sleeping bags and closed our eyes than Vera felt the irritation crawling around her left eye. I took our flashlight and shined it onto the eye. There were tiny little bugs crawling back and forth. For the next two hours I carefully swept them to the side of her eyeball with the corner of my handkerchief while she held the eyelids apart. All in all I removed more than 20 of the little creatures. Only then did the itching stop and Vera was able to sleep.

The bug problem was history by morning, and we discreetly moved our sleeping quarters to a public parking space. We explored the old city of Jerusalem from this Church to that Dome and on to the Wailing Wall. Jerusalem is a treasure trove of things to see, and we made the most of the day.

We were able to sneak back into our favorite olive grove for another night. Whether it was the very Garden of Gethsemane where Christ spent his Last Supper, we don't know—and nobody else knows, because there are at least four olive groves on the Mount of Olives that claim the honor.

An early start south to the "Rose-Red City of Petra" found us dipping our toe into the Dead Sea, followed by an all-day drive through rugged desert terrain. Occasionally, the road descended to a barely moist riverbed bordered by oleander bushes in gorgeous bloom. As dusk approached, we reached the village of Wadi Musa, gateway to the ancient Nabataean city of Petra. Vera insisted that we drive far enough through the village to avoid a gathering of the curious.

We stopped beside an olive grove and unwound ourselves from a long day of being bounced around in our little VW on a badly maintained road. Vera had begun to cook our supper of spaghetti when the first faint call, similar to that made by a bird, sounded from somewhere nearby. An answering call from another part of the darkness was followed by a third. Suddenly, we had the company of a dozen men with an assortment of firearms, not the usual crowd of hungry children and curious women.

Without looking up from her pot of soon-to-boil water, Vera complained that we should have driven farther from the village. I quietly explained that these were not our normal visitors. They were obviously not friendly, and from their demeanor I realized that we had some explaining to do. I held up my hand in greeting and called out that we were Americans. After some heated discussion there stepped forward a young man, named Allah, who asked in broken English who we were and why were we here. My explanation was followed by further heated discussion. Some seemed to accept our explanation, while the majority felt we were those intruders from Israel who periodically came to steal their sheep and goats.

Eventually, they allowed me to drive back to the village, where there was an encampment of Royal Jordanian Army soldiers who could confirm our status. They would hold Vera hostage until Allah and I returned. I protested this condition, but there was no alternative.

Allah and I drove back to the village together, located the army headquarters, explained the situation and followed a truck full of soldiers back to our olive grove. Vera and I gathered up our belongings and spent the night sleeping within their compound.

Allah agreed to take us into Petra the next day. A short way past our olive grove, the road suddenly ended at the edge of a sheer drop onto a dry creekbed. There were no barriers or signs warning "End of Road," "Danger," or "Stop." I don't know whose "God" (or Allah) was watching over us, but, as luck would have it, we had stopped just in time.

Petra was worth every bump on the long detour south from Amman and the Dead Sea. The entranceway was a quarter-mile gorge 100 feet deep that narrowed at times to a mere dozen feet. It opened onto an extraordinary temple of red, orange and yellow sandstone carved into the living rock.

From there, one entered a secluded and protected valley filled with ruins dating back to the early centuries of the Christian era. It served as a safe stop on the caravan route stretching from the southern ports of the Arabian Peninsula north-northwest to Jerusalem and Damascus. We camped for two days under an outcropping of sandstone. We hiked the valley floor and searched for shards on a massive mound of ancient rubbish.

It was this latter folly of searching, bareheaded, for souvenirs that caused me to have severe headaches on our trip back north. They became so bad that I relinquished my driving responsibilities to Vera. Upon arrival in Amman, I could do nothing but crawl into bed and receive medication from a doctor that Vera managed to locate. This slowed us up a bit until I was in good enough shape to continue north toward Damascus.

Arriving at the outskirts of Damascus, we stumbled on a series of cave-like openings in the sandstone cliffs that apparently were the home for many families. These otherwise homeless natives welcomed us, and, for a small contribution, we were able to use one of the caves during our stay.

Our friend from Beirut, George, was in town and invited us to dinner. We were able to clean up a bit and change into our fancy outfits in the bathroom at a gas station nearby. At the time I was still a bit woozy from my heat exhaustion, so I remember little of the restaurant, food and after-dinner entertainment.

From Damascus, we traveled north toward Aleppo and then west toward the Turkish border. Our intention was to visit the coastal plain at

Issus where Alexander won his first great battle against the Persians under King Darius. We were still in Syria when the sun began to set. We turned onto a dirt road and climbed into a forested area we thought would be out of sight and safe.

Night came quickly, and we were cozily asleep when suddenly shouts close by awakened us. It was a squad of men in military uniforms. They were brusque with us, but not violent nor even threatening. The phrase "Americans," the showing of passports and the lack of drugs, firearms or other suspicious baggage upon inspection all seemed to satisfy them, and they left. Our sleep was over for the rest of the night, but it occurred to us that we were safer because of the incident. Those soldiers were there looking for someone—drug traffickers or smugglers—who might have dealt with us differently if they had been the ones who found us.

The road zigged and zagged through rough terrain until the Syrian border house came into view. Before crossing into Turkey, we exchanged a $20 American Express traveler's check into Turkish drachmas with the Syrian custom guards. Then we went through to the other side of the border. We told them how many drachmas we were bringing into the country, but not the exchange rate. I mention this because we found out later, while under investigation for dealing in the black market, that the rate we got in Syria was 10 times the official rate. We should have known, or at least suspected, that was the case, because the $20 lasted us all the way across Turkey.

It was still morning when we entered Iskenderun on the coast. I had to brake suddenly, and, in so doing, the horn started to blare loudly and wouldn't stop. A crowd gathered, some irritated by the noise and others who thought it pretty funny that we didn't know how to turn our horn off. I was in a bit of a panic mode because I had no idea what to do. I dug out our VW maintenance manual and was poring over the hieroglyphic-looking details of its electrical circuits when a young boy indicated that he knew how to stop the noise. With much bravado, he stood on the front bumper and jumped up and down—and, with that, the honking ceased.

I was relieved, but I didn't feel much like a macho American fighter pilot in front of all these young Turks. The cause of the honking turned out to be the wiring under the front hood. It had frayed and then shorted when it settled against the metal. Jumping up and down moved the frayed section off the metal and solved the problem temporarily. (It reminded me of my flight over Alameda when the aft fire warning light came on while I was pulling too many G's.)

I knew something about the Battle of Issus, in which Alexander the Great defeated a much larger Persian army. The site was just north of

Iskenderun on the road to Adana. I was interested in learning more about it but, unfortunately, the Turks seemed totally indifferent to its significance and, without maps or a guide at the site, it was hard to know what we were looking at.

We slept outside Adana, a bustling port town, and then resumed our trip north, up through the historic Cilician Gates connecting the high plateau of central Turkey to the Mediterranean Sea and the Middle East. My diarrhea had been acting up again, and around noon, we stopped to rest by a good-sized stream flowing alongside the road.

It was a warm summer day, and I took off my clothes except for my shorts. A Turkish soldier, in full uniform with rifle, suddenly appeared, shouting in a manner that was clearly unfriendly, even threatening. With hardly anything on, I felt rather exposed. That I explained I was American didn't impress him, and he motioned me to follow him back up to the road.

From her vantage point, Vera saw what was happening and was also unsure what to do. At this moment, a car came around the bend in the road and stopped when Vera signaled she was in need of help.

The driver was a young man about our age who spoke English and had just returned from California, where he had spent a year at Davis, the agriculture campus of the University of California. He understood the problem immediately. The soldier was shocked at my "nakedness" and was determined to take both Vera and me back to his army encampment for violating the Muslim code of morality. The man in the car was able, although with some effort, to explain our situation. Reluctantly, the soldier allowed us to continue our trip.

My condition was not good, and when we reached the town of Pozanti, near the top of the pass, we visited the doctor, recommended to us by our "Good Samaritan." The doctor shot me full of vitamins and told me to take it easy for a day or two.

That soldier was our first exposure to a certain unfriendliness of the Turks, which continued as we drove through the country. We thought it might be a language problem, but we decided that it was a basic characteristic. When we finally left Turkey and entered Greece, the difference in attitude was night and day.

In Konya, the capital of the Central Highland, we found further evidence of a surly attitude toward us "foreigners." We engaged in conversation with a group in which a little German and English were spoken. The result was like the visit to the refugee camp outside Baalbek. We decided not to stay longer in Konya, but to continue on our way west.

The next stop on our schedule was Sardis, home of King Croesus;

another untended pile of ruins dating back to 700 B.C.. There was little to show for all Croesus' assumed riches but piles of rubble indicating that many people lived here long, long ago; it was not worth a foot of film. Our disappointment was ameliorated by our taking as a souvenir a 10-lb. chunk of marble engraved with the classic floral design (which is now part of a stone hut I built many years later on our property in Newtown).

Our next stop was the port city of Izmir on the Aegean Sea. It was formerly called Smyrna and was reputed to be the birthplace of the poet Homer. Whether that is true or not, Smyrna goes back a long time and had been subjected to successive waves of occupation by Anatolians, Lydians, Aeolians and Ionians, all before Alexander the Great came along in 334 B.C.

Here, too, there was very little left to see. We arrived dirty and tired, to be met by Colonel Morrison, the father of Jim Morrison from the 496th FIS. He was assigned to the NATO Headquarters in Izmir. We had dinner with him and the publisher of the *Izmir Demokrat*, with the result that a story about us, complete with photograph, appeared on the front page.

Ephesus was just down the coast from Izmir. Like the other places we visited in Turkey, there was little security and much indifference by the attendants. It was one of the 12 cities of the Ionian League during the Classical Greek period. In the Roman period, Ephesus had grown to a population exceeding 250,000. It was an immense site where we were able to become invisible until closing time. With one eye open most of the night, we slept in the ruins of the Temple of Artemis, said to be one of the Seven Wonders of the Ancient World. We left early the next morning without confirmation.

It was then north to the ruins of Pergamum and Troy, both lying along the coastline leading up toward Istanbul (Constantinople). Pergamum was interesting, and Vera was talked into taking a ride on a camel. At Troy it was difficult to fathom just what we were looking at; the ruins were scattered with little definition, hardly enough to film for posterity. My diarrhea had now gotten to the point where I was having difficulty holding down food.

The pace we were keeping was taking its toll. When we arrived in Istanbul, it became clear that I should get some medical attention. We decided that Vera should stay at the Istanbul Hilton while I went to the American Hospital. I stayed there for three days while they fed me glucose and saline solutions intravenously. They prescribed a diet of yogurt and goat's cheese for the next two weeks. It finally got my digestive track operating normally.

Aside from this interruption, our stay in Istanbul was memorable. The Mosque of Saint Sophia was an extraordinary sight, the city was teeming with life, full of exotic outfits and strange accents. Its hills and water lines were as picturesque as those of San Francisco. The hot, sultry atmosphere made one lazy and reluctant to move on. But move on we did, driving northwest to the border with Greece.

Edirne, standing as sentinel between two continents, offered our last glimpse of Asia Minor and four fascinating countries of the Middle East. It was a miniature Istanbul, with its picturesque mosques and riverfront views, but we barely slowed down in our anticipation of entering Europe again with the magic of Greece as our first stop. Vera would be revisiting her birthplace, and I would be experiencing the wonders of ancient Greece and the birthplace of Western civilization. Carefully adhering to my Spartan diet, my insides had settled down and were behaving themselves. I was up to traveling again, and both Vera and I were anxious to regain the schedule we had roughly outlined back in Landstuhl.

Our travels through Greece became the highlight of the trip. (We returned the next summer for a long week of island-hopping on Mykonos, Naxos and Santorini (Thera). We traveled third class on tramp freighters, rode broken-down motorcycles the length and breadth of Rhodes, slept for the second time under the stars at Sounion, and survived one frightful night at sea during the height of an Adriatic storm.)

What made Greece so special? There was the weather: day upon day of cloudless skies, hot in the daytime, cool at night, little humidity. The variety of landscape: quickly changing from snow-clad mountains high in the distance to long stretches of level plains to close-ups of white sand and azure-blue waters. And the people: Their friendliness was so natural and welcoming. There was a language barrier, but it was easily overcome. Often, we would run across those who had family in the United States, even some who spent half the year on a temporary visa working there. They loved the Americans. The Truman Doctrine had helped them in focusing their political views, and the Marshall Plan was critical to their economic recovery from the war.

It was so different from our experiences elsewhere. Arab countries: cautiously curious, but suspicious and critical. Turkey: unfriendly, aloof. Italy: everyone was lively and friendly, but always wanting to sell you something. Added to all this was the fact that my few days of rest and a new diet had me running again on eight cylinders.

While Greece might appear small on the map compared to Turkey, the number of interesting sites to visit was overwhelming. We spent a whirlwind three weeks trying to fit everything in.

From Edirne we drove non-stop to Salonika. Turning south, we were surprised by a brand-new highway, courtesy of the Marshall Plan, that encouraged maximum speed. It was a beautiful asphalt highway, straight and level through the valley of Larissa. It was the best since Switzerland, with only one problem: every once in a while we would encounter a large pothole that bounced us almost out of the car (until we put the top up). Finally, we left the level plain and began to twist and turn up through the passes bringing us to Athens.

Vera had been to Athens many times while flying for Swissair. Her schedule always provided a 24-hour layover and her German/Swiss education had made Athens one of the highlights of her time as a stewardess. She became our tour guide, and we enjoyed our few days of luxury camping in a youth hostel close to the center of the city.

There were also those sites within a day's drive that were musts, like the plain of Marathon, where I became tour guide and pontificated on what I had read in Sir Edward Creasy's The Fifteen Decisive Battles of the World: From Marathon to Waterloo. There was the spring at Delphi, out of which its famous Oracle issued prophesies, and down the road an ancient "Olympic" size stadium. We camped out overnight beside the temple of Poseidon at Sounion, located on a promontory with three sides looking over the Aegean Sea. And just outside Athens, the beautifully designed, perfectly scaled, well-maintained Byzantine church at Dafni.

We drove down to the Peloponnesus via Corinth, known for its Doric temple in honor of Aphrodite, and then on to Mycenae with its Lion Gate and burial site of Agamemnon. From there it was a short drive to Argos. Here we found little more than a village remaining from those glorious times around 800 B.C. when it dominated the likes of Tiryns and Mycenae. Just to the south we visited a circle of small villages, Myloi, Nea, Kios and Nafplion, with views of the Aegean. We stopped and spoke with the natives, who were friendly, curious and anxious to tell us of relatives living in the United States. Epidaurus was next on our list of musts.

There, we experienced one of the more memorable evenings of the trip when we saw the play Medea by Euripides presented in Greek with the traditional chorus chanting its woes and wisdom. The theatre, slightly larger than a half-circle, held 15,000 and was famous for its acoustics, which allowed every viewer to easily hear what was being said on stage. Our seats were high enough up and far enough to one to side to prove the claim.

We planned to remain overnight and had found a spot for our VW in the woods a short way from the public parking lots. When we got back to the car, the top had been ripped and the insides ransacked. They found our American Express Traveler's checks and my Baretta "safely" hidden behind the dashboard. It was now quite dark and, admittedly, a bit scary. We immediately got out of there.

We didn't stop driving until the remains of the fortress of Tiryns loomed off to the right. These gigantic pieces of white cut stone seemed a safe place to hide and became our newest campsite. In the morning, we explored this ancient fortress. Later we found a "store" with tables by the side of the road. Vera had her espresso and I my yogurt and goats' cheese. We debriefed our stupidity and narrow escape for the third time.

Back in Athens, we went to the American Express office and had no trouble getting replacement traveler's checks. Their policy was to satisfy the traveler with a legitimate story of lost or stolen checks. (Later on in New York, the American Express office would have me come in to verify the counter-signatures appearing on the checks presented for payment. None of them remotely looked like mine but had been accepted by AMEX as necessary to maintain their acceptance by the local banks.)

Another day in Athens and suddenly we felt the press of time. We raced our little bug almost non-stop the 1,200 miles to Venice, where our campsite gave us easy access to the city. Venice, with its canals serving as streets, felt like it was floating like a lily pad on the edge of the Adriatic Sea. Again, Vera's Italian allowed her to converse easily with passersby and waiters.

Our trip was not over, but the more adventurous part was—if uncertainty and risk are an important part of the term. We entered Switzerland via the Stelvio Pass into the high valleys of the Engadine and onto Davos, the city of many fond memories. Silly us; stopping at a roadside crèche, with a slight rain falling, we readjusted some of our baggage and left behind the small vase found by Francesco in the field by the temple at Paestum. It joined the two beautiful alabaster vases we received as replacements for the fake artifacts returned to the dealer in Luxor—they did not survive the bumpy trip back to Cairo.

We stopped off in Basel for two days to visit Vera's mother and relatives living nearby (seven in all). They listened intently to our adventures but had to be wondering what was in store for Vera in America. Vera was the only child of the seven Rheinberger siblings. She would be leaving shortly to live in a country far away, a country they little understood or appreciated. It must have been a sad day for all of them.

We had a month or so of traveling ahead of us, beginning with Landstuhl AFB. It was nostalgic time for me, feeling that I probably wouldn't see most of them ever again. It had the usual pilot talk about their last trip to Wheelus, the 496th winning the gunnery competition, dogfights with the Canucks, squadron gossip. Their life seemed tranquil, with the normal alert duty, sports and squadron parties.

There was nothing in the air to suggest the coming Hungarian revolution and the Soviet reaction. (Vera and I were safely in the United States when the Soviet troops entered Hungary. It happened Friday evening while the pilots were enjoying a typical evening at the Officer's Club. The entire wing at Landstuhl deployed immediately northwest to Hahn AFB. I was told that a lot of 100% oxygen was consumed on the way.)

From Landstuhl, we drove to Paris and set up a newly purchased tent in the Bois du Boulogne. Vera's Aunt Lillie and husband, Herr Doktor Notz, drove from Basel for a visit. We dressed up as best we could and met them at nice restaurants. The second night it rained heavily, and we returned just as the water was entering our tent. Our hastily constructed moat of dirt was a dismal failure, and we were forced to retreat to our bedroom in the Bug.

It was now on to Merry England, first London to Oxford and then tracking J.B. Priestley's *English Journey through the Cotswolds*, the Potteries (Stoke-on-Trent—love the name), Birmingham to Liverpool. Here we met up with my uncle Norman, who was staying with relatives. My weight was still below 130 pounds, so they insisted I have some tests for amoebic dysentery. The tests were negative, but everyone's advice was to slow down. Even Vera was not in good shape. While in the Cotswolds, we woke one morning to find that the field we had chosen for our camp was the private stomping ground for a very large and unfriendly bull. In our haste to exit, Vera wrenched her already-bad knee while vaulting over a fence.

Our plans were to leave the car in Bremerhaven for transport by ship to the United States and then take the train from there to Rhein-Main Airport. This took us back to France, up through Belgium, The Netherlands, Denmark and back into Germany. Our method of camping out still worked most of the time, but we also found youth hostels increasingly available and inexpensive.

Nothing special remains from this part of the journey. The changes in landscape, manner of dress and language told us which country we were traveling through and how small they all are. I have a few, admittedly insignificant, vignettes still in my memory bank: the guard at the disembarkation center in Dover who, in the midst of a heavy downpour at night, guided us by foot (no room in the car) for a good quarter mile, chin up, to the exit gate, without complaint (and minimum tip), and a parting "Enjoy yourself, mate, while in England"; the law in Copenhagen that allows the bicyclists (to your right) to turn left when the stop signal turns green; dining in a three-star restaurant housed in a riverboat tied to the shore of the

Hamburg See, which had an imperceptible motion to it. Both of us became seasick and we left in the middle of the main course.

Upon leaving our four-wheeled companion at the docks in Bremerhaven, our trip was officially over. What an experience! What a "getting to know one another" for two newlyweds from diverse backgrounds. Those shared adventures—challenging, exhilarating, surprising, some unique, some dangerous—all contributed to shaping our relationship. For the most part, we were in agreement on major decisions, but, as the reader might have gathered, our record was not perfect. Witness the time in Normandy when Vera got back into the car and drove off for a couple of hours, leaving me to reconsider the position I had stubbornly taken about an issue I have forgotten.

Spending five months together in which no third party was available for advice or precedence to guide us helped in keeping our marriage on good footing. As for the experience itself, we had the luck of youth and a confidence in ourselves to handle strange situations. Would we do it again? in the same manner? As a matter of fact, we did do it again, when we returned to Greece the next summer. Would we encourage our children do the same, or even let them? At the time, of course we would have, but, then, we had no children—and the world was different.

With our own funds depleted and credit lines exhausted, we bade farewell to Europe, Swissair and the United States Air Force. It was time to get on to new adventures: for Vera, life in the United States; and for me, the beginning of my career at Weeden & Co.

Before I leave these five months of travel and adventure, I want to talk about Vera and me. Until now, she appears in these pages not so much as a lover and newlywed, but more as a friend and companion. In a way, she had become a replacement for the relationship I had with the men of the squadron, or earlier with my Zete house brothers and even earlier with the neighborhood gang in Alameda.

The sex we enjoyed together was a new ingredient that created a tighter bond than previous relationships, but did not dominate. This latter point, I believe, was shared. What was appealing to both of us was the glamour associated with each other's uniform; our physical attractiveness; and the challenge of testing, absorbing and adjusting to someone from a totally different culture. But that deeper love, as I have come to experience it, was not part of our relationship then, nor did it change much as we moved into the early years of our marriage. Unfortunately, for reasons that I suspect were the responsibility of both of us, that deeper love never fully blossomed in the way it does in more enduring marriages.

Our relationship had begun in Geneva, when I was met by a very attractive Swissair stewardess at the top of the stairs on a late-night flight to London. It blossomed during hurried weekends of skiing at Flumserberg, Davos and Megève and found us hastily committing to marriage during a dinner in Rome with my mother. It was a romantic relationship that was hurried along by nothing more than each of us deciding it was time for marriage.

I had made the decision not to request a regular commission and to return to New York City and employment with Weeden & Company. Marriage and a family seemed a logical companion to starting my business career. As for Vera, life as a stewardess had provided her with considerable independence from the unwelcomed demands of her mother and the overprotectiveness of her aunts. And while she looked forward to the longer flights to places like New York, flying had lost its initial charm. I offered a suitable replacement.

It was Vera's idea to visit the places of antiquity in those countries to which she had flown, and I was wholly in agreement. We saw it as that "Grand Tour" before settling into being adults and parents.

New Year's Eve 1954 at Swissair HQ, Kloten, Switzerland (left to right): Vreni Engel, Don, Vera.

With Vera Knauer, soon to become Vera Weeden.

At Wallasea, near Liverpool, England, end of Mideast trip (rear, left to right): Don (weighing about 135 pounds), relative of Don's, Uncle Norman Weeden; (front): Vera's mother — Hildegard Rheinberger — and Vera, 1956.

Vera and Don on wedding day, September 30, 1955, Basel, Switzerland.

Chapter 11
New York City, 1956–1960

The flight from Frankfurt-am-Main to New York City was uneventful. The Weeden & Co. apartment on West Ninth Street was available for us to unwind and begin adjusting to the Big Apple. I knew most of the employees at Weeden from my summers working there. I was more than eager to get started.

Vera was in charge of finding us an apartment to fit my new salary of $400 a month (down from $525 in the Air Force). Conventional wisdom allocated 25 percent of one's salary for rent, making $100 a month her target. I bought a Sunday *New York Times* and the two of us sat cross-legged on the living room rug highlighting every rental close to $100. Unfortunately, there were not many that weren't at the far end of a subway line or in a questionable neighborhood. Vera spent her mornings on the telephone and then visited what was still available. The subway took her into every borough of the city (including Staten Island by ferry), and she immediately became far more familiar with the city than I was or would be.

We settled on a one-bedroom apartment for $110 a month in the Cobble Hill section of Brooklyn, a blue-collar neighborhood across Atlantic Avenue from Brooklyn Heights. I preferred the Heights, being closer to Wall Street and more upscale, but we couldn't afford it. Even at $110, the apartment was not ideal. It was a fifth floor add-on to a four-story brownstone; the owner, Nick Carlucci, had done the work himself after World War II.

The apartment had no inside partitions except for the bathroom, a sway-back linoleum floor throughout, and a heating system controlled by a thermostat in the hallway two floors below. But no complaints. It was better than our little VW, which was five flights below nestled beside the curb.

My Weeden's monthly salary of $400 was no bargain, but it came with lunch and a good chance for advancement. Vera could practice her Italian with our landlord and learn Spanish from the renters below us.

My career path was now set, and I began to think seriously about Weeden. The first order of business was to refresh myself on the back-office routines: confirming, clearing and settling trades made by our traders. As it was in San Francisco, I enjoyed the action that built to a frenzy as we approached closing time for deliveries. Everyone in the cage (an old-style name for the back office) helped to turn incoming deliveries into outgoing deliveries before all windows closed for the day.

In 1947, when I worked in the San Francisco office, this frenzy happened only occasionally. In the New York office 10 years later, it was a daily occurrence.

When I arrived, my brothers Jack and Alan were working in the New York office. Jack was in charge of operations, and Alan managed our Municipal Bond syndicate bidding and oversaw our trading in New York. Jack lived on East 12th Street in Manhattan. Alan lived in Larchmont with his wife and two small boys. Both had been with the firm for five years.

My father, Frank (now 63), and his brother, my Uncle Norman (now 59), had established Weeden & Co. in 1922 as a partnership. In 1928 they converted it into a publicly held corporation with an offering of $300,000. Both were still active and ran the firm with the help of three long-standing partners working in San Francisco and Los Angeles. The five of them constituted the board of directors. My father, uncle and mother were the three largest shareholders, collectively owning over a third of the outstanding shares. The rest of the shareholders were either employees or friends and amounted to fewer than 100.

The firm remained profitable during the Depression (except in 1932 and 1937) and throughout World War II, and it normally paid a healthy dividend. Weeden shares were sought after, especially by employees. When shares came into the market for sale, Frank would suggest a fair price, buy them and parcel them out to those employees he felt most deserving.

I renewed my relationship with my brothers and we began to meet informally for dinners at the Downtown Athletic Club. We mainly discussed the business. I learned that Alan had had some differences with Frank over the direction of the firm and allocation of resources. Their relationship had become so testy that they weren't on speaking terms for a while. This surprised me. I thought Alan mild-mannered and relaxed, but it seems he was anxious to shift the direction of the firm from San Francisco (all five board members lived on the West Coast) to New York and to give the younger producers more say.

Alan later told me that Frank had been quite upset with me back in 1953 for committing to a full four years with the Air Force. He said that three of his sons had already served in the military and my going was not necessary. He complained that he had already worked a long time in the business and had put us all through college. He asked Alan to talk to me about it. At the time, Alan had begun to write me a letter to that effect, but he never sent it, feeling that I ought to be able to do what I wanted. None of this ever became a discussion between Frank and me.

Meanwhile, Vera was settling in. I realized later that she was not as happy as she thought she would be living in New York City. Among her complaints, she felt the neighborhood was beneath her social status. There was no one in the neighborhood she felt comfortable with. At one point she wanted to apply for work with the United Nations as a guide or translator. I was against it, insisting that the bread-winning responsibilities were mine. I suggested that, if she were lonely, she might become involved in something artistic, in which she had both interest and talent. She started a course in sculpting given by Vincent Glinsky at New York University. Later she joined his studio located in Greenwich Village.

A miscarriage during our first year in Brooklyn was also a downer. Another problem was the relationship that developed between Vera and Alan's wife, Barbara. With my mother living in Alameda, Barbara quite naturally had assumed the role of family matriarch, East Coast, and had made that very clear. I was oblivious to the subtleties involved and tried to assure Vera of the contrary. In retrospect, I should have talked with Alan about it.

To supplement my present income, I responded to an advertisement by the New York Air National Guard looking for pilots with jet experience. A squadron of F-94Bs, Lockheed's all-weather interceptor aircraft, was being delivered to Floyd Bennett Naval Air Station for use by the Guard. By July 1957, I had completed the preflight paperwork and schooling and had successfully made my first solo flight. I began spending weekends flying with the 102nd Fighter Interceptor Squadron, getting to know the peculiarities of the aircraft (slower and heavier than the F-86D) and integrating myself into squadron life again.

It wasn't long before the operations officer, a Captain Blake-Loeb, a World War II fighter pilot, suggested we go up and do a little dogfighting. I flew his wing out past the eastern end of Long Island, where we split up before turning back to engage. Youth won. My acceptance by the rest of the old-timers was secured.

I began getting as much flying as I had time.

Vera and I continued to adore our little VW. We spent many weekends driving all over the Tri-State area looking for the ideal place to raise a family. We would start out early Saturday morning, with map and the *New York Times* Real Estate section, looking at homes for sale in New Jersey, Connecticut and Long Island. Toward evening we would find a secluded spot in a forest area or near the shore and use the Bug as our motel, just as we did before. This continued until Elizabeth was born on August 1, 1958.

With a car in New York City and no garage space in our budget, we had a late-evening ritual of moving the car from one side of the street to the other to avoid ticketing the following day. Our Bug was shorter by 6 inches than most American cars. This offered spaces for me to squeeze into, a challenge which I enjoyed. The downside was the height of the Bug's front and rear bumpers: 3 inches lower than those on most American cars. The result was smashed front and rear hoods when those parked next to us maneuvered their way out from the curb. After paying for repairs twice, we left the crushed metal as a sign of indifference to the next New York driver who climbed over our bumper.

Before we moved to Brooklyn, we experienced an even more seamier side of the city. My mother had flown East to welcome Vera, and we moved over to Jack's apartment on East 12th Street. Jack invited Mom over to dinner and then walked her home while Vera and I prepared to retire. As I was brushing my teeth, still clad in trousers and T-shirt, Vera called from the front window that a man was being beaten up across the street. When I looked out, I saw two burly-looking white men roughing up a slender black man in the step-down area in front of the brownstone across the street.

The Good Samaritan (I thought I was going to be) raced down the stairs, grabbing a broom that stood in the hallway. When I arrived in the street, I told the men to stop. I was ignored and then told to "beat it." I took the broom and tapped one of the men on the shoulder. Still struggling with the black man, one of the men mumbled that they were plainclothes cops and showed me what he said was a badge. At that moment, the black man managed to escape; he ran away. I thought, "Mission accomplished."

I was soon disabused of that idea when the two men turned on me and proceeded to make an arrest. Vera had appeared at the scene and explained who we were. It made no difference. The charge, as told to the sergeant at the 9th Precinct police station and to the magistrate judge the next morning: "While engaged in the act of arresting a known male prostitute, Weeden, presumably a customer of said prostitute, knowingly hit said officer two dozen times on the head and shoulder with a deadly weapon." Having lost their man, they at least had me, and their story remained firm, even two weeks later when we all appeared before a grand jury to hear my case.

I was fortunate enough to know Charles Grimes, lawyer and uncle of my close friend Chuck Kelly. I had stayed in his house for part of my summer working as a lifeguard at the Piping Rock Club on Long Island. Early in his career, Mr. Grimes had served on Tom Dewey's team when Dewey was district attorney for the City of New York. Grimes knew the man who represented the city before the magistrate judge; they arranged for a transfer of my case to the grand jury.

I was relieved temporarily from a public trial. I had to defend my actions two weeks later before 26 citizens whose role is determining whether there is sufficient evidence to require a public trial. Their decision was dismissal without prejudice. The entire matter, including fingerprints, was scrubbed from the records.

Several years later, I met the father of Don Stone, a good friend of my brother Alan's. When he was introduced to me, Don's father said that he already knew me from my appearance before the grand jury. He said my testimony was so compelling it resulted in the only unanimous vote he remembers during all the years in which he served on the grand jury.

To Vera, the whole experience was inexplicable, sordid and frightening. She had been in America less than a week. It underscored what she had been brought up to think of America: a land of cowboys and Indians, uncultured and violent.

As for me, my initial confidence turned to concern and second thoughts. During my overnight stay in the Centre Street jail, among a collection of drunks, druggies and panhandlers, I started thinking that I might have erred in what I did—not the intention, but to mistake for bullying what was really plainclothes policemen doing their duty, while I stubbornly insisted they cease and desist. If convicted of the felonious assault charge, it would have damaged my career and my relationship with Vera, even my relationship with my family. It has remained a scar on my own personal evaluation chart.

In December 1959, we bought a 16-(plus or minus)-acre property along a dirt road in the northwest corner of Newtown, Connecticut, an 80-mile drive from our apartment. Elizabeth was 15 months old and Vera was pregnant with Frank. We had concluded that Long Island was too crowded and would become even worse with the continued expansion of the Long Island Expressway, and New Jersey was a collection of too many nondescript towns all squashed together. Connecticut seemed to offer something different—harder to get to, but less dense, more relaxed, New England. In Vera's mind, maybe more European.

The house was little more than a cabin. It sat on a meadow close to a year-round running brook with plenty of forest all around. Interstate 84 was just being finished around Danbury, with Interstate 684 on the drawing boards. They would substantially reduce the two-hour drive from Brooklyn.

My father, after visiting the property, advised against it as being too remote. He was right: It was isolated, but I felt we did not want country club–style weekends. My normal day at Weeden was intense and included after-work drinking and some dinners with traders and customers. I was looking forward to weekends of rest and family.

As for Vera, her attitude toward life in the U.S. was not improving. My flying, the business, irritation toward Barbara (and Mother, after an extended visit while having an operation on her knee in California)—it all contributed to Vera's unhappiness. More than anything, Vera was uncomfortable socially. People spoke too quickly, had different upbringings, parroted American attitudes and seemed to know little—or care little—about her European culture.

I thought I understood this, and I wanted to protect her. Spending the weekends on Pond Brook Road in a family-only environment would be an opportunity for both of us to be with the kids and maintain the closeness we had enjoyed on our Grand Tour.

Vera had told me a few months after Elizabeth's birth that she was not happy in the States and felt she would be better off living in Europe. (She had known a German pilot with Swissair whom she cited as having the kind of lifestyle she preferred.) I responded with the arguments that it might not be as she hoped; that living in the U.S. would be better for her and the children. I also said that I would be totally a fish out of water in a European environment, even if there was some work I could do, and that she should allow more time.

Vera continued to feel strongly about this. I finally suggested she should return and find out. So she and Elizabeth spent the better part of the summer of 1959 visiting her relatives and staying in a quiet resort town, Savognin, in southeastern Switzerland. She came back refreshed and feeling better about things.

Most of my flights with the National Guard were plain vanilla: getting to know the territory, some instrument weather flying with an occasional cross-country flight. Night flights were a little tricky, as I was normally just coming off a hectic day at the office and my mind had little time to adjust to the business of flying a jet fighter at night and the necessary landing requirement.

I did have a couple of unusual flights that I remember clearly. After one in particular, I was happy to finally get down safely. It happened early one Saturday morning in summer when the only people on the field were the Air Base officer, my crew chief and me.

It was an absolutely beautiful day, not a cloud in the sky, a slight wind from the south, active Runway 12. I took off, climbed to altitude and spent the time lazing around the sky, not paying much attention to what was happening below. A cloud bank had developed offshore during the night and had been drifting slowly onshore, eventually covering about a third of the active runway with a ceiling of zero, visibility zero. When I returned and asked for instructions from tower, I was told the active runway was 30, which was the only runway with ILS (Instrument Landing System) capability. I requested Runway 12, which was clear of fog for the initial two-thirds of its length, but I was sternly refused.

Even though I considered myself a pretty good instrument pilot, I found myself too high and too fast each time I made my ILS approach. After the second effort, I said "Enough of this," and I told the tower I was going to land VFR on Runway 12 whether he liked it or not. With only minimum fuel left, I pulled up to about 100 feet, leaving gear and flaps down, made a 180-degree teardrop turn, landed and turned off the runway before entering the fog bank. Suddenly, there seemed to be a very large crowd waiting for me as I shut down.

For some reason, this experience solidified my reputation and led to my later being chosen as one of the pilots to ferry our F-94Bs out to Tucson.

Back home, there were other indications of Vera's unhappiness. One afternoon she brought home a blond-haired dog that we guessed was part cocker spaniel and part Spitz. She had found it shivering on the catwalk of the Manhattan Bridge. When I inquired why she was walking there, she told me of her unhappiness and loneliness.

We made room for "Queenie," the name I suggested because she looked very much like the dog I had when I was little. Queenie was very friendly and took to Vera. The only problem was walking Queenie up and down four flights of stairs each time she needed to go out.

A few months later, we visited Alan and Barbara in Larchmont. We brought Queenie along. Unbeknownst to us, she had just come into heat. In the evening, we let her out for a moment and she ran up the street. Before we could catch her, she'd found a boyfriend or two—or more; the whole neighborhood was howling. Queenie gave birth to seven puppies: four blond and three black. We kept them in our tiny bathroom with the apartment's only door. We finally placed all the puppies, but it was not easy.

I had flown almost three years with the 102nd FIS when the aircraft was retired and replaced by the C-119, a twin-engine propeller-driven cargo plane also used for parachute drops during World War II. We were initially told that we would be getting the F-86H, capable of flying through Mach 1 in level flight. When this did not happen, I helped to ferry our F-94Bs out to Davis-Monthan Air Force Base outside Tucson, Arizona, and then resigned.

Brother Alan thought it would be fun to go with me and suggested that with his being in the active Naval Reserve, they might allow him to go as a passenger in the radar observer's seat. And sure enough, they did.

After briefing Alan on the bailout procedure, we took off in clear weather heading south-southwest. The weather called for a frontal condition along our route, but our destination, Pope AFB in North Carolina, was calling for broken (IFR condition) visibility good. I climbed to 37,000 feet and leveled off in the clear.

Between Washington, D.C., and Richmond, Virginia, the aircraft's electrical system failed. I turned off whatever I could to conserve battery power and passed a note back to Alan "to pass up the maps" of the terrain below. Lacking communications with air traffic control, I turned left and away from the commercial flight paths.

After a few minutes, a hole appeared in the undercast and we spiraled down until we were under the clouds. We were at 2,000 feet and over water. It turned out to be the Chesapeake Bay, not far from the Patuxent River Naval Air Station. I executed an emergency landing procedure and landed without further incident. Dinner at the Officer's Club was shared with a member of the Navy's Blue Angels aerobatic flying team whose plane also needed repairs. The conversation was lively, with Alan recounting his experiences in his underwater demolition unit and we pilots exchanging our own war stories.

Two weeks later, on July 3, we started off again from Floyd Bennett in another aircraft just out of a major overhaul. Believe it or not, Alan was still up to the ride. As soon as we were airborne, I lost radio contact. Complicating matters, my instrument check showed both oil and fuel pressure gauges reading "zero." The engine sounded OK. I presumed the problem was not the engine but the alternator, which operated the two instruments. We were now 100 feet off the ground and climbing. Our destination was Wright-Patterson Air Force Base in Dayton, Ohio. It was the USAF headquarters for maintenance. What better place to fix whatever needed fixing?

I continued climbing to altitude. It was a beautiful day and very quiet without a radio (it turned out that the maintenance crew had rewired the main antenna improperly). When approaching Wright-Patterson, there was a big thundercloud ahead of us. We spiraled down from 35,000 feet remaining VFR (in the clear) until we entered the runway landing pattern. We were now close enough to the tower so that radio communication was restored.

The rapid descent had caused the inside of the canopy to frost up. I had to scrape the ice off to see. I asked Alan to watch out for aircraft as we descended. Alan was having a problem unsnapping the plastic sun goggle attached to his helmet. The combination of frost and sunshade made it difficult for him to see anything outside. While I kept saying, "Keep your eyes open for any commercial aircraft," he kept saying, "I can't see a goddamned thing."

The next three flights had us stopping in Kansas, Colorado and Utah to refuel before our leg into Alameda Naval Air Station. We had some fun on the way: I did a little low-level flying. Alan kept reminding me of wives and children back home. Our evening flight plan into Lowery AFB, Denver, was several times distracted by thunderstorms. They kept pulling the automatic direction finder (ADF) arrow away from the Denver radio beacon.

I wanted to buzz the stone cabin at the top of Muir Pass, but low fuel argued against it. Much to Alan's credit, he was composed throughout; he even enjoyed it. Said he would do it again. He offered to reciprocate by taking me scuba diving. So far, I have never found the time.

Frank was on the tarmac to meet us. He looked pleased and proud of his two sons, although it was not his style to say much. We spent the evening together with Mom, and then I continued my trip to Davis-Monthan alone. Two weeks later, I flew another aircraft to Tucson for mothballing.

After going through ground school for the F-86H, orders were changed and C-119s would be arriving instead. I had no interest and was transferred back to the Air Force Reserve, Inactive. According to my flight record, that concluded my flying time with the United States Air Force and New York Air National Guard: a total of 1,066 hours spread over six years.

Late in 1957, I learned that Weeden was considering ending its market-making in municipal dollar bonds. These are tax-exempt revenue bonds normally issued to finance large government-sponsored infrastructure projects like dams, toll roads and bridges. The issues were structured mainly with a very large long-term maturity, carrying a high rate of interest. They were attractive to both institutional and individual investors. The bonds were actively traded in the secondary market with considerable competition.

Weeden did a good business in them but was finding it difficult to turn a profit. The competition was keen, the spreads were narrow, and we did not have a captive list of retail clients. Hearing that we might stop trading them, I argued that it was an important part of our image on the street and that a more aggressive marketing effort might help. Alan was supportive and persuaded Frank and others to let me take over the trading responsibilities.

162　　　　　　　　　　　　　　　　　　　　　　　　　　*As Luck Would Have It*

I knew little about trading, so I took a seat directly across from Bill Simon and Bob Tighe, both of whom had recently joined Weeden from Union Securities when their firm was acquired by Eastman Dillon. They guided me until I began to feel comfortable doing it by myself. I also began visiting the many small, regional brokerage houses that specialized in selling tax-exempt bonds. They were ideal customers for Weeden because the size of their orders was small and they did not drive a hard bargain on price.

My trading style was to satisfy every inquiry so they would come to rely on us as their preferred dealer. Profit per trade went down a bit, but volume rose substantially and we were again profitable. We even began to intrude upon Salomon Brothers' dominance of the institutional business. Within a year we were considered one of four dealers that dominated the municipal dollar bond market. With increased volume, I could justify hiring one of the better municipal bond brokers, freeing me to spend additional time on the road.

My added traveling did not help Vera's sense of loneliness. When we purchased the property in Newtown in December 1959, I made the decision, welcomed by Vera, to devote every weekend to the family.
Except in the harshest of winter weather, we traveled the 80 miles to Pond Brook Road every weekend. This was done first in our little bug and then, as the family grew to four and then five, in a VW combo.

Henry Frank was born in May 1960. Shortly after, we moved from Cobble Hill to the Concord Village Apartments, ninth floor, looking west directly at Lower Manhattan. The apartment had just enough space for the four of us. Vera began to meet other young mothers whose husbands worked on Wall Street or were lawyers or accountants. One young man from Norway, Jacob Stolt-Nielsen, had already created his own shipping company, which became one of the earliest to specialize in moving cargo by containers.

After the move, Vera's attitude toward America improved greatly, and our life settled into a routine that was satisfying for both of us. I was now finished with flying. One or two days a week, I would stop off at the Downtown Athletic Club and play a game of squash racquets (enough to win the Class B championship one year). Routinely, Jack and Alan (they used the club for swimming) and I would meet for dinner. There were also stops for drinks with our traders and/or customers and then back home. Vera, meanwhile, had developed a keen interest in sculpting and spent one evening in Manhattan while I babysat. Our weekends were always spent on our property in Newtown.

My 30th birthday came and went. I am not big on birthday celebrations, particularly my own, but I did believe there was something special about the 30th. It was a moment of transition. Up to then I was learning, looking, testing and experiencing possible paths to a suitable lifestyle and a career within Weeden.

Our move to Concord Village and our purchase in Newtown completed our decision to remain in New York City. A casual investment in National Semiconductor Corp. eventually drew me into the world of Silicon Valley. At Weeden, I was soon to begin my involvement with its struggle with the New York Stock Exchange.

The first had the effect of isolating our family from the life of many with similar backgrounds, careers and social interests. The second provided me with liquid assets that changed our economic status and gave me a special insight into how the technology would affect Wall Street. And finally, I found something to do at Weeden that engendered passion and focus.

The Weeden house at Duck Hollow on Pond Brook Road, Newtown, Connecticut, 1961 (above). Don's first crack at building something (below).

Queenie, Elizabeth, Vera and baby Henry Frank (Frankie), 1960.

Don at home with Frankie, 6 months, and Elizabeth, 2.

Chapter 12
New York City, 1961–1965

Christine Anne arrived in March of 1962. Concord Village was a two-bedroom apartment buildng overlooking Copley Square, Brooklyn Heights and the Lower Manhattan skyline. The Chase Manhattan building was in mid-construction. Vera and I moved into the smaller bedroom and began to think about a larger apartment.

There was a park across the street. From there, it was a short stroll to the promenade on Brooklyn Heights. I had easy access to the Brooklyn Bridge, which provided a pleasant walk, over soft wooden planks, to Manhattan. The office became an easy stroll of 20 minutes.

Elizabeth, not yet four, was already a very confident little girl. Several times, I let her walk the long block to the grocery store by herself. I would sneak downstairs before her and watch from across the street. She would march down the sidewalk with her little purse clutched tightly in her hand and then return with her purchases.

When the grandparents invited her to California, we were quite comfortable in sending her alone on a Pan Am flight to San Francisco. In the month before I arrived, her grandfather had been teaching her how to swim. On her fourth birthday (August 1) she swam the entire length of our 20-yard pool without stopping or taking a breath.

Our social life had picked up considerably. Concord Village was filled with young couples working in and around Wall Street. They were a diverse lot and fun to be with. During good weather there was often a "bring your own bottle" get-together on the roof of one of our buildings. Most of the couples had children and belonged to the same babysitting club. The rules were quite complicated, depending on number of children, their ages, day of the week, number of hours, and whether it was day, evening or late night. We were fortunate that our kids and their ages dovetailed with the mother in charge of making the rules.

My good friends Chuck Kelly and Jack Smith were also married now and living on Manhattan. The Jack Smiths would invite us over to their apartment on East 49th Street, where he would bring his telescope up to the roof and the six of us would peer into Arthur Miller's apartment on East 50th for a glimpse of Marilyn.

Friday evenings found us driving to Newtown for a quiet family weekend on Pond Brook Road. There was plenty of space outdoors, lots of nature to explore, a brook to wade in and books to be read in the evening.

In 1961, I turned over the municipal dollar bond desk to others and joined our stock desk to learn that side of Weeden's business. This is a good time to explain how the firm entered the business of trading stocks the same way we traded municipal bonds. Over the years, we noticed that our customers, institutions and non-member broker/dealers, began to recommend/use listed stocks in their accounts. As their interest moved from low-risk preferred stocks to utility common stocks, and then to industrial common stocks (the latter happening after World War II), Weeden followed along, making markets net of any commission. This fact made our net bid or offer more attractive to institutions and non-member brokers than the total cost of a trade done through a NYSE member broker. Our revenue came from the spread between our bid and offer. The trades were mainly in small amounts. By the time I joined the firm in 1956, this business had grown significantly, although we were still below the radar of the regulators and the NYSE.

Instead of being made a trader, I was given some "you can do no harm" accounts in Akron, Toledo and Columbus, where I could practice my sales pitch to "use Weeden when buying and selling listed stocks." Unfortunately, the local banks had little in the way of orders, and even less interest in saving a few dollars for their trust accounts. This last point is important, as it represents the dilemma we had marketing this business. Weeden was not a member of any exchange and did not charge an additional commission as required by members of all exchanges. This gave us a significant price advantage when dealing with institutional accounts.

Akron became an exception to the "you can do no harm" theory. While in town, I visited the treasurer's office at Firestone and Goodyear, the two biggest tire and rubber companies. Both had major pension funds and stock repurchase programs handled by Chase Manhattan's trust department in New York. When I explained the savings in commissions that could be achieved if the trade were done with Weeden, they asked whether Chase used us on their pension fund orders. I said that Chase certainly knew us and executed listed stock orders with us, but I did not know whether they were doing it for their company's pension funds. I silently hoped they would ask Chase, and that's exactly what they did.

When I returned to our office, I was met by our head trader, Eddie Sinclair, who wanted to know "What the hell did you say to those people out in Akron?" He had received a call from Tommy Cahill, the head of the trading desk at Chase, who wanted to know who this guy "Weeden" is who is telling one of our best accounts that "we aren't doing our job properly. We are getting hell from our senior VP, Charles Simon, who covers those accounts." I thought for a moment and then told Eddie that in no way did I say anything other than Chase knew about us and did business with us. Period! I then said I was willing to meet with Mr. Cahill and Mr. Simon in person to go through my conversations in Akron—I even insisted on it. They accepted my story. No harm was done. Slowly, our business with them increased.

Why do I mention this incident? It is interesting because Chase, like so many of the banks (and other institutions for other reasons), tended to ignore our markets in listed stocks because (1) it was accepted practice to do the business on the NYSE, (2) they felt no fiduciary responsibility to seek a better price, and (3) they had become used to using the commissions given to exchange member brokers to attract commercial deposits for their banking department.

I assume that Chase had never bothered to explain to their clients in Akron the possibility of receiving a better price away from the NYSE. They were embarrassed and uncomfortable for not having done so. I was beginning to understand how the real world operates.

About the same time, the First National City Bank (now Citibank) stopped using our net markets in stocks listed on the NYSE. Over time they had become a good customer of ours. Foster Cooper, their head trader, phoned my father and said that he had been directed by top management not to do business with Weeden in NYSE-listed stocks. Exchange officials had convinced them that many of their members with significant deposits of cash with the bank were complaining about the trust department diverting business away from their exchange to firms like Weeden. They implied that some were considering withdrawing their balances from the bank. The argument the bank management relied upon was "the uncertainty of getting the best price away from the central market may expose the trust department to liability."

Frank did not argue with Foster but countered with the suggestion that they continue to do their odd-lot purchases and sales at a net price 1/8th or a quarter point away from the next trade, that being the same price as if it had been done on the exchange floor. By doing it that way, it would "always" save the trust account the full NYSE commission. Foster was delighted with the suggestion, and each day forward we would execute dozens of odd-lot (less than 100 shares) transactions with the First National City Bank. Soon after, the Irving Trust Company also stopped trading with us for the same reason. This made it clear to me that we had a real fight brewing with the NYSE that could not be avoided.

There were other signals that the NYSE was no longer passive about our small but growing penetration of their marketplace. Back in 1959, they had indirectly challenged us by pulling their ticker tape from the offices of Municipal Securities Corp (MS), an over-the-counter broker in Dallas. They also ordered their member firms to disconnect any direct telephone wires they had with MS. The NYSE then declined to give any reason for their action and Silver, the owner of Municipal Securities, sued them under the Sherman Anti-Trust Act that "prohibited conspiracies in restraint of trade." In the meantime, Municipal Securities had gone out of business.

I was trading dollar bonds at the time. Frank asked me if any of my classmates at Yale Law School would look into the matter. I asked Bob Beshar to keep us informed of its progress through the courts, which he did. After a mixed set of decisions in the lower courts, the case came before the United States Supreme Court. In May 1963, the court decided by a vote of 7 to 2 in favor of Silver. (I have described the saga of its trip through the courts in a book titled Weeden & Co., the New York Stock Exchange, and the Struggle over a National Securities Market, published in 2002.) Our interest was obvious: If the NYSE could do to others what it did to Municipal Securities, without any explanation, hearing or due process, then Weeden's business was in jeopardy.

During this same period, the Securities Exchange Commission (SEC) Special Study of Securities Markets, an investigation into whether the SEC's rules for national securities exchanges and associations sufficiently protected investors, was authorized by Congress (May 1961). It was the result of their investigation of a specialist firm on the American Stock Exchange that exposed a series of "egregious acts of fraud, misrepresentation and self-dealing." The study encompassed all aspects of trading on all stock exchanges and trading in over-the-counter stocks in the United States.

This study was of obvious interest to Weeden, although the release made no mention of our special market in which listed stocks were being traded in the over-the-counter marketplace. It did highlight shortcomings in the industry's self-regulation practices.

While this Special Study was being conducted, I was learning the art of quoting a market in a security where the market, price and volume were dominated/controlled by the NYSE specialist. It was quite different from what I had experienced while trading dollar bonds, where the playing field was level and everyone had an equal chance of doing the business. Our head trader, Eddie Sinclair, let me trade a few of the chemical and drug stocks. I quickly got the gist of how much you were at the mercy of what was happening on the NYSE floor. I did not do well, but I learned a lot.

Rather than trying to master the art of trading individual stocks against the near-monopoly of the NYSE specialist, I found myself thinking about the larger picture. It troubled me that the NYSE specialist system had evolved in a way that first squeezed out competition from other members and then from other exchanges.

Over the years, the specialists came to dominate the NYSE, had gained a trading monopoly for each one in their assigned stocks, and were able to direct the exchange to do whatever was necessary to prevent any significant competition from developing. As one who was trying to compete, I saw their willingness, legally and illegally, to squash competition as a misuse of power. I saw them as bullies, plain and simple, misusing their size, just like the bully at the top of the seawall. It stirred up similar feelings I had when crossing 12th Street with my broomstick in hand.

In 1961, Bob Beshar had arranged a meeting with David Silver, who was clerking for the District Court judge handling the Silver case. Over a dinner of crab au gratin at Whyte's restaurant on Fulton Street, I described our business and pointed out why the action of the NYSE had anticompetitive implications.

Sometime later, David went to work for the Special Study, where he described our business in listed stocks. Eventually it was studied along with the other two markets, listed and over-the-counter, treating it as "the Third Market," with its own chapter. Frank and I helped staff members of the Special Study design a questionnaire that would show exactly what firms were active, who they did business with, and why the institutions and non-member firms found our markets useful, competitive and advantageous to their clients. This was far more exciting than trading a bunch of stocks.

I was also introducing our net markets to the European banking community. Two of our most active clients were Swiss Bank Corp. and Credit Suisse, both with a branch in New York City. They acted as agent, or broker, charging a commission on each transaction. On stocks listed on the NYSE, they would add an additional commission on top of the NYSE member firm's commission charged to them. By trading with Weeden, they were able to retain part, or all, of the member-firm commission for themselves.

Many more European banks were obviously doing the same thing, only not at a level to justify a New York office. After I cut my teeth in Akron, I made my first business trip to Europe. Officers at Chase Manhattan Bank, J.P. Morgan and First National City Bank wrote letters of introduction and I began a series of trips described by the movie title "If It's Tuesday, This Must Be Belgium." I would fly over on the weekend and spend the next week visiting five cities, a minimum of six banks per day, with a dinner to boot.

At 32 years of age, I was up to it, although barely. I found enough interest to justify our opening an office in London.

It was May 1963 when I signed a 99-year lease, standard in Britain, for modest space on the Lower Ground Floor of Warnford Court. It was just off Throgmorton Street in the heart of the financial district and close by the London Stock Exchange. Two months later, the U.S. Congress passed legislation creating an interest equalization tax on foreign purchases of U.S. bonds. I had just obligated myself personally to paying rent for 99 years for an office that overnight had far less business potential.

As it turned out, the tax created greater opportunities by shifting considerable underwriting business from New York to London. Weeden became one of the leading dealers in dollar-denominated bonds of American corporations. They were traded in London and Zurich, with delivery and settlement in Luxembourg or Brussels. Our active dealing in bonds and our third-market business grew impressively, and I found myself spending a fair amount of time visiting clients and hosting dinners.

Vera would join me upon occasion and enjoyed the attention and the four-star accommodations when we traveled together. One of those trips coincided with an extended stay in Switzerland with Elizabeth and Frank in tow. While in London, we stayed at the Connaught Hotel and arranged for a separate room for the children. Richard Durlacher, the largest jobber (specialist) on the London Stock Exchange, had invited us for dinner and we were anticipating a late evening. About 7 o'clock the next morning, we were awakened by a call mentioning that there were two children about the ages of three and five who had arrived at the dining room in their pajamas. "Could they be yours?"

On one trip to Amsterdam with my brother Jack, we went to visit the Bank Krayenhagen on Three Kings Street. I thought I knew where it was but as we approached the vicinity where I thought it should be, I turned to a passerby and (impressing my brother with my command of the German language) inquired in German if he knew "Vo der Drei Koenigen Strasse gestanden, bitte?" ("Where is Three Kings Street, please?") The gentleman was very gracious in his instructions which, we soon discovered were directing us in the opposite direction. We concluded he knew very well where the street was but he was doing his little thing to annoy a couple of Germans who had the audacity to return to Amsterdam after the war.

When we began doing business out of London, we would telex all the banks with our two-sided markets in the 50 to 60 stocks popular in Europe and traded on most European exchanges. Our market was usually a three-eighths or half-point spread around the NYSE closing price on the previous day and was good for up to 500 shares. They were much appreciated by the banks executing on behalf of their customer and who only wanted to earn the normal commission. Others were active as traders and resented our net markets for undermining their practice of providing much wider spreads.

Jack set up the office and insured that the operational and regulatory aspects ran smoothly. He ended up spending the better part of six months in London. I continued my trips to the Continent, visiting clients who were located in most of the major cities. In the summer I would dovetail the trip into Vera's visit with our three children to Savognin, along with members of her family.

I was still part of our stock desk but did little in the way of trading. It was during this period that I began a mental transition toward defending and then advocating for Weeden's Third Market business.

When I first returned from the air force, I learned that a Weeden Bros. Partnership had been established by my father for his four sons. The purpose was to consolidate in one investment vehicle the small amounts of money being distributed to each of us from the estates of relatives, most of whom had lived in England. The accumulated funds totaled $43,000.

Initially, we piggybacked on arbitrage deals in which the firm was an active market maker. There was little risk, and we made some money. At our dinners at the Downtown Athletic Club, I suggested that because three of the four brothers were making a living through short-term, low-risk trading, the Weeden Bros. partnership should invest in long-term venture plays that had the possibility of large gains. I saw it as a hedge against our daily business. Jack and Alan went along and left it to me to learn how to get involved. Don Lucas and his colleagues at Smith Barney were doing much the same, and I followed along. Weeden Bros. invested $5,000 in two startups, Applied Dynamics and Allied Research, which eventually were sold at a modest profit.

In 1959, Don Lucas showed me a startup that came from Smith Barney's Minneapolis office. They were eight engineers and physicists leaving Sperry Rand in South Norwalk to start a new company. They named it National Semiconductor Corporation. The Midwest Technology Fund was investing $250,000 of $500,000 being raised. Its director, Bud Ryden, had helped start Control Data Corp., which at the time was a high flier in the new electronic technology. Weeden Bros. invested $25,000, and I invested $5,000 personally.

A story has since been told that someone at Smith Barney called the venture capital and private equity firm American Research and Development Corporation (ARDC) to ask their opinion on the future prospects of

As Luck Would Have It

the semiconductor industry. ARDC was run by Georges Doriot and had an excellent reputation for knowing about the new technologies. They were the first major investor in Digital Equipment Corp. when it was still operating out of a garage in New Hampshire. They knew nothing about National Semiconductor but thought the industry in general had "matured" (this was five years before the first integrated circuit was built).

The investment in National was completed in the summer of 1959. At the time, Vera and I had focused our house-hunting on Connecticut after eliminating Long Island and New Jersey. We were looking for a getaway and summer retreat rather than a primary home. We liked the area around Danbury, known as the Hat City of the World, although its economy was suffering from a secular trend away from men wearing hats. Poor access by auto and train gave it a "back eddy" flavor that kept real estate prices low in comparison to areas with the same driving time from New York City. In December we closed on 16 acres, more or less, located on the outskirts of Newtown, one town farther east from Danbury. The price was $25,000.

The men who left Sperry Rand to form National Semiconductor Corp. rented a building in Danbury for their first factory. On the weekends I would drop by and get to know them, learn what a semiconductor was and how they were made. In 1962, a vacancy occurred on the board. Bernie Rothlein and Ed Clark, members of the board, along with Don Lucas, recommended me. I remained on the board until 2000, when I reached the mandatory retirement age of 70.

National grew rapidly and needed capital to expand. I discussed it with Frank to see whether Weeden & Co. would make an investment. Frank came to Danbury to check out the facility and meet the team. He remembered the story about an oil distributor in which friends had made loans, collateralized by its inventory of oil drums. When hard times came and they went to collect the barrels of oil, they found the barrels empty. After hearing Bernie's pitch on how well they were doing, Frank asked to see the inventory. With some reluctance, Bernie finally opened one of the drawers of his desk and said "Here it is," while explaining that the diodes crammed into the drawer would sell for a lot of money.

Frank agreed to Weeden lending $75,000, as part of a $250,000 loan, which had warrants attached, convertible at $10 per share. The original investment had been at $1 a share, an indication that National was seen as an interesting play in a growth industry. By regulation the shares would only be sold to a sophisticated investor with the intention of holding them for a minimum of two years. Over time, this requirement was breached by many of the early investors in Minneapolis, where several over-the-counter brokers made markets in its stock. Its price became quite volatile as news about the industry fluctuated, and trading activity rose to the point where the paper formalities were all but forgotten and ownership became widely distributed.

At the time National was incorporated, Sperry Rand brought a lawsuit charging National and its eight founders with stealing trade secrets. Our lawyers believed the lawsuit had little merit. In 1964, the Connecticut State Court agreed with Sperry. Besides the shock of losing, we learned that in Connecticut, Sperry was entitled to secure the assets of National by closing us down pending determination of damages. The market price per share returned to $1.

Members of the board, local counsel, Tom Ramseur from White & Case, and Bob Beshar, a guest of mine, who was counsel for Weeden, held a meeting at the Red Lobster Inn in Bridgeport attended by. Bob was awkwardly kept waiting outside. Sperry had asked for $1 million in damages and agreement from National to stop making the alloy transistor, the technology it claimed had been "stolen" from Sperry. We were willing to give up the alloy transistor, having moved on to another technology in the interim, but we had no way of paying the $1 million. Our assets, especially liquid assets, came nowhere near that amount. The assembled lawyers had no solutions to offer except bankruptcy.

I left the meeting and explained the situation to Bob. He believed the only chance of survival was to request the Federal District Court in New Haven to place National into "voluntary" receivership until the matter of damages was resolved. Absent any better suggestion, the board voted to do just that and appointed Bob to make the overture to the District Court.

The rest is history. National went under the protection of the Federal District Court in New Haven, a receiver was appointed, and we continued to do business. Cash was tight, employees deferred salaries, and the landlord took stock in lieu of rent. The firm continued to produce diodes until Sperry settled for $300,000, payable over five years. A new round of financing was now possible with Bob Beshar's friend Peter Sprague as lead investor, but only if the prior convertible debentures would convert into shares.

Frank represented the lenders informally and I informally represented the company informally. We were back and forth on determining the appropriate "new" price of conversion, with Frank holding the stronger hand. The company agreed to $2.25 per share and National never looked back. In the early 1970s, the value of Weeden's position in National stock rose considerably, but its price volatility affected quarterly earnings to the degree that we felt compelled to sell it.

As Luck Would Have It

The success of National earned a lot of money for Weeden, Weeden Bros. and me personally. It had been my suggestion to invest in venture startups, as was the idea to open a London office. I should also mention the turnaround in the profitability of our dollar bond trading. In combination, they began to change the relationship I had with the firm, my father and my two older brothers.

I had always been that cute younger brother following in my older brothers' footsteps, from Sadler School through Stanford. At Alameda High School I was elected student body president, just like Alan and Jack. In sports, I swam backstroke because they swam backstroke. Socially, I ended up joining the same high school fraternity and the same fraternity at Stanford. Even my four summers working at Yosemite National Park were the result of Jack working there before me.

With Jack, and especially Alan, I had a strong, almost "hero worship" relationship. We were all competitive, but, for the most part, it didn't overlap. I felt no jealousy toward either of them and admired what they did. There was no physical violence that developed scars among us. The three years of separation prevented any adversarial relationship developing. Outwardly, I could well have given the impression of lacking initiative and independence.

I see my upbringing differently. While my parents had a strong and supportive interest in all of us, witness Frank's coaching, their intensity naturally diminished when they got around to me. The Depression and World War II complicated their focus and absorbed much of their time away from the "boys."

At the same time, I was active, quick and well coordinated, did well enough in school, and managed to stay out of trouble. I had a lot of self-confidence and made the best of the independence afforded me. If I was dependent on anyone, it was the neighborhood gang. It was a large part of my daily life up through high school, and it was where I was an acknowledged leader.

The one time Jack, Alan and I spent time together for an extended period was in 1947. We spent three weeks hiking the John Muir Trail. It began to alter my view of a relationship that previously reflected our differences in age. I began to view the three of us as equals.

My working on the Norwegian freighter, Yale Law School, the Air Force and my Middle East adventures further developed our new relationship. When I returned to the family fold, it was with greater self-confidence and a more objective view of them. At our regular dinners together at the Downtown Athletic Club, when we played the role of Weeden's shadow board of directors, my opinions began to receive equal weight. Just how far our relationship had changed is illustrated by a dinner some time before I had taken responsibility for the stock trading desk.

Alan was critical of Frank's reluctance to shift control eastward and was still smarting from Frank's sale of precious Weeden stock to Bill Simon and Bob Tighe, both of whom reported to Alan. Alan wanted to put an ultimatum to Frank regarding a change in management control to the three of us. Weeden had been a public corporation since 1928, but voting control was in the hands of Frank, Norman and Mabel. Jack, Alan and I held small amounts.

I was surprised at his tone of urgency and told him so. I agreed that it should take place eventually. As for me, I was in no hurry, having been on board for a shorter time than either Alan or Jack. Knowing Alan's indifference to our "Third Market" business, I might have been concerned whether he was up to overseeing all aspects of the firm. I assumed that with any change Alan would become the president. Jack did not say too much one way or another, but I sensed that he also felt this was not the time to press Frank. The discussion went on through dinner without resolution, which meant we would do nothing. Alan was upset, but the more we talked about it, the firmer became my arguments against it. Essentially, I had made the decision on what the three of us would do.

It was Friday, November 22, 1963, when John F. Kennedy was assassinated. I was on the trading desk making my markets in the chemical and drug stocks when we heard the news. Once reality set in, the stock market went ballistic on the down side. Everybody wanted to sell; something, anything, everything. The ticker tape recording last sales on the NYSE, our guide in determining the market we would quote, was unable to keep up with the volume of selling occurring on the floor. Once we realized we were buying shares at prices above where trades were taking place on the floor, we engaged the odd-lot specialists to tell us the most current trade.

I remember the trader at Hartford National Bank asking for a market in ACD (Allied Chemical). I quoted him 32-33, when the last sale reported on the tape was 35. He was a seller and told me I was off my market. When he came back a few minutes later, I quoted him 31-32, based upon my latest information from the floor. He sold me his 1,000 shares at 31. The ticker tape ran until 7 o'clock in the evening before it finished reporting every trade done on the NYSE. Total volume exceeded 16 million shares. The average volume for the year until then was just over 4 million shares.

I encouraged the desk to keep making markets despite the difficulty in knowing what was happening on the Exchange floor. Because we were

As Luck Would Have It

usually below the reported last sale, we didn't do that much business, but we were generally lauded by our customers for hanging in and not freezing under difficult circumstances. I felt it was an ideal time to demonstrate some independence of the ticker tape (this issue became important in the ensuing debates about the competitive value of the Third Market).

By 1963, the die was cast. We were in a real fight with the NYSE. Unbeknownst to everyone except the NYSE, this fight had started in the late 1950s when the NYSE noticed that off-board volume in stocks listed on their exchange was increasing faster than their volume. A good portion of this increase was due to their members going off board to firms like Weeden, where they found a better price than was available from the specialist. In 1959, the NYSE completely revised its rules, including the paragraph numbers. One of the new rules, the significance of which was missed by the SEC, required a member to obtain permission from a floor governor before going to a dealer like Weeden. This had the effect of ending the practice, but it did not stop the growth of the Third Market.

The SEC Special Study, published in 1963, quantified the extent of Third Market growth. Frank had spent considerable time with members of the Special Study, helping to design various questionnaires submitted to users and market-makers. They included everything about the users—who, why and how—and the market-makers—spreads, volumes, capital used and stocks traded. Frank felt the more that was known, the more comfortable the SEC would be that we provided competition, added liquidity and acted properly. He also thought it would help legitimize the practice and encourage others to use us.

Neither Frank nor I, in our many meetings with the staff, exhibited the usual Wall Street attitude about the SEC as being inept, uninformed and anti-Wall Street. The SEC Special Study provided the Third Market with valuable publicity and solidified the NYSE's determination to put us out of business.

On the personal side, Christine's arrival in March 1962 was not without some last-minute excitement; "trauma" might be a better word. I had wanted to be in the delivery room throughout the delivery, which was seldom permitted at the time. Our obstetrician, Dr. Macgregor, arranged to have the birth take place in a Lutheran hospital about 20 minutes away, easily reached via the Gowanus Expressway. We prepaid for the usual six-day stay.

The predicted day arrived. It happened to be the same day that John Glenn was being honored with a ticker tape parade up Broadway to City Hall. I was home and relaxed, as was Vera. The cramps began slowly during the parade and then slowed during the afternoon and early evening, when they came at shorter and shorter intervals. Past experience suggested that there was plenty of time. It was close to midnight, and both of us did not want to use one of the six days by arriving 5 minutes before midnight. Suddenly the water broke and the labor pains came at increasingly shorter intervals.

Our car was parked in front of the building. We were on the Gowanus Parkway headed east in no time at all. It seems that in a third childbirth, the whole process moves along more quickly than prior births. The pains became sharper as we sped down a bumpy Gowanus Parkway. Upon arrival, Vera was hustled into the delivery room while I parked the car. By the time I had put on my gown and mask and entered the room, the baby had already been born. I registered us in at 12:05. By the fifth day, Vera was fed up with staying longer and we returned to Concord Village. No rebate.

Our search for a new apartment stretched out to the end of the year. A strike had closed down the New York Times, making the search more difficult. Finally, an estate sale became available to our broker. It was on the southeast corner of 72nd Street and Park Avenue. Our cost: $33,000.

The apartment had been the residence of Mrs. Meyer, widow of the president of the Hanseatic shipping line based in Hamburg, Germany. She and Mr. Meyer purchased it in 1913 when the building, 755 Park Avenue, was built. Both were ardent opera lovers and patrons of the Metropolitan Opera Company. We were told they hosted many late-evening parties that featured performers including Enrico Caruso.

The apartment was designed for nine rooms, including kitchen and servant quarters. The Meyers eliminated the walls separating the living room, library and master bedroom, creating an expansive area for entertaining. It was said that the arias heard coming from Apartment 1A often equaled those heard in the old Opera House.

We kept the library and living room together and had a wall built, re-creating the master bedroom. The three children slept in the two rear bedrooms. The apartment had the original paint from 1913. Rectangular black smudges of grease and soot on the walls marked where paintings had hung for 50 years. We painted every wall with subdued colors from the Williamsburg collection and sanded the floors.

Everything went smoothly, except when I applied a new coat of water-soluble paint on the ceilings of the two rear bedrooms. The original coat was an oil-based material. The moisture loosened the bond underneath and the ceiling began to sag in large folds. Another mistake was to use duct tape on the glass doors between the dining and living room. They consisted of small plates separated by wood molding. Removing the duct tape was far more difficult than just removing the paint from the glass.

My parents thought our move into a nine-room apartment in the heart of the elite Upper East Side of Manhattan, plus a 16-acre Connecticut hideaway, was living pretty high on the hog. It also separated us from our new-found friends in Concord Village. It tended to isolate us as a family. We were the only family with young children in our building of 48 coops. To complete the transition, I joined the Racquet and Tennis Club on Park Avenue and 53rd Street for their squash racquets facilities. My sponsor was Charlie Grimes, son of my savior in my cop-beating incident. Three of those seconding me were partners of specialist firms on the NYSE floor; they must not have read the SEC's Special Study.

Weeden's annual report for 1963 reported the 14th consecutive year in which gross sales increased over the previous year, going from $154 million to $1.1 billion. Net income had not been as consistent, as one would expect for a dealer firm. It rose from $208,000 in 1950 to $911,000 in 1963. If one took our bottom line over the 14-year period, the result would show $1.25 of earnings for every $1,000 of sales, a rather low margin for a firm taking substantial inventory risk on a daily basis. This exposure caught up with us in 1962, when the stock market dropped precipitously and unexpectedly due to a confrontation between President Kennedy and the steel industry. Our losses in the second quarter were substantial. By the end of the year, we had returned to profitability.

A strength of Weeden was the efficiency of its back office. Efficiency was almost an obsession with Frank and was passed down to Jack, who was given overall responsibility for operations a few years after joining the firm. Like most firms in those days, we did all our own clearing and settling of trades. What distinguished us from most of the brokers was this attention given to the back office by top management. Much of our business was in small trades, with customers on both sides, often handled by two different offices. Securities had to be received, shipped and delivered quickly to reduce the cost of borrowing in a period of relatively high interest rates. It called for creative management and constant oversight.

Weeden made a point of hiring young women and giving them positions of responsibility. We always paid well, established a broad-based bonus system, instituted a profit-sharing trust in 1946 (one of the earliest on Wall Street) and treated all our employees as part of a family. Our Christmas parties were known for the skits put on by every department that poked fun at every level of management.

One of Jack's responsibilities as head of operations was acting as master of ceremonies at these parties held in each of our offices.

With the publication of the SEC's Special Study, Weeden's reputation on Wall Street took a spurt upward. Our cooperation with the staff had proven valuable, witnessed the Study's conclusion: "Under existing conditions, it appears that the over-the-counter market for listed stocks has been beneficial to investors and in the public interest."

The study was careful not to reveal names of the firms behind the statistics reported. We could see that Weeden & Co. accounted for over 50 percent of total activity done by the eight firms defined as the "Third Market." In a Fortune magazine article titled the "The Ten Most Powerful Men on Wall Street," Frank was cited for leading the largest Third Market dealer.

From our new home on Park Avenue, the family would drive to Pond Brook Road every weekend. Our dull beige VW combo sped us there 30 minutes faster than the trip from Brooklyn. Our route took us on major highways until we exited off the new Interstate 84 to Pond Brook Road, a dirt road that curved and bumped for a mile and a half.

The property turned out to be closer to 30 acres than the 16 acres, more or less, described in the original deed. It was shaped like a sausage, stretching for a quarter-mile along both sides of a free-running brook that flowed even in the driest of summers. The brook made a long ninety-degree loop after entering our property. An abandoned single-track railroad bed followed the brook, with the remains of two stone bridges at each end of the property. It had been part of the Shepaug Valley Line, running north from Danbury to Southbury, which had stopped operating some years before; the tracks and ties were removed, leaving the roadbed clear for easy walking.

Our driveway ran 200 yards off Pond Brook Road to a small cabin overlooking a meadow that sloped gently to the brook. It was picturesque, quiet and protected.

The land was nestled into an isolated corner of Newtown. My father's remark "It is much too lonely for me" was one of its charms. From our property, Pond Brook continued for a mile into the Housatonic River, now a full-grown lake behind a recently constructed dam. Our Pond Brook retreat changed my lifestyle. I took to those tasks required when one owns 30 acres of untouched woodlands and overgrown meadows. There were fallen trees to butt up and then split into firewood, brambles to clear and vegetable gardens to plant. The cabin was nice and cozy, but one bedroom was hardly enough for the four of us. Tina was not yet born. Later, when the series of mother's helpers from Germany came along, it was overcrowded, even with an added bedroom.

Elizabeth Smith, a friend of the family, came to visit and remarked that another bedroom would be nice. The upshot was my deciding to build a stone house myself at the other end of the property, on higher ground,

As Luck Would Have It

with a view of the brook where it made its wide turn below. During my hikes along the brook, I had run into some interesting stones at a spot downstream where the railroad bed ran very close to the brook. It had been shored up with tailings from a local quarry. Many of the tailings had one or more flat surfaces at 90-degree angles. They were of manageable size and weight. What better than a hut built with native stone and timber from the property?

I planned a simple one-room stone hut, 10 by 18 feet on the inside with walls 18 inches thick. There would be a fireplace at one end, two windows on one of the long sides, and a door opposite. It would have an attic reachable by a pull-down ladder. The stones would come from my treasure trove along the railroad and the wooden floor from the large downed oak tree nearby.

It took me two years working on the weekends, hauling the stone tailings in the back of my Vauxhall station wagon (won in a lottery at a municipal bond club outing), mixing the concrete and fitting the stones neatly together. The surfaces both inside and out came out relatively flat. By the time I had finished my work of art, wiser heads had prevailed elsewhere. Two new rooms had been professionally added to our cabin below.

I had only one fright throughout the effort. Frankie, barely three, started up the ladder to the attic and lost his balance just at the top rung. My back was toward him, but instinctively I turned and caught him just before he hit the concrete floor. It was the first of several close calls for Frank over the next few years.

My next big project was clearing underbrush and planting seedlings indigenous to the region: walnut, chestnut, hemlock and ash. These were available from the state Department of Agriculture. Our land was covered mainly by scrub, or swamp oak, also referred to as piss oak because of its smell when cut. For several years there was an infestation of gypsy moths that fed off the spring growth of oak leaves, leaving our forest looking "winter-like" in June. To minimize future damage, I, along with the kids, planted more than 2,000 seedlings of hemlock.

Other projects that would keep me busy during the years ahead included installing a grass tennis court and building my dream house with the help of a U.S. Government pamphlet titled "How to Build Your Own Wood Framed House."

From the beginning, I wanted the weekends to be devoted to the family. During the week I was busy in my own world of business. Often it extended into the evenings spent with customers, employees, friends and brothers. There was almost no entertainment at home except for times when Mother came to New York City. While at Pond Brook, I rested, recovered, did my outdoor activities and played with the children.

It was a perfect environment for interacting, observing, encouraging and steering them away from trouble. I made up stories about rabbits and snakes, water skitters and frogs, and a friendly dog named Bowser. I read them Winnie-the-Pooh, Watership Down and the Tolkien trilogy, to mention a few. There was nothing special about those weekends, just being together as a family. Brushing up against one another throughout the day felt comfortable and satisfying.

There were moments when my mind would migrate to my work. It was then left to Vera, the kids down the road and my children's creativity to keep them busy. Vera set the daily schedule, brought us together for lunches and dinners, and shared in the family activities.

By the end of 1963, the opening of an office in London and trips down to Washington kept me off the stock trading desk—not the best thing if you are a junior trader trying to master the art. This was especially tricky when your main competitor, the NYSE specialist, is controlling the fluctuations in pricing. The good traders on our desk were watching every tick, looking for trends, talking to our larger customers, deciding whether the specialist was long or short, and many other inputs that would help him determine whether to be on the long or short side. You had to be there every day to do it right and make a profit.

I had little interest in the minor price movements of stocks, watching every tick up and down; this attitude extended to the longer trends of the market. What I kept seeing was a NYSE trying to put us out of business, like they did to Municipal Securities. It was the issue I took home and thought about on the weekends. I'm sure some were questioning my value to the firm, especially those on the desk who spent full time making markets. Being the boss's son, having two older brothers in the firm, plus a strong self-confidence, helped overcome any self-questioning.

The firm's business continued to grow for the next two years, driven mainly by an increase in our Third Market trading. We enjoyed a 25 percent increase in revenue despite a slower and lower bond market. My move from bonds to stocks had come at a propitious time for me, and it neatly rounded out the three younger Weedens' involvement in the firm: stocks, bonds and operations.

A new development occurred in 1964 with the listing of Chase Manhattan on the NYSE. Back in 1929, the price of listed bank stocks fell precipitously. The general public became concerned about the safety of their deposits. It was the consensus that bank stocks should not be traded on a public exchange. Over time, banks withdrew their listing on an exchange and moved to the over-the-counter market. Several of the Street's well-capitalized firms competed as market-makers. M.A. Schapiro & Co. was the largest. His trading activity was akin to that of a wholesaler in which he limited his business to recognized institutions and registered retail securities' brokers.

In 1964, the equity market was growing rapidly; the 1929 Crash was now an historical event viewed with curiosity rather than concern. The banks were growing and wanted to benefit from a broader distribution and improved stock price they felt was obtainable by relisting. Chase Manhattan Bank was the first to apply for listing on the NYSE, and their application was quickly approved.

Morris Schapiro was concerned—not so much with having an additional competitor, but with NYSE Rule 394, which prohibited its members dealing away from their floor in any stock listed on the Exchange. This meant that Merrill Lynch and several hundred other long-standing and satisfied customers of his could no longer do business with him in Chase's stock. Morris knew quite well that Chase's successful listing would open the floodgates for further listings.

In their informal discussions together, the NYSE suggested if M.A. Schapiro joined the Exchange and became a specialist firm on the floor, they would assign him the exclusive trading of Chase. But with respect to further listings, he would have to stand in line with other specialist firms for additional assignments. Bottom line: He would have a monopoly of their members' orders in Chase but would be excluded from dealing when other bank stocks were assigned to other specialists.

Morris saw this as a clear violation of the Sherman Antitrust Act; "An Agreement in Restraint of Trade" was the applicable language. The NYSE offer was not only unacceptable to this strong-minded, independent giant on Wall Street, but it was repugnant to his every legal and moral sense of right and decency. For over 40 years, he had nurtured a strong, close relationship with brokers who were members of every exchange across the country, and to have the NYSE able to prevent their doing business with him even in one single bank stock was just not right.

One of his first calls was to Weeden, and I went to see him, along with Bob Beshar. That first meeting included George Reycraft, a partner of Cadwalader, Wickersham & Taft. It was the same George Reycraft with whom Bob and I met when he worked in the Antitrust Division of the U.S. Department of Justice when the Silver (Municipal Securities) case was before the Supreme Court. Our views were similar to Schapiro's in that Rule 394 was a violation of the Sherman Antitrust Act, but our situation was quite different: In Schapiro's case, the NYSE was taking business away from him, while in Weeden's case, we were trying to take business away from the NYSE.

We both agreed that the NYSE Rule 394 being "a conspiracy in restraint of trade" should apply equally to both firms. Nevertheless, Schapiro's case was very straightforward, whereas in our situation the issue of "injury" was less clear and might be more difficult for the court to rule against the NYSE. Bob Beshar, plus all the family, felt uncomfortable in joining Schapiro in a lawsuit. And ultimately, after much to-do and a full-page statement in the *New York Times*, Schapiro eventually decided not to sue.

Our business was growing nicely. The institutions were more willing to check our prices and our market share was rising. We saw little reason to get embroiled in litigation that cost money and usually loses some friends along the way. Besides, my father and uncle had a general distaste for lawyers and courts. We were also at a point in the growing confrontation with the NYSE where Frank strongly felt that our complaint over Rule 394 could be resolved without lawsuits, hopefully with the intervention of the SEC. He pointed to the Special Study and its conclusion that our markets were in the public interest. The SEC commissioners would undoubtedly find a solution to our liking.

I went along with Frank, although my own feelings were somewhat different. I saw the NYSE as determined to continue doing what they were doing, and they would use whatever influence they had over our customers, our bankers, the corporations who listed on their Exchange, as well as the SEC, to see to it that the Third Market would be contained, if not eliminated. They would even go to Congress if need be. I thought Schapiro's case was so clean and persuasive that the courts would throw out Rule 394 using similar arguments as were used in the Silver case. Over the remainder of the year and well into 1965, the SEC took on the role of mediator, the NYSE modified Rule 394, and Schapiro ended up not suing.

Meanwhile, my family was settling into our rather commodious new living quarters and enjoying the amenities of Manhattan's Upper East Side. With three young children (ages 5, 3 and 1), being close to Central Park was a windfall. It was clear that Vera could use help, and she soon arranged through her relatives in Basel and Lörrach, Germany, for a series of mother's helpers to live with us over the next few years.

My earnings at Weeden, plus some luck in investing, allowed for our new lifestyle. The fancy address placed us in the middle of New York's rich and famous, although we must have appeared out of place to our doorman. Often, our bulky beige Volkswagen bus, suffering the dents and scrapes of one who couldn't afford a parking garage, would end up squeezed into the space just in front of our entranceway.

The first year, 1963, was a busy one, scraping and painting the entire apartment ourselves and accumulating furniture to fill seven rooms. Elizabeth would be 5 in August and entering kindergarten. Choosing the right school and then having our child accepted was a lot more complicated than back when I was sent to Sadler School in Alameda. A public school was not considered. I'm not even sure there was one at a reasonable distance from our co-op. But there were a dozen or more private schools, each having its own personality and social status.

I was taken aback by the high tuition and turned off by the social considerations involved. Vera decided we could avoid both problems by enrolling Elizabeth at the Lycée Français de New York. It was just a block and a half toward Fifth Avenue. It was coeducational and the classes were conducted solely in French, a practice which pleased Vera. Monsieur Galy, its director, hired teachers only from Paris. Both Elizabeth and Frank became fluent in "Parisian" French, which had a distinct dialect recognized throughout the world as being the only "pure" French.

Elizabeth would remain with the Lycée Français all the way through the 12th grade, when she received her baccalaureate. On the way she spent several years at their school located on 72nd and 94th streets and two years at the École Français in the mountain resort town of Villars above the east end of Lake Lucerne in Switzerland. I can remember many dinners when Elizabeth or Frank would ask Vera, in French, for help on some problem raised in class, and Vera would reply in German. I thought this was something special, since I was so bad at languages.

It wasn't long before I became involved in the less-attractive side of Upper East Side culture. There were three banks of elevators at 755 Park Avenue. Since it was a cooperative, I did not own my apartment. I owned shares in a corporation, which owned the entire building, which entitled me to use a specific apartment. The building had a board of six directors, two representing each of the elevator banks. My bank had been short a director, and I was approached about filling the vacancy not long after moving in.

After Vera and I met everyone on the board, I was formally elected. I was quite a bit younger than the other five, all of whom I found interesting and full of lore about New York. State Senator McNeil Mitchell, who was the other director from my bank, was particularly interesting, having sponsored the Mitchell-Lama Housing projects and who always had a basket full of stories about New York politics.

After a couple of innocuous meetings, we were presented with a potential sale of shares by one of the apartment holders who had found a buyer named John Lowe. Mr. Lowe owned a firm in the apparel business and was married to a very attractive woman who owned a shop on Madison Avenue. He had graduated from the West Point Academy. Along with the normal financial information, he had submitted 50 letters of recommendation. I, who could barely round up five letters, was very impressed and ready to vote for his acceptance. Surprising to me, each of the other directors voiced concerns about his financial condition and seemed prepared to vote against. It was decided to adjourn without taking a vote.

The next night, Senator Mitchell invited me up for a drink and explained in a fatherly way that the problem, plain and simple, was the fact that Lowe was Jewish. His becoming a shareholder would upset the unwritten rule that the co-op would have no more than one-third of its shares owned by Jews. We talked about the policy, its history and the reasons for it, at some length. I suggested that a solution might be that I not attend the next meeting and they could vote as they wished without my presence.

That is what happened; they had their meeting and voted unanimously to "accept" Mr. Lowe's application. I was quite surprised at their decision. At the next annual election of the board, I was not on the slate for reelection.

Early in 1965, a crisis concerning our head stock trader could not be ignored and I took it upon myself to resolve it. Eddie Sinclair had joined Weeden in 1946. In 1949 he was asked to quote markets for us in a few industrial common stocks listed on the NYSE. He turned out to be very good at it and eventually became our head trader. Frank liked Eddie very much and thought of him as a very decent person.

Unfortunately, Eddie had a drinking problem. Over the years it began to creep into the hours of trading and his decision-making. This was silently tolerated by everyone in the New York office. It became obvious to me sitting on the trading desk, especially when he took a break in mid-morning to get a drink downstairs. I liked and respected Eddie, but his drinking was beginning to jeopardize the discipline and morale on the desk. Finally, I decided his condition could no longer be tolerated, and I told him that when he goes to lunch he need not return for the rest of the day. The next morning, the two of us discussed the matter and Eddie decided to quit. I explained the situation to my brothers and then my father. As a result, I was now in charge of the stock trading desk.

I thought it was a strange way to obtain a promotion, but it was Frank's style. He didn't like controversy or confrontation. I never considered whether this change was accepted by the other traders because they recognized my leadership talents or because I was the boss's son. Nor did I sit down with everyone and talk it over. Eddie left and I took over, and that was that.

On the home front, with the mother's helper on board, Vera was able to continue to do her sculpture classes and I would stop off at the Racquet and Tennis Club and play a game of squash. By 1965, Elizabeth was attending the Lycée Français and Frank was in kindergarten at their 72nd Street facility.

When summer vacation arrived, everyone shuttled off to Newtown. I would work the week in New York and then begin the tedious train ride to Danbury by way of South Norwalk. There I would change onto the "Toonerville Trolley," an ancient single car that often broke down. Whether it was a train or bus that finally arrived in Danbury, there was still a 20-minute drive to Pond Brook Road.

At the same time, Bob and Christine Beshar, with their three daughters, were spending their weekends at Gypsy Trail. It was located in Carmel, New York, not too far from our place. We began seeing them a fair amount and, as families, we became quite close. Bob and I had lots to talk about, with Weeden's growing involvement with the SEC and the NYSE, but conversations were not limited to business. Everyone joined in when we discussed the "no-nos": religion, politics and social issues.

Christine and Vera had their own strong opinions, while the children listened and contributed theirs.

Christine Beshar (née von Wedemeyer) and Vera Weeden (née Knauer/Rheinberger) were of strong German ancestry, but with quite different backgrounds. Christine came from the landed aristocracy in Pomerania, where the von Wedemeyers lived on a large estate with many full-time tenants. Her family was close to and finally bound by marriage to the von Bismarcks, who came from the same region.

Both of Vera's parents were from Leipzig, also in the eastern part of Germany, and represented the typical upper-middle-class managerial and manufacturing set. Bob met Christine during his time at Yale, when Christine was a student at Smith. To finish Christine's remarkable résumé, while having four children (the last one a son) and living on the west side of Manhattan, Christine began working in the law library of Davis Polk. After five years, she took the bar examination in New York without attending law school, passed it, and joined Cravath, Swaine & Moore. She eventually became Cravath's first woman partner. Quite an accomplishment! Some of my fondest memories are the days and evenings at Gypsy Trail filled with games, food, drink and long discussions about all sorts of things.

Vera and I also visited my brothers Alan in Larchmont and Jack on 12th Street, and entertained the parents when they were in town. Uncle Norman was often available as he traveled between his home in Alameda and his cousins and friends in England. Vera found him to be the one source of understanding and sympathy for her discomfort with my intense focus on the business and how it dominated the family discussions.

Being alone in the city during the week freed me to spend the evenings entertaining customers and drinking with my colleagues at Weeden. There were also friends around town from Stanford days, and always a game of squash to fill in the gaps. I was very comfortable with the arrangement and felt that Vera, also, was comfortable in being away from the noise and tension of Manhattan life.

In 1965, there was an election for mayor of New York. The Republican candidate was John Lindsay, a young, charismatic Congressman representing the 17th District, my district. It ran from 14th Street to 96th Street, from Central Park to the East River.

I was interested in his candidacy, but it was not until mid-July that I became involved. I was strolling along Madison Avenue and came across one of his storefronts with all his volunteers inside having a good time while the voters were walking by undisturbed. When I dropped in and began looking at the campaign literature, nobody paid any attention. I left thinking that it was a poor way to get people interested in their candidate.

I mentioned this to Bob Beshar, who put me on to Bob Sweet, another associate at his law firm, who was high up on the Lindsay team. Bob Sweet passed me on to Chuck Leedham, in charge of the Manhattan campaign. Chuck thought I might be helpful and sent me down to their storefront in the East Village, which seemed dead in the water.

What I found was a storefront strategically positioned at the corner of Avenue A and Seventh Street in the heart of New York State's 67th Assembly District. The district ran from 14th Street on the North to Houston Street on the south; and from the Bowery and Third Avenue on the west to the East River. The population was around 100,000, composed mainly of remnants from the many waves of immigrants that had arrived in the late 1800s and early 1900s: German, Irish, Italian, Greek, Polish, Ukrainian and Jews from several Eastern European countries. They were the old and the slow who never quite made it to a better neighborhood.

After World War II, Blacks and Hispanics arrived from the southern states and Puerto Rico. Then came the hippies from all over the country who found the East Village rents affordable, the lifestyle informal, and a high tolerance for their music and their drugs. Tompkins Square Park ran from Seventh to 10th, from Avenue A to B, plunk in the middle. It was a mini Central Park with numerous benches, a central amphitheater, and quiet nooks and crannies providing space for everyone.

When I arrived at five o'clock, Avenue A was almost as crowded as Madison Avenue, but the storefront was completely empty except for a Miss Richardson sitting at a desk in the back. She was in her 70s, nicely dressed with elegance in her face and demeanor. For most of the locals, she must have appeared haughty and forbidding. Bottom line, Miss Richardson was not attracting anyone and didn't seem to care. I learned later that she was a descendant of the family who owned the Herald Tribune. She had fallen on hard times and ended up living alone in a small apartment on 12th street off Second Avenue. Miss Richardson was a fish out of water, recruited as the only non-Polish, non-Ukrainian Republican in the district.

The other district coordinator was a middle-aged lawyer of Irish-Ukrainian descent active in the Reform Democratic Organization who had grown up on the corner of Avenue A and 10th Street. He had the perfect credentials for getting out the vote. His problem was the changing population mix. He wouldn't walk east of Avenue A without a .32-caliber pistol in his shoulder holster.

I reported that their problem was the co-leaders. Chuck asked me to talk with Jim Phelan, the coordinator in the neighboring district to the south. He was an officer of Chase Manhattan Bank, with as little experience in politics as I had. Jim's district was made up mostly of Italians and Chinese. He said, "It's not easy, but doable. Get to know the people. Get to know what they want from City Hall and then go to Lindsay's headquarters in the Roosevelt Hotel and get the mayor's commitment." I thought that was good advice.

I told Bob and Chuck I would take on the task of rejuvenating the campaign effort in the East Village but would need help: bodies with political savvy, ethnic diversity and election experience. Meanwhile, I began to walk the district.

It's interesting to see people's reaction to a challenge. Lindsay's race for mayor was a considerable challenge with odds unusually long. Except for Manhattan, New York City was mainly a blue-collar town. Lindsay was the epitome of the elegant English hierarchy, born to wealth, the product of prestigious universities and Long Island country clubs. He was no Fiorello La Guardia or Abe Beame.

The 67th was Democratic by a large margin. Maybe 15 percent were registered Republicans (almost all Polish or Ukrainian), with a lesser number of liberals. Duke di'Viggiano was head of the local Democratic clubhouse and well known for getting out the vote. If there was a district that seemed the antithesis of what Lindsay represented, it was the 67th.

There were young people at Lindsay's headquarters who saw the challenge of winning a district that had always voted Democratic: Phil Schacter, a media expert; Geoff Stokes, an English professor; and Ray Santini, owner of Chumley's bar in the Village, signed up and brought their friends and contacts.

Meanwhile, I spent my first two weeks walking and talking, asking questions and noting what people wanted from the city. Many of the answers were obvious: reduce the crime, improve the garbage pickup and install better lighting in the housing projects. Others were more specific: a vest pocket park on Sixth Street. Remove the druggies from the vacant house on Avenue B. And then there were broadly held concerns by business, older residents and the new younger element. They included the Lower Manhattan Expressway and the Cooper Square Development Plan. Both were enormous projects that would raze major portions of the district and its sister district to the south.

We developed a list for approval by headquarters and Lindsay's public commitment. Some were ignored and some turned down. The most helpful was his opposition to the Cooper Square Development Plan. It would have razed nine full blocks going south from Ninth Street and east from the Bowery. Useful, but later disappointing, was his promise to remove the Lower Manhattan Expressway from the city's planning maps.

Our storefront began to fill with volunteers. Pamphlets were distributed under doorways and on street corners. Building by building, visits began, even east of Avenue B. Young, non-political residents, new to the neighborhood, joined the effort. Evenings found the storefront jumping with activity. It became an exciting project and I was into it foursquare.

I was still working full-time at Weeden, but as soon as the closing bell rang, I was on the Lexington Avenue subway bound for Avenue A. In September the family returned from Pond Brook Road. The children were busy with school, and Vera had no objections over the time I was spending away from Park Avenue. I had enlisted some of our friends and even people from the office to join the effort. The campaign had grown in intensity, and the polls indicated that Lindsay had a chance.

Campaigns at best are disorganized, short of funds, subject to hiccups, and dependent on volunteers who may or may not show up—and we experienced all of the above. As we got closer to Election Day, it became more and more chaotic. The reputation of the local Democratic Party machine, led by the Duke, was well known and in full force.

In the evenings, we would place posters around the district, and the next morning, they would all have been taken down. Of greatest concern were the shenanigans expected on Election Day at the 52 polling places scattered throughout the district.

I needed to round up enough lawyers, or the equivalent, to cover every polling place from 6 a.m. to 9 p.m. They would carry the latest voter list and a copy of the election laws to prevent improper refusals, dead men voting, double-counting and intimidation of voters. It was not an easy task, but somehow we did it. Many of the law students I had met at Yale were New Yorkers and associates at the leading firms in the city. Many went on to become significant partners. Non-lawyers, like Nicholas and Sarah Pileggi, Nora Ephron, and other notables, or soon to be notables, joined in the effort.

When the polls closed, everyone came back to the storefront, relaxed, and waited for the results. Ever so slowly, it began to look like Lindsay might win citywide. Beer and potato chips arrived and a party ensued. A call came down from headquarters inviting us uptown, but no one bothered as we waited for our own returns, slow to come. Cases of Budweiser arrived and were consumed long into the early hours of Wednesday.

When we finally locked the door, I looked back onto a sea of discarded brochures, voting lists, "Lindsay for Mayor" placards and hundreds upon hundreds of empty Budweiser cans. They covered the tables, were scattered on shelves, overflowed the wastepaper baskets and littered the floor. The final count had Lindsay winning our 67th by 300 votes out of 21,000 cast.

After wishing everyone good night, I wandered aimlessly toward the Astor Place subway stop, drinking in the elixir of victory. It was the 67th I had in mind. It was extraordinary what we did. It was less than three months from my first walk around the district. It was less than two months that a team had been put together. That team was not my doing: Some were sent down to shore me up; some drifted in from the neighborhood; others heard about something going on in the East Village.

It happened because we convinced the voters that Lindsay was on their side on those things that mattered: no more bulldozing the neighborhood, no Lower Manhattan Expressway, make the streets safer, create vest-pocket parks. As they say, "Winning the war is not enough, there is also the peace to be won." That crossed my mind; we had to make sure Lindsay came through.

I found it hard to let go. Lindsay's victory and our success made the hard work, long hours and many frustrations worthwhile. It also solidified a relationship that had developed among the core of volunteers. We had come from a variety of backgrounds, wealth and education. Some had grown up in New York City; others, like myself, were newcomers. We were all young and energetic, full of idealism. Together we pulled off the impossible: a Republican winning a majority in a Democratic stronghold. What next? Bob Sweet had the answer.

As Lindsay's newly appointed deputy, Bob would have the important responsibility of keeping the citywide Lindsay-for-Mayor organization together. Unlike traditional campaigns, Lindsay's had had to create storefronts in every district in the city, independent of the Republican clubhouses which in many districts did not exist.

Bob Sweet's solution was to keep the storefronts open and rename them "Civic Improvement Associations (CIA)," with the aim of building a permanent Lindsay presence. A CIA seemed a good way to stay in touch with the neighborhood. I saw it as a way to remind the Lindsay Administration of the promises we had made during the campaign.

This was another new experience for me. During my time in Brooklyn, living in Cobble Hill, I used the subways daily or walked the Brooklyn Bridge to work, all the while thinking only about the business. The transition to Park Avenue, the Racquet and Tennis Club, and entertaining at Upper East Side restaurants was no different. When I was overlooking Tompkins Square, I felt I was truly part of a neighborhood.

There was also the hard core of volunteers. Keeping them together was as important as keeping pressure on the new Administration. If done correctly, we could create a bottom-up link, as opposed to Bob's top-down vision. We might actually do some good. With everyone's agreement, we incorporated under the name The Lower East Side Civic Improvement Association (LESCIA). IRS approval as a 501(c)(3) nonprofit arrived in June 1966.

My post-election letdown was soon dispelled by the birth of our fourth child, John, on March 29, 1966. The presence of a mother's helper reduced the added burden on Vera. Elizabeth was in third grade and Frank in kindergarten. Vera continued her sculpting while I refocused on Weeden and problems at National.

National had not recovered from the lawsuit and needed funding. There was a growing concern over the relaxed management of Bernie Rothlein, exemplified by the pee-wee golf course he had put in just outside the main entrance to the factory. The board decided a change was necessary, and I was chosen to convey this to Bernie, largely because I was thought to be the closest to him and his wife, Rena.

It did not go well, and many years passed before Bernie and I spoke again.

At Weeden, the stock trading desk made the adjustment from Eddie Sinclair's informal style to my off-the-desk oversight. Meanwhile, a troublesome problem arose from our too-successful bond trading in Europe. We had become one of the most active dealers in the growing market for Euro-dollar bonds, bonds issued in Europe instead of New York by U.S.-based corporations.

Our competitors were European and more loosely regulated with respect to their capital requirements. They had no haircut on capital for trades outstanding beyond normal delivery date. Under National Association of Securities Dealers (NASD) regulations, "fails to deliver" carried additional risk. The longer a trade remained outstanding, the larger the haircut imposed.

European traders operated mainly from the short side of the market. Absent any regulatory compulsion to settle trades, they were indifferent to meeting the normal delivery date. When we would demand that they deliver what they had sold us, they would say, "Sorry, old chap, but we're short the bonds."

The fact that most of their fellow dealers were also short created a "daisy chain" of short positions and made it almost impossible to unwind. As our "fails to deliver" increased and lengthened, we began to run out of required capital. Bottom line: We stopped trading in London, slowly reduced our fails and never went back.

As 1966 unfolded, Rule 394, which effectively prevented members from taking their orders off board, became the focus of intense discussions involving the NYSE, the SEC and Schapiro. Peripheral but important were the interests of the Justice Department and Weeden.

Eugene Rotberg, SEC staff member, conducted a confidential study that concluded Rule 394 was a classic violation of the Sherman Antitrust Act and Schapiro should win his case, if brought. By the end of the year, the NYSE proposed modifying Rule 394 to allow brokers to execute a trade away from the floor of the NYSE, if they followed several complicated steps. The SEC was satisfied that it eliminated the antitrust issue, and Schapiro agreed not to sue. Chairman Milton Cohen convinced Frank that it was the best they could do and it was in our interest to go along.

I felt differently and voiced my reasons, namely: (1) the new rules were more intimidating to the broker because they now involved both the specialist and a governor in the process of getting permission to go off board, and (2) it discouraged Third Market dealers from quoting a price because the broker was required to show the specialist our price and allow him to meet it (in street jargon, this was no different from "shopping a bid"). Nevertheless, I was determined that its failure would not be the absence of better prices available from Weeden & Co.

Adding to my after-the-market-closed activities, LESCIA was formed with a board of 20 members representing the district's diversity and was soon operating. Lindsay moved fairly quickly to create several vest-pocket parks out of abandoned vacant lots. We got the city to take over the Christadora House on Avenue B and Ninth Street, stop its use by the druggies and begin plans for refurbishing it for use by the community. We reached out to the large Hispanic community and encouraged their participation in LESCIA. We established a storefront where people from the neighborhood could come with their grievances and requests. We would then direct them to the people at City Hall who could help. We would even intercede if necessary.

What won the 67th for Lindsay was our obtaining his written opposition to a 1959 proposal by Robert Moses' Slum Clearance Committee to bulldoze a swath of low-income residential buildings from Ninth Street south to Delancy and from Second Avenue to the Bowery. When I first "walked the neighborhood," I became convinced that the Cooper Square Alternate Renewal Plan (CSARP) was a far better solution. It called for careful replacing of individual buildings deemed beyond repair, renovating others and maintaining the character and multi-purpose qualities of the neighborhood. The plan followed the concepts of Jane Jacobs as set forth in her 1961 book The Life and Death of Great American Cities.

LESCIA aligned with CSARP to keep the pressure on the Administration for the next four years. Eventually the Moses plan was discarded; the area blossomed and turned into an important tourist destination. Today it stands as one of the few tangible examples of progressive community-based planning in New York City.

LESCIA also sponsored the Tompkins Square Park Summer Festival under the direction of Martin Ewenstein and Phil Schacter. Martin was new to our group. He was an economist for CBS and a member of the Liberal Party. For us, he was Sol Hurok bringing popular entertainment to the East Village. Phil Schacter had key to organizing the volunteers and much more. They instituted a summer-long series of free entertainment every Wednesday at 8; Martin found the acts, Phil organized the volunteers and I supplied the fliers. The Parks Department contributed lights and sound, and the performers their time.

Over the years, we drew the likes of Pete Seeger, Richie Havens, David Amram, the Fugs, the Feenjon Group (from Israel), Joe Lee Wilson,

As Luck Would Have It

a group of Slavic dancers from the Soviet Union, the Blues Project and the Melatones (African American).

There were many other performances, but one that sticks vividly in my memory was by the Sirovich Day Center Symphony Orchestra. The center was on 12th Street at Avenue A. It catered to senior citizens over 70 living in the surrounding area. Many of them were retired musicians who had played with various orchestras in the city, including the Philharmonic. They were ecstatic about the opportunity to perform again in public. Wednesday evening arrived, and Martin had no idea what to expect.

The performers arrived on foot, carrying their instruments. The men were dressed in tuxedos, the ladies in long white dresses. They came in twos and threes, struggled onto the stage beneath the clam-shaped backdrop, and began to tune their instruments. The neighborhood drifted in with folding chairs and umbrellas in case the slight mist in the air turned heavy. The stage was barely able to accommodate the 40-odd musicians assembled. When the maestro raised his baton, promptly at 8, the Park grew quiet with anticipation. And for the next two hours, Ukrainians and Poles, Puerto Ricans and blacks, sat or stood together and, along with the younger people newly arrived in the district, listened appreciatively while the predominantly Jewish orchestra played their favorite German music.

Note: The formation of LESCIA had the effect of extending three month's campaigning for Lindsay into a four-year involvement in the 67th.

In late spring of '68, I took a temporary leave from Weeden to run as the Republican candidate in New York's 19th Congressional District. That exposure resulted in my being asked onto the board of trustees of the City Club of New York, an organization devoted to good government. I became its president in 1974. Through the years, I continued to oppose the Lower Manhattan Expressway (LME). When it was finally removed from the drawing boards and the extraordinary transformation began of the area known as Soho, there was still the street-level congestion it was meant to cure.

The combination of a bad conscience, a desire to find solutions to difficult problems and a timely rise in the value of my National Semiconductor stock encouraged me to create the Manhattan Auto Study. This two-year study was completed in 1976. At the end of 1977, due to troubles at Weeden, I resigned from the City Club, withdrew from all outside activities, and stopped smoking and drinking to concentrate on saving the family firm.

That is a short summary of a turbulent period in my life that had me running in a number of different directions—most with good intentions, some poorly considered, one enormously satisfying and one that complicated my marriage.

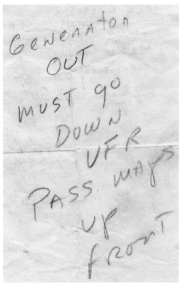

Note to Alan from Don on first leg of flight to Davis Monthan Air Force Base, Arizona, to retire the aircraft, an F-94B. Don was member of 102nd Fighter Interceptor Squadron, NY International Guard, flying out of Floyd Bennett Field, Long Island.

Elizabeth at Duck Hollow, 1960.

Elizabeth and Frankie on Brooklyn Bridge, April 1962.

Elizabeth heading to San Francisco to visit grandparents Frank and Mabel Weeden, July 1962.

Frankie's first time on skis, December 1962.

As Luck Would Have It

Vera and baby Christine Anne (Tina), 1962.

Frankie, Tina and
Elizabeth at Saranac Lake,
Adirondacks,
visiting the Sprocks, 1964.

Frankie, Elizabeth and Don
on a hike at Duck Hollow, 1964.

Tina trying on Don's shoes.

Frankie (front row, second from right) in kindergarten class (1965), Lycée Français, Manhattan.

Oma, Frankie, Tina (in car) and Elizabeth at the World's Fair, New York City, 1966.

With Oma at Duck Hollow.

Frankie, Elizbeth and Tina at Rockefeller Center rink.

Chapter 13
New York City, 1966–1969

My assuming leadership of Weeden's New York stock trading desk was never announced formally but was accepted as fait accompli in the New York office. The stock traders and salesmen outside of New York were mostly old-timers and still looked to Frank for guidance. I continued my business trips, including Europe, and oversaw requests for markets from member brokers. It was not time consuming, but it precluded any meaningful role as a day-to-day trader.

Frank was making fewer trips away from Alameda. He installed a teletype machine in his closet at home which connected with the firm-wide circuit over which the firm's daily activity flowed back and forth real time. He was now able to remain in daily touch while teaching the young children in Alameda how to swim.

Alan continued to badger Jack and me to join him in giving an ultimatum to Frank on turning over management to the three of us and bringing control to the New York office. If Frank rejected the idea, Alan's risk was minimal. He was well respected throughout the municipal bond community and would surely be reemployed. Jack was also well known for his grasp of the industry's operational issues. I was just beginning to be heard on the Street, but not in a way that would help my résumé. Yet I agreed. So did Uncle Norman, which helped in getting Frank to agree.

The timing seemed right. Weeden was growing fast and the business had clearly shifted east and away from the offices that populated our board of directors. Alan was elected president and CEO while Frank remained chairman of the board. Jack and I were elected vice presidents. An informal office of the president was created that included Jack and me. Frank called the new arrangement "The Troika."

In November 1966, Frank spoke at an American Management Association meeting on "The Third Market: Past, Present and Future." I had his remarks printed up and widely distributed. It was a good first step in telling our story to the public: matter-of-fact, no editorializing, bland. In July, Frank was featured in an *Institutional Investor* magazine article that provided added exposure to the Third Market and to Weeden.

The article pointed out that the percentage volume of the Third Market relative to the NYSE had increased 50 percent between 1960 and 1966.

Meanwhile, the NYSE's modified Rule 394, now called 394(b), was cleverly designed to satisfy the SEC. It proved to be a non-starter despite our efforts to accommodate to it. I meticulously recorded the few, meager efforts by member brokers to use our markets. I had the results printed in a full-page ad in the New York Times. This was my public "shot across the bow" to both the NYSE and the SEC. Frank went along reluctantly, while I was warming up for a no-holds-barred fight.

Financially, my situation had taken a giant leap forward. National's change in CEO in 1966 coincided with its acquisition of Molectro Science Corp., a start-up company located in Silicon Valley (Santa Clara). Molectro was producing some of the first integrated circuits in the industry: two diodes and a transistor on the same sliver of silicon. It was a breakthrough in technology that attracted two men from Fairchild Semiconductor: Dave Talbert, with manufacturing know-how and Bob Widlar, a circuit design engineer.

Not long after they arrived, they mentioned to Charlie Sporck, VP of manufacturing at Fairchild Semiconductor, that National could use a strong CEO. The call caught Charlie at just the right moment. He was fed up with their parent, Fairchild Camera and Instruments (FCI), based on Long Island. Despite the enormous profitability of its semiconductor business, FCI made no effort to include them in the company's stock-option program. As a consequence, Charlie was secretly flying to London from San Francisco on weekends to negotiate with Plessey, a large electronics company, about joining them along with a group of his Fairchild colleagues. At the last minute, Plessey's general counsel mucked up the deal, leaving Charlie high and dry.

Charlie called Don Lucas, board member and founder of National. Don had left Smith Barney to join Draper, Gaither & Anderson, an early venture capital firm located in Palo Alto. Don was interested and called Peter Sprague, National's chairman. Charlie flew to New York and met Peter and me at the Racquet and Tennis Club. General agreement was reached on his becoming CEO.

That evening, we met for dinner at Le Steak on Second Avenue and 58th with Jack Hegarty and Bob Beshar to explain our decision to Jack. Jack was immediately on board, if he could exercise his unvested stock options received when he became CEO. Toasts were made all around, with the details to be filled in by Bob. Charlie flew back to San Francisco to organize the team that would join him. When word seeped into the market, National stock rose to $20 per share.

The year 1968 was a federal election year for president, one-third of the U.S. Senate and all members of the House of Representatives. My 67th Assembly District lay entirely within the 19th Congressional District for New

York State. The 19th covered an area almost four times the size of the 67th district. It started at 79th Street on the west side of Manhattan and ran south along Amsterdam Avenue through Lincoln Center, Clinton, Chelsea and the West Village, where it swung east taking in all of Lower Manhattan, Chinatown, the Lower East Side and then north to 14th Street.

The Manhattan Republican Party began to look for a suitable candidate, almost anyone who would take on a historically impossible task of winning this predominantly Democratic district. In the last election, the Republican candidate had received slightly over 10 percent of the vote cast.

On being asked, we at LESCIA suggested a young Puerto Rican on our board with political aspirations. His candidacy was rejected by the Ukrainian and Polish Republican Clubs, even though they had no alternative to recommend. Eventually, my name came up. The idea had not occurred to me, but I was not averse to meeting Vincent Albano, who ran the Republican Party in Manhattan. I found him to be mild-mannered and a straight talker. His problem was finding someone, almost anyone, who would take the time and spend a little money.

Another name that bubbled up was Barry Farber. He had his own radio talk show and lived on the Upper West Side. Barry had better credentials than I, being Jewish and knowing several languages, but had little in the way of personal resources to bring to the table. I was offered the job after committing to run a strong campaign and spending some of my own money. There was no primary. The last time I ran for an elective office was in 1946 at Alameda High School for president of the student body.

The family had some questions, voiced skepticism but offered no strong objections. I said I would remain in touch; that my responsibilities were not such that I had to be available on a daily basis. And there might even be some positive fallout with respect to our customers and people on Wall Street. Whether the last point held any water doesn't matter. I remained on the Weeden payroll during the six months of active campaigning.

Having made the decision to run, I approached the job the way I had in the Lindsay campaign: Learn the concerns of my constituents and what they wanted from their congressman.

Finding a campaign manager was first on my list and, as luck would have it, Peter Sprague was interested. Peter and I were seeing a lot of each other after his investment in NSM and becoming our new chairman. He lived in Lenox, Mass., but was spending most of his time in New York City, where he owned a home on Sutton Place South, an extension of East 58th Street. The house shared a garden that overlooked the East River. He was interested in politics and saw this as a way of getting his feet wet. His willingness to do it was a big load off my mind. And we happened to think alike on most issues.

Peter was 10 years younger than I and had the energy of two and the ideas of three normal people. These qualities came packaged with an enormous self-confidence, a lively personality and strongly held opinions on almost any subject. As the only son of one of two brothers who founded Sprague Electric, there was an aristocratic air about him that belied a strongly liberal bent. Peter brought to the campaign a great deal of energy, creativity and ways to spend money.

It was a time of political and social turmoil in America. The overriding issue before the nation was its involvement in Vietnam. The war had become unpopular, especially with the youth who resented being drafted to fight a war in which they saw little purpose. President Johnson's determination to escalate our involvement, in Texan macho style, and "beat the little commie buggers" was fast losing support. In early 1968 he decided not to seek re-election.

This threw the presidential election open to each party to choose a candidate who wanted to pursue the war to victory or the most honorable and earliest way out.

My own thinking on Vietnam was evolving. I first saw it as another Korea, a Communist effort to expand their hegemony; the only difference being that Korea was an overt attack, while in Vietnam, it was more covert through infiltration.

I then read Marguerite Higgins's book *Our Vietnam Nightmare*. Her views reminded me of *Thunder Out of China*, Jacoby and White's 1945 analysis of the political situation then. Their views on what should be done were totally contrary to our country's official policy, one that 20 years later had us still refusing to recognize the government of the largest country in the world.

Ms. Higgins detailed the history of Vietnam from the time it became a French colony. She described how little the West understood the Asian mind and how the United States government had so interfered in the politics of Vietnam that it had assumed ownership of the war.

I was also influenced by my time in the Air Force. I had read in the *New York Times* that a Captain William Leitch had recently returned from Vietnam, having flown 500 combat missions over South and North Vietnam in a Skyraider (a propeller-driven, low-level ground support aircraft). Could it be the same Bill Leitch from the 496th FIS?

I finally found Bill in the bowels of the Pentagon. I visited him in Washington, where we spent a very long evening reminiscing and catching up. Yes, he had flown 500 missions between 1964 and 1966 and had some very strong opinions on what we should do: "Either send an additional million troops over and finish the war, or get out." Whether we had a moral right or duty or justifiable reason for being involved was not Bill's business. When I finally decided to run, I took the position that Vietnam was the wrong war, in the wrong place, at the wrong time, for the wrong reasons.

The challenge facing my candidacy would be formidable. Leonard Farbstein, the incumbent, had been 12 years in office, preceded by 24 years as a New York State assemblyman for the Lower East Side. His margin of victory in elections had always been substantial. I became one of four challengers. The others were a woman representing the Conservative party, a stockbroker from the Liberal Party, and David McReynolds, running as a Peace and Freedom candidate. Except for Mr. Farbstein, who defended President Johnson's policy in Vietnam, all four challengers were against continuing the war.

There were other strikes against me in which I enjoyed exclusivity: (1) I didn't live in the district; (2) I was a Wall Street name wanting to represent a very low-income district; and (3) my English/Swedish background was almost non-existent in the district. I would make up for these deficiencies with a slick, aggressive media program and by spending more money than the other four candidates combined.

There were other issues, but the war dominated. Of 10 full-page ads placed in the *Village Voice* and reprinted for distribution, four were related to the war: "Let's Get Out"; "After Chicago, What?"; "and the War goes on" and "I don't want Nixon or Humphrey either." Others spoke to the issue of my running on the Republican line in a largely Democratic district: "Don Weeden. The First Republicrat" and "Now Is the Time for All Good Democrats to Vote for a Republican."

If I hadn't been in trouble with the Republican Party from the get-go, my ad on Nixon and Humphrey did the trick. My name was removed from every Republican clubhouse posting of their candidates. I was cast adrift. The real reason could have been the absence of any money available from our campaign.

By far the largest voting bloc was Jewish. It was concentrated along Grand Street in the Lower East Side and near Lincoln Center on the Upper West Side. Three of my opponents were Jewish. The controversial 1967 war in Palestine was still fresh in everyone's memory. "You don't have to be Jewish to support Israel" was a theme I spoke to wherever I campaigned. It didn't help, since I received the fewest votes cast in the Grand Street polling booths. One of our ads had a title that was almost as long as the body of the text: "Maybe we should call it the Leonard Farbstein Memorial Lower

Manhattan Expressway." It reminded people that the LME was still on the drawing boards since 1946 and that Farbstein had never objected to its being there during his 24 years as assemblyman and 12 years as congressman.

In the end, I received slightly over 34 percent of the total votes cast. The other three challengers received over 5 percent each, and Farbstein a tad over 50 percent. Farbstein lost the Democratic primary in the 1970 race for Congress to Bella Abzug, who then won handily in November. True to my colors, I placed an ad in the Village Voice just before Election Day that read "Bella is Better."

After his election in 1966, Major Lindsay began to waffle on his promise to kill the Lower Manhattan Expressway and in mid-1968 proposed his own "cut and cover" tunnel that would have also devastated an area affecting half of the 19th Congressional District.

I continued my opposition to the LME and became part of a small group that met periodically at Ratner's restaurant on Delancey Street to strategize. It included Harold Harmatz, owner of Ratner's, and several from the Cooper Square group. Occasionally, Jane Jacobs would join and update us on similar meetings in the West Village. LESCIA eventually contributed a study by a group of traffic and land use planners that undermined the conclusions of the Expressway supporters. To my personal satisfaction, Governor Rockefeller effectively killed the project.

As my 1968 campaign developed under the direction of Peter Sprague, it became filled with the usual pressures of deadlines, confusion and disorganization. There was the added excitement of novices experimenting with new ways to create attention to a candidate starting from scratch and riding a poor horse. Sprague created mobile theatres that wandered through the district displaying multiple photos of me, my family and my positions. We held a parade that toured the district with me waving from the back of a convertible. We spent lavishly on advertisements and handouts.

Here are few of my better—or worse—memories.

• The nice old Jewish lady on Grand Street who asked me if I were one of the Wedeens, a nice Jewish family in the Bronx? "No. I am a Wedeen from Alameda, California." She said, "You seem like a nice boy and the Wedeens are a fine people. Mazel tov."

• While standing at the top of a subway entrance on Houston Street, suddenly realizing that all the people I was handing literature to lived outside my district.

• Peter's bright idea of making up "Weeden for Congress" bumper stickers with industrial-strength glue on the backs. The night we placed them around the district, we had a beer party at our headquarters before sending out the volunteers. They were meant to be placed neatly on lampposts, but some ended up diagonally on store windows and were almost impossible to remove.

• The evening when I spoke at the local ironworkers union headquarters on 14th Street. In the middle of my speech, realizing no one was listening, my mind went blank. After a few awful moments that seemed an eternity, I managed to end my little speech with the plea, "If you're against the war, I would appreciate your vote."

There were other issues besides the war. Drugs had been spreading rapidly among the youth and veterans returning from Vietnam. During the Lindsay campaign, soft drugs were available around Fifth Street and Avenue C. Now they seemed to be available everywhere. I believed that marijuana was no more destructive than alcohol and should be legal. "Take the criminality out of its use; lower the violence connected with its purchase; make it available for taxing like cigarettes; reduce corruption of the police, courts and politicians; and eliminate the cost of incarceration." I also argued for the use of methadone by heroin addicts as a medicinal and safe replacement for that dangerous and costly drug.

I took the side of the low-income Puerto Ricans who were evicted when their buildings were torn down to build the Masaryk Towers, a moderate-income housing project. The law gave them first claim on a portion of the new apartments without having to put down a deposit. When the rental office opened, those evicted found that they were required to put up $5,000. I challenged this. When I was ignored, I began to lend the $5,000 to those families who were displaced. The requirement was rescinded.

The district formed a narrow inversed "J," with a high density of shops, vehicles and people. This made it difficult to move about quickly. To solve the problem, I bought a Yamaha 90-liter motor scooter. I often arrived at our next event before my advance people.

The experience was enormously challenging; I had to be knowledgeable, plus have an opinion, about the war in Vietnam, cases pending before the Supreme Court, all the way down to the concerns of a very local nature. The 19th district was a widely disparate community. I had to be able to verbalize my ideas and solutions in a natural and sympathetic way. It did not come easily.

We ran an energetic campaign, but we were not well organized. We spent money that wasn't necessary and didn't spend money that would have been useful. We were right on with almost every issue, and I have no regrets or second thoughts. It was a race that couldn't be won and therefore allowed me to say whatever I believed was right. Except for a very few people, the volunteers and staff have dropped out of sight. The individual voters whose hands I shook are faceless, but as a group they remain unforgettable.

The campaign had suspended my normal family activities. During the summer, they were all busy at Pond Brook, with occasional visits by me. When everyone was back at school, they got caught up in the excitement and publicity of the campaign, although Vera wisely kept the children's involvement to a minimum. There had been photos taken of our life on Pond Brook and now photos on the grass in Tompkins Square, strolling down Grand Street in the Italian sector and meeting prospective voters at a subway entrance. Following the election, I spent a quiet week in the Caribbean with Vera, relaxing and licking my wounds.

Unplanned fallout of my political activity was an affair with one of the volunteers; a younger woman, single and living uptown from the East Village. Ann had grown up in Queens as an only child; her parents were now living in Florida. She was attractive, personable and one of the LESCIA volunteers. Our affair began slowly, rather innocently, after the Lindsay campaign. It turned serious, leading to the eventual coming to her apartment and consummating a strong physical attraction for one another. It then blossomed into a relationship that was intense and absorbing. It continued for almost five years, when Ann concluded that I was determined to remain married to Vera.

Ann was not only a wonderful bedmate; she filled a vacuum in my life that I can only describe as loneliness: a strange way to think of my time with her. My life was already filled to the brim with relationships: a good wife and mother; four wonderful children; a firm full of great people; brothers and a father with whom I constantly interacted; challenges and responsibilities enough for two.

You may say it was the normal weakness of a highly charged male taking advantage of a sweet, innocent girl. Maybe that's the way it started. Over time, it became more, especially for her. This was something I had not thought of, or if I did, I was unable to give her up.

Shortly after Election Day, I was in Washington, D.C., testifying before the SEC at their hearing on the stock exchange commission rate structure. Our testimony was requested, since our Third Market activity directly affected the viability of that structure.

I updated the commissioners on our Third Market business since the Special Study report. In 1968, Weeden had $19 million in capital, of which well over half was used to finance overnight inventories in NYSE-listed stocks. Our listed overnight inventory averaged more than $29 million and was turned over once every five trading days. This was over three times the overnight inventory carried by all the specialists on the two floors of the Pacific Coast Stock Exchange.

I pointed out that Rule 394(b) was equally unworkable as its predecessor, Rule 394, and was the principal cause of what the NYSE referred to as "fragmentation." I suggested they follow the recommendation of the Justice Department: recognize it as a violation of the Sherman Antitrust Act and have the NYSE remove it. The SEC did nothing. Rule 394(b) remained in effect.

An interesting question from one of the commissioners to me: "What would your reaction be if the SEC decided to abolish fixed commissions?" I replied: "While it would cut into our business substantially, we had no standing to object. Our margins would narrow considerably, but we believe we would remain competitive." (This opinion was not held by everyone at Weeden.)

My campaign for Congress had the effect of increasing my name recognition on Wall Street. My position on the war was popular with some, and I received modest contributions from those who shared it. I participated in the moratorium held in Washington, D.C., the following year. I also joined Ben Buttenwieser, senior partner of Kuhn, Loeb & Co., and Sinclair Armstrong, executive vice president at the U. S. Trust Company, in heading a committee from Wall Street against the war in Vietnam. In 1969 the three of us spoke at the Trinity Church, located at the foot of Wall Street, calling for a moratorium.

Even though I lost the election, 34 percent of the vote was a moral victory. I also believed the experience more than offset the time and money expended. I was more comfortable and confident before most any gathering, friendly or hostile. My public speaking had improved, and I had more assurance when challenged or heckled.

Market structure issues were now gaining greater attention with the Street, the regulators and in the press. Being the largest Third Market maker made Weeden the logical firm to represent the entire group. I began making our case at public hearings, in speeches at industry conferences, and before members of Congress and their staff.

I explained how institutions moved their bond business into the over-the-counter market from the exchange-auction market when they became active in the 1920s; they preferred a competitive dealer environment with significant available capital and the opportunity to privately negotiate trades.

I also explained how new technology would improve how business was conducted; how it would reduce costs, increase transparency and would allow for centrality through better communication links. I told about Frank's upbringing on his father's three-masted freighter, where he learned the importance of efficiency and innovation. Even in his 80s, we would still find him wandering through the "cage," checking on how things were being done and thinking about how they could be done better.

Jack was imbued with the same genes. As head of Weeden's back office, he was incorporating the latest technology into our daily handling of deliveries, transferring stock certificates and moving securities from one office to another. Meanwhile, I was learning about the latest innovations as a member of National Semiconductor's board. It was clear that semiconductor technology would dramatically change the way Wall Street handled its business.

Weeden was already using electronic systems that supplemented the NYSE ticker tape: Scantlin's Stockmaster, Ultronics and then Quotron. They reduced our dependence on the NYSE's ticker tape.

Weeden was an early investor in and user of electronic systems that communicated large buy and sell interests to our institutional clients. AutEx was one of those systems. For Weeden, it was a time-saving improvement. For smaller firms, it expanded their coverage. For the institutions, it reduced need to manually keep track of offerings made by the Street.

The NYSE had developed a similar system called Broker's Automated System (BAS), but was only available to member firms. It was designed to maintain the specialist as the center of the market, while AutEx's design recognized that the institutional investor had become the real center of the market. This difference would eventually cause AutEx to be the favored system. We were the second firm to sign onto AutEx. Then we invested $300,000 in their next round of financing. Within two years, BAS was discontinued. In 1975, AutEx was sold to Itel and Weeden enjoyed a handsome profit.

In 1969, after some debate, Weeden also invested in a trading system called Instinet. It was far more radical than AutEx. It allowed institutions to trade directly with one another anonymously—in effect, to become an electronic exchange. It threatened the traditional exchange as being obsolete and the broker as unnecessary. Frank and Alan had opposed the investment, and our salesmen and traders saw it as a system that could eliminate their jobs.

Jack and I felt differently. We reasoned that the technology was there. It would eventually replace some of the business now being done by brokers through exchanges. Yet it might also increase the total pie because it made executions cheaper, quicker and more efficient. By owning a piece of Instinet, we believed Weeden would realize a capital gain far greater than any profit lost from our regular business.

Instinet was slow in gaining users. Its radical nature not only turned off Wall Street, even the traders at the institutions saw it as threatening their jobs as well.

I went on the Instinet board as the fifth member, becoming the tie-breaker if the two founders, with equal representation, had a falling-out. That happened almost immediately. I made the decision to back Jerry Pustilnik over Herb Behrens, as being the smarter and more committed of the two. Over the next eight years, in a series of investments at diminishing prices ($10 down to $0.25), Weeden & Co., my brothers and I ended up owning 92 percent of the company. In 1987, Reuters acquired Instinet for the equivalent of $22 per share.

The younger Weedens felt it was time to share with the SEC our views on the future of the stock market. I was again full-time at Weeden and laid out the issues and discussed them with Jack and Alan. Alan did the writing and I signed the letter as executive vice president. The letter was 15 pages long.

The essence came down to this:

"The central marketplace today is no longer a geographical concept. It is a *communications* concept" (emphasis added).

We ended on a sober note.

"The combined system for trading listed stocks which we envision should be more efficient and less expensive than the present system. A lot of fat in the present system would be eliminated. Marginal producers and well-established firms, including ours, might find the going so rough that merger or liquidation becomes their only course... The system the Exchange seeks to perpetuate is moribund. The forces acting on the marketplace for listed stocks are irreversible and will ultimately prevail. We urge the Commission to resist the temptation to compromise in favor of the status quo."

My letter was dated December 19, 1969—10 days before the end of the decade. It was prescient in several ways:

• In 1969, the minimum commission on the exchange was $44 for each 100 shares of a stock selling at $50. Today, brokers are charging as little as $8 a trade—a reduction of 82 percent on 100 shares. If the trade involved 10,000 shares, the commission would still be $8, as opposed to $4,400 under the old rules.

• Ten years later, Weeden Holding Corporation merged with another firm to avoid bankruptcy.

• Electronic technology radically changed the market, making it far more efficient, less costly and more transparent.

The commission vacillated on market structure for 30 years.

W hile the '60s contained important studies, hearings and disclosures on the stock market, it was left to the '70s to implement the changes being considered. It was the '70s when the gloves came off and the protagonists, mainly the NYSE and the Third Market, presented their cases before Congress, in the public media, at industry conferences, and with the staff and commissioners at the SEC. The disappointing result of Frank's efforts to convince Manny Cohen on removing Rule 394 shifted the firm toward a more aggressive strategy. I became its lead strategist and spokesman.

Weeden's strategy now expanded beyond writing letters. When the SEC accepted NYSE's Rule 394(b), we changed our approach from a frontal assault to an encircling movement via the regional exchanges. We became members of all the regionals which traded NYSE-listed stocks and had NYSE-member brokers in their membership.

Sharing of commissions was allowed between two members, a practice that the NYSE had no control over. This allowed an institution to distribute commission revenue to non-NYSE members. Some of those trades were crosses involving two or more institutional orders. The majority involved Weeden acting as a net dealer on one side, even though the broker was a NYSE member. In effect, the trade bypassed Rule 394(b). It was a trade that satisfied everybody: the institution, the broker, the regional exchange and Weeden, not to mention the ultimate trust account or mutual fund holder.

In 1969, we joined the Cincinnati Stock Exchange (CSE) as their odd-lot specialist in 112 NYSE-listed stocks. Over the next two years we were asked to join the Detroit, Philadelphia, Boston and Pacific Coast stock exchanges. Third Market volume surged from 5.5 percent of NYSE volume in 1969 to 8.3 percent in the third quarter of 1970. Regional volume climbed from 12.1percent to 14.2percent, due largely to the availability of our markets.

As fallout from my campaign, I was invited in 1969 to join the City Club of New York. It was formed in the 1890s as a good-government movement to oppose Tammany Hall, which at the time controlled City Hall. The members were an energetic and knowledgeable group of strong-minded

As Luck Would Have It

liberals, mostly Jewish, concerned about the city. They held Friday round-table luncheons and published a monthly, *City Club Comments*, edited by I.D. Robbins.

The next year, I was elected to their board of trustees. Joel Harnett was president. Joel and his wife, Lila, and I became good friends, a relationship that continued after their move to Phoenix in the early '80s.

In 1974, I was elected president and Joel became chairman. My first initiative was to change the bylaws to allow women members. I also financed a two-year research project, the Manhattan Auto Study, which offered solutions to the street congestion south of Manhattan's 59th Street.

Also through my campaign I met Louis Kelso, a lawyer in San Francisco. He had co-authored a book titled The Capitalist Manifesto. Kelso's thesis: The means of production was not only labor, as Marx believed and Keynes accepted, but included capital. He called it "The Two-Factor Theory of Economics." He predicted that the second factor, capital, by investing in labor-saving technology, would become a larger and larger percentage of our national income. Unless hourly wages kept up with productivity, the earnings from these capital investments would accrue to a limited number of people.

I had learned at Stanford that Keynes equated investments to savings, and savings equated to earnings not spent on consumption. Keynes' definition of earnings is a bit fuzzy, but he recognizes that most people in the laboring class have little money left after their consumption needs, that most of the savings that turn into investments are provided by those who earn considerably more than their ability to consume or who have assets against which they can borrow.

After making the point that most investments increase the earnings of the few with extra cash or the ability to borrow, Kelso points out that, if the trend continues, the need for labor will decrease further, less will be consumed, and demand for investment capital will decrease.

The idea was contrary to Say's law, which says "Supply creates its own demand." That is not what happens when technology creates more supply and less need for labor, causing a reduction in labor's contribution to the consumption function. A way must be designed to increase labor's participation in the investment process and the profits that ensue.

Kelso designed what came to be known as an Employee Stock Ownership Plan (or Trust). A corporation or large shareholder (usually the founder) would contribute shares to the trust that would serve as collateral against which the corporation could borrow, with the earnings produced going to the workers. The incentive for creating the trust would be newly created tax advantages. Kelso convinced Huey Long, U.S. Senator from Louisiana, to sponsor the needed legislation, which became law in 1969.

I invested a small amount in Kelso & Co., whose business would be advising corporations wishing to finance using ESOPs. I was asked to join their board. The ESOP was not perfect. To implement one fairly and correctly, it took a lot of time and effort on the part of the corporation. Nevertheless, within 10 years, more than 10 million employees were participating in an ESOP.

Unfortunately, Kelso was mainly interested in marketing his economic theory rather than in finding paying clients. After several years, Kelso & Co. was turned over to others. I had supported Louis throughout, and as a consequence, I was not asked to remain on the board.

Kelso, ESOP and Two Factor Economics dropped out of my mind until I received a letter in 2007 from Patricia Hetter, who had been the secretary, then second wife and then widow of Louis Kelso. Kelso had died in 1990. She reminded me how long it had been since the first ESOP and how glacially slow the idea of Two Factor Theory was being understood and accepted. She mentioned that Harvard Business School Press had recently published *Equity: Why Employee Ownership is Good for Business*. She ended by reminding me about "your being such a loyal friend to Louis through thick and thin. I don't know how we would have pulled through without your support."

Gilbert "Gil" Kaplan was another interesting, creative and successful individual who entered my life. I first met him in 1967, when he came to my office with his idea for a new magazine. Gil had worked at the American Stock Exchange, where he learned about Wall Street and the emergence of the institutional investor. He visualized a magazine that would pull together everything of interest to those people working at the institutions and those on Wall Street who serviced them. He wanted to do it through a high-quality, full-color monthly magazine.

When Gil completed his pitch about his *Institutional Investor* magazine, I immediately committed to a full-page ad that would appear monthly inside the front cover.

His magazine became must reading. Every month, there would be an article on a major issue confronting the industry, as well as a portrait of a leading personality from the buy and the sell side. His annual conference was the highlight of the year, held at the New York Hilton and drawing attendees from around the world. I was asked to be a principal speaker or panel member a half dozen times. It was always about the Third Market and its struggle with the NYSE. Weeden usually reserved one of the penthouse apartments to entertain our institutional clients, our out-of-town employees, and even our competitors.

At one particular conference, a large and boisterous crowd had gathered as the evening wore on. A line of windows faced south, with full view of the Equitable Building across the street. It was mostly empty of people at this late hour, except for the occasional cleaning lady. On this particular evening, on the floor slightly below ours, there appeared a couple who, unaware of anything but themselves, proceeded to make love on top of one of the desks. As the scene unfolded and news spread, the eyes of more than 100, mostly men, became riveted on the spectacle. The male member of the twosome eventually looked up to see the audience he was entertaining. The lovemaking now having ceased, the gentleman helped his lady friend recover her dignity and then, with great poise, lightly nodded in our direction as they made for the elevator.

I was not there at the time, unfortunately, but received several calls complimenting Weeden on their choice of entertainment.

Gil and I became good friends, helped by his strong anti-war position. His magazine was tremendously successful, went public and was eventually acquired by others. Gil then devoted himself to his real love, conducting Mahler's difficult Symphony No. 2 before any orchestra, anywhere in the world, that would invite him to be guest conductor. Reviews were not always complimentary, and the accusation was sometimes made that he bought his way onto the podium. But who cares? That is what he wanted to do, and he had earned the money to follow his passion.

Frank and Mabel.

Weeden family in Sun Valley, Idaho, 1967, celebrating 50th wedding anniversary of Mabel and Frank (standing, left to right): Don, Norman, Jack, Vera, Bill, Bill's wife Patty, Bill's son Charles and daughter Barbara, Alan's sons Don and Robert, Alan's wife Barbara, Alan; (seated, left to right): Alan's daughter Leslie, Tina, Frank, Mabel, Elizabeth, Bill's son Billy, Frankie.

As Luck Would Have It

Family photo for Don's 1968 Congressional race:
Vera holding Johnny, Tina, Elizabeth, Frankie, Don.

Headlines from full-page ads in *Village Voice,* 1968.

Vera and Tina at home at 755 Park Avenue, New York City.

Vera, Tina and Johnny at Duck Hollow, 1968.

Paris, 1971.

Vacationing in Savognin, Switzerland, 1970.

Scotty (left), Tina, Johnny, Duck Hollow, 1971.

Chapter 14
New York City, 1970–1978

Change was in the air as we entered the new decade. For me personally, it meant being elected chairman of the board of Weeden & Co., replacing my father, Frank, who retired from active management after 45 years. The transition was not without tension within the family. Jack had come down with a bad case of hepatitis and had to give up his management of operations.

Alan and I disagreed on which of us should assume Jack's responsibilities. I felt I knew more about the back office than Alan and had more time available. Alan disputed both points. I suspected he was mostly concerned about his image within the firm and on the Street if I were to assume additional responsibilities. There was also my increasing advocacy of the Third Market. He felt it undermined the firm's excellent reputation among the bond trading community and the member brokerage firms with whom we did substantial business.

Uncle Norman's good counsel suggested that Alan assume the additional role, Frank retire as chairman while remaining on the board, and I become chairman. Alan was conciliatory and assured me that he would pass the torch of CEO to me after five years. I reluctantly agreed. At the same time I was comfortable with the new title and enjoyed my present freedom from day-to-day responsibilities. Frank was disappointed that he could no longer joke about the "troika" and had no intention of giving up his back-corridor snooping.

Volatility was not far behind. In 1966 the stock market touched 1000 in the Dow Jones Industrial Average after an uninterrupted climb from 550 in 1962. Daily volume doubled. By the end of 1967, the market retreated to 770 on higher daily volume. A surge in buying, led by mutual funds, returned the DJIA to 1000, and daily volume soared to 15 million shares. Suddenly, the market ran out of steam and retreated 35% to a low of 631 in 1971. Wall Street was still physically clearing trades. The exchanges were forced to close on Wednesdays to catch up on their deliveries. In the same period, 10-year U.S. treasury yields rose from under 6% to over 8% and then returned to 5.5%.

The effect on Weeden was mixed. In the four years bracketing the end of the decade, Weeden's sales volume soared from $3.7 billion to $8.7 billion, while earnings went from $2.23 per share in 1968, collapsing to minus $2.61 in 1969, followed by profits of $3.25 and $3.84 in 1970 and '71. The loss in 1969 was mainly from the 33% rise in interest rates affecting our large inventory in bonds.

In 1970, Donaldson, Lufkin & Jenrette became the first NYSE-member firm to issue shares to the public. At the urging of the younger Weedens, our firm was close behind. In two underwritings headed by Bache & Co., Weeden raised close to $20 million. The capital allowed us to better serve our institutional customers through larger inventories and the non-member brokers through additional offices.

As an aside, in 1970, one other Wall Street firm went public: Lehman and Company (not to be confused with Lehman Bros.), a market maker in over-the-counter stocks, which raised $300,000. The firm was owned by Ted Lehman. I knew nothing about the firm, or Ted, until the early 1990s when I met him in Moscow at the office of my partner, Mark Mariska. Ted and I became good friends over the years when we worked together on a startup involving Russian and German technology.

Ted had had a fascinating life: He grew up in Gdansk, Poland, where his father was the correspondent for Reuters. He was 12 when the Germans invaded Poland. In time, his whole family ended up in concentration camps, including Auschwitz. Ted, the only family survivor, was young, healthy and quick-witted enough to be useful to the Nazis as a translator (German, Polish and Russian) in the Krupp factory, which made long-range Howitzers. In keeping with the chronological format, I will have more to say about Ted later on.

The continuing growth of the Third Market (35% increase vs. minus 3% at the NYSE), our public statements, full-page advertisements in the New York Times, my committee participations and letters to the SEC, coupled with our regional exchange memberships, all were of serious concern to the NYSE. In no order of importance or chronology, the NYSE upped the ante with a series of strategic moves: engaging William McChesney Martin, former chairman of the Federal Reserve Board, to prepare a report on market structure; achieving the appointment of William Casey as the new chairman of the SEC; and hiring Jim Needham, recently a commissioner of the SEC, as their new president.

They also were successful in lobbying the board of directors of the NASD to reverse a decision that would have included listed stocks on NASDAQ, a soon-to-begin electronic system for centralizing the over-the-counter market.

These initiatives of the NYSE had us constantly reviewing how to react. The "us" included Jack, Alan, Bob Beshar and Fred Siesel, my executive assistant. Fred had joined Weeden in 1970 from the American Stock Exchange, and prior to that he had worked at the SEC. We all agreed our game plan must reflect Weeden's limited resources and be sensitive to the culture of the Street. We had previously excluded legal action as inappropriate, expensive and uncertain. We also had deferred on requests by the regulators and class-action lawyers to join them in bringing action against institutional investors who had ignored our markets.

I spoke at industry gatherings and visited corporations listed on the NYSE. Our monthly full-page ad in the *Institutional Investor* magazine was very effective. My book, *Weeden & Co., The New York Stock Exchange and the Struggle Over a National Securities Exchange*, written in 2002, spells out our efforts to expose, argue for and detail changes that would allow for full competition among competing market-makers and exchanges.

This is probably as good a time as any to ask why Weeden was getting involved as deeply as it was, especially on the issue of eliminating fixed commissions. Weren't fixed commissions the key to making our net markets so attractive? Wouldn't Weeden lose its advantage with the institutions and find its Third Market business dwindling?

These questions were raised within the firm and hotly debated, especially among the family. I argued that our strength came from our willingness to make markets, take positions, assume risk, operate efficiently, work on narrow margins, establish strong relationships with our customers and handle their inquiry with integrity.

Our daily contact with the institutions would continue to give us a leg up on the specialists, who lacked the same direct contact and were not used to taking large risks. We did not underwrite equity issues and we did no research. We would not be viewed as a competitor by the member firms. They normally shunned risk-taking and could well become good customers of ours, given the opportunity. The issue was out of the bottle and our comments should reflect consistency on the value of competition.

One tactic used by the NYSE brought us close to breaking our rule against litigation. The story begins in early October 1970, with letters from the NYSE and the AMEX to the NASD, asking it to reverse its agreement to include listed stocks on NASDAQ. Gordon Macklin, president of the NASD, and previously a partner of a member firm, then spoke privately with SEC Chairman Hamer Budge (an ex-Congressman from Idaho) and received assurances that the Commission would not challenge a reversal.

On October 20, the Executive Committee of the NASD, all six members being partners of NYSE firms, voted unanimously by phone to reverse the agreement made in 1968 by an overwhelming majority of the NASD membership. On Saturday, October 23, the full Board of Governors, a majority of whom represented member firms, approved the reversal by a voice vote on no more justification than the requests from the two Exchanges.

J.R. Smith, an officer of Weeden, just happened to be one of the 21 members of the Governing Board. He immediately notified me of the action taken that evening. On Monday morning, thanks to Bob Beshar's sharp pen, Gordon Macklin was in receipt of a letter putting the NASD on notice that Weeden would not stand by and "let them push us around." On October 27, Jack and I presented our case to Macklin and his board chairman, Gordon Teach (member of the NYSE). This meeting was followed by a meeting with SEC Chairman Budge. The outcome of our letter and meetings was an agreement by the NASD to develop a pilot project on NASDAQ involving 50 listed stocks that eventually led to a full listing of stocks traded in the Third Market. I was very pleased with the support of the family and others to litigate if necessary and relieved when we reached a compromise that avoided it.

The whole experience reinforced my feelings about the depth of NYSE's concern, their closeness to the SEC and their willingness to fight tough and dirty. I kept seeing that guy at the top of the steps.

In November 1970, I spoke about the "Central Market vs. The Single Market" before the National Investor Relations Institute. Then in March 1971, in Minneapolis, the title of my talk was "Keeping the Power Spread Around." Then "Competition: Key to Market Structure" before the Western Finance Association gathering in Vancouver, B.C.

I was asked to appear before the Securities Industry Association (mostly NYSE-member brokers) at their annual get-together at the Greenbrier. And I went into the lion's den itself when the NYSE asked me to spell out my ideas before its membership, gathered in its richly paneled Board of Governors Room.

At the same time, Andrew Melton, partner of Smith Barney and president of the Investment Bankers Association (IBA), was organizing an industry-wide committee to find a solution to the "seriously fragmented state of our secondary market" (meaning the stock market). Ironically, the secondary market in bonds, in which the IBA members were all heavily involved, moved off the exchanges into the over-the-counter market in the 1920s. The committee, absent a voice from the Third Market, met several times over the next few months. They were unable to make serious headway without input from the principal cause of the fragmentation.

Gordon Macklin was asked to suggest someone from the Third Market and he asked me to be their representative. He explained to me that some on the committee would not be happy and suggested that I refrain from any long-winded pontifications on competition, the interests of the public investor, etc. – in fact, the less I said, the better. "Fine with me," knowing that little would be accomplished whatever I said.

I attended several meetings. I was always placed at the end of the table out of sight and, as I had expected, out of mind. I kept myself busy and my mouth quiet, by smoking cigarettes that were available in great quantity in front of me. I was not a smoker until then, but I soon grew addicted. It took me almost 17 years to kick the habit.

The committee disbanded when the spotlight shifted to the SEC's call for public hearings on market structure. These hearings were the first important initiative by the newly appointed SEC Chairman William Casey. Casey was a tough-minded lawyer, ex-head of the CIA, and had close ties to the Wall Street community. He was a good friend of Bernard J. "Bunny" Lasker, chairman of the NYSE and a floor specialist. At the time, Lasker was slated to be the finance chairman for President Nixon's re-election campaign in 1972. We were naturally troubled by Casey's appointment.

I read Casey's initial speech as chairman in which he emphasized his concern for the small investor. I wrote him an eight-page letter emphasizing our concern for the small investor. I explained why Rule 394 was not in their best interest. I explained in great detail the history of 394, emphasizing how it eliminated competition and prevented member brokers from seeking best execution. It was a good letter that ended with some rather florid language, thanks to Bob Beshar:

"If the Surgeon General required cigarette manufacturers to warn smokers about the health hazards in smoking, and the Food and Drug Administration made physicians warn their patients about possible side effects when recommending drugs, and the Federal Trade Commission compelled advertisers to document their product claims, why shouldn't the Securities and Exchange Commission require member firms to warn their clients that they might not be getting best execution?"

If Casey had not known of Weeden before, he did now.

Other studies were focused on market structure: an SEC study of institutional investors in the marketplace; Mr. Martin's study and two Congressional studies, one in the Senate and one in the House of Representatives. The latter two were begun in 1971 as a reaction to the paper-crunch problem on Wall Street.

Meanwhile, everyone and his brother were testifying at the SEC hearings. There were the usual suspects: the Exchanges, the SIA, the IBA, the Association of Stock Exchange Brokers, and an association representing NYSE floor brokers. There were also 30 individual member firms testifying.

Weeden was the only firm from the Third Market, and we made our usual points in clear but nondescript language. I couldn't help but think that by sheer weight of numbers, the new chairman would find a way of curtailing our activities. (Our testimony enjoyed some notoriety when I spilled a jug full of water while pouring myself a drink during brother Alan's introduction of Jack and me. The three of us were at the table before the commissioners and a roomful of interested parties. Alan quickly explained that his younger brother always wanted to be the center of attention.)

Our fear was reinforced a few weeks later when Chairman Casey hosted a dinner for the members of Andy Melton's committee to thank them for their work. It was in his spacious home on Massachusetts Avenue. After cocktails and a sumptuous dinner held at a monstrous circular table, we retired into the smoking room for brandy and cigars.

After some discussion, Casey turned to me and said, "Well, Don, what do you say to all this?" I replied amiably, but seriously, "I like your choice of cigars, Chairman, but I am sorry to say that these meetings have not changed my position. Eliminating the Third Market would not be right, nor would it be in the public interest."

Mr. Martin's report had been made public shortly before the hearings. His past role as president of the NYSE drowned out any objectivity learned as chairman of the Federal Reserve Bank. He called for a return to a centralized market based on the NYSE with the regional exchanges remaining, but only in a secondary role. As for the Third Market, he blatantly called for its elimination.

As it turned out, the word "elimination" was an emotionally charged word for most economists, whether they were left-leaning or conservative on economic policy. Jim Lorie, professor at the University of Chicago Graduate School of Business, appeared at my office unannounced shortly after the Martin Report was made public. A man of few words, Lorie asked me what he could do. I suggested he write to the SEC, expressing his views on the matter. And that is just what he did. In fewer than two pages, he excoriated the whole concept behind Martin's proposal for a central market. He ended the letter by pointing out that Martin would:

"increase the monopoly power of the NYSE and defend the public interest through self-regulation by the Exchange. This is a little like having the rabbits guarding the lettuce."

The letter was co-signed by 19 of the "21 especially well qualified academicians," ranging from Milton Friedman on the right to Paul Samuelson on the left. (Of the other two: one agreed but didn't sign; the other was unavailable.) It was the kind of letter Bill Casey had to respect.

Jim and I became good friends, especially during the National Market Advisory Board meetings held from 1975 to '77. Along with visits to his summer place in Tesuque, N.M., I enjoyed his great sense of humor and raunchy stories. He also introduced me to Victor Niederhoffer, his prize student at the Chicago Graduate School of Business and several times the National Single Squash Racquets Champion. My most memorable athletic experiences were the squash games I played with Victor. He was living in New York City. We would alternate between the Harvard Club and The Racquet and Tennis Club. He would spot me 10 points in a 15-point game and then adjust two points, depending on who won. The handicap generally ranged from 8 to 12. He would play in his stocking feet and I would demonstrate my quickness by retrieving his shots until he wore me out.

Finally, the SEC released its White Paper on Market Structure in February 1972. Written by Phil Loomis, long-serving and well-respected staff member of the SEC, it was unanimously approved by the Commission. In it, the Third Market was fully recognized as an important part of the market and in the public interest. Martin's vision appeared dead. The Commission had made their decision. Rule 394 was about to disappear. For us at Weeden, it was almost too good to be true. And so it was.

The firm's attention now shifted from the SEC and the Justice Department to the halls of Congress. The need to close the exchanges on Wednesdays in the early 1970s was costly and embarrassing to Wall Street. Many member firms had to close or merge. Tens of thousands of their clients found their securities misplaced and their cash on deposit lost or misused. Wall Street called on Congress for help, similar to the FDIC (Federal Deposit Insurance Corporation) established to support bank customers during the Depression.

Congress was willing to cooperate. In return, they voted to make their own studies of the industry and market structure. From now through 1977, my attention was primarily directed toward insuring that both the House and Senate members and their staffs understood the issues from our perspective.

The continual shuttle trips to and from Washington, D.C., and the overnight stays fell to Fred Siesel and me. Jack joined us occasionally, and Bob Beshar contributed his insights.

It was also a time when my family was becoming more complicated and scattered. It began with Vera's decision that Elizabeth and Frank spend a year at the Ecole Français in Villars, Switzerland, and her desire to move to Pond Brook year-round. Both ideas made sense. The first would increase our two older children's exposure to Switzerland, to Vera's family in Basel and to the European way of life. The move to Pond Brook was more complicated. I knew of her continuing discomfort over the pressures and unpleasantness of the Big City and Johnny's refusal to learn the French language. There was also unhappiness with the whirligig life that I had evolved into after my race for Congress and my heightened involvement with the business.

Vera and I had been considering the adoption of a black child. It was a time in which race was on everyone's mind. This would be a way to demonstrate our commitment to racial equality: sharing our family with a black child who could benefit from our economic and social status. We discussed the pros and cons at considerable length. In the end, both of us felt quite comfortable with the idea; we were willing, capable and excited. It may well have been our way, unknowingly, of keeping our marriage together, and reestablishing a closeness that had been lost in the demands each of us had placed upon ourselves. The decision to move ahead was made late in 1970, and the adoption was finalized in time for Vera's move to Pond Brook.

The reaction to our adoption of Scott (we called him "Scotty") from my family was muted by the fact that it was a done deal when announced. I had assumed it would not be well received. To their credit, the family accepted the reality of this 18-month-old African American boy becoming a Weeden. One light bit of humor that bubbled up was the photo of a football player on the UCLA roster, black as the ace of spades, with the last name of Weeden. By July 1972, when the Weeden clan gathered in Canada's Jasper National Park to celebrate my parent's 65th wedding anniversary, Scotty was there in the front row of our formal family portrait.

Ann, whom I was still seeing, was totally unprepared for the news. Her reaction was to take an overdose of sleeping pills. I was called at home on a Saturday morning by a girlfriend of Ann's who said that she was at the hospital and resting peacefully. She told me I was the cause of it. I was overwhelmed by the news and uncertain what I should do. I was 40 years old, married with four young children. My relationship with Ann was close and strong, but in my mind, it had not reached the point of considering a breakup with Vera and spoiling a happy family.

Ann perceived it as a permanent rejection of any long-term relationship involving her. However I tried to explain my thinking, it fell on deaf ears. I should have realized that having continued the relationship for such a long time implied something to her that I had not yet contemplated. Having unintentionally misled her is something I continue to regret. I wanted to keep in touch. She moved to California, eventually married, had two children and subsequently went through a divorce. My concern for her continued for many years, and we met from time to time when I traveled to San Francisco, but our intimacy had ceased with the news about the pending adoption of Scotty.

Before Frank and Elizabeth went off to Switzerland, Frank and I went on a 10-day hike into the High Sierra. It was the end of August 1971. With us were two of my early Alameda buddies, Warren Musser and Bill Davis, and Davis's 14-year-old son. The trip was a perfect way to reengage with old friends from Alameda and to get to know Frank better. It was strenuous for all of us, but especially for an 11-year-old.

We started at Florence Lake and trudged up the trail until we hit the John Muir Trail and the South Fork of the San Joaquin River. We made another jog upward to Evolution Valley (9,600 ft.), where we made our base camp. We traveled higher, including Muir Pass (11,600 ft.) and fished for golden trout in several of the small lakes well above the timber line. I was impressed with Frank's determination and toughness throughout, even when he suffered a bit of altitude sickness on the way up. Coming down, the two of us became separated from the others and were still walking at dusk along the river bank trying to find the John Muir trail. Finally, we gave up looking, made camp on a sandbank, cooked our meal and bedded down, with me reading "Hamlet" by flashlight to Frank until he fell asleep.

In early August, President Nixon had announced the government's intention to go off the Gold Standard, and the stock market instantly surged higher. The NYSE had difficulty opening many issues, and, in the case of General Motors and Ford, failed to open them all day. The next day found them still having difficulty. Finally, Weeden decided to open them on the Philly Stock Exchange by shorting into the buy orders collected there. The NYSE then opened both stocks shortly thereafter at the same price. In light of the discussions over market structure, it was a poke in the eye to the NYSE's contention that they were indispensable. The *New York Times* reported the event on their front page. And it was of sufficient interest in Washington that an upcoming Senate hearing on market structure would want to explore the details.

A week after my return, I went to Washington to listen in on those hearings. When I arrived, I made myself as inconspicuous as possible. At the urging of Vera, I had not yet shaved from the trip. I squished myself quietly into a corner seat in what became a rather crowded chamber.

Among those testifying was Elkins Wetherill, president of the Philadelphia Stock Exchange. After an introductory statement, Elkins was asked to explain how the Philadelphia Stock Exchange was able to open both General Motors and Ford before New York. It was a technical question, and Elkins was not familiar with the details. Steve Paradise, Chairman William's administrative assistant, leaned over and, pointing in my direction, whispered something to the chairman. Chairman Williams then announced that there was someone in the audience who might be able to answer the question.

After being sworn in to tell "nothing but the truth," I commented that I would have shaved this morning if I had thought I would be testifying today.

Senator Brook, the Republican senator from Massachusetts, assured me that my presence was welcomed, with beard or without, as long as I told the truth. I then proceeded to explain what happened. I was comfortable with the beard (it balanced my bald head somewhat). I have merely trimmed it when needed ever since. At the time it was the only beard south of Fulton Street and added to my growing reputation as a maverick.

The year 1972 found Weeden as one of the top 25 Wall Street firms showing over $30 million in capital. We had 550 employees, of which 340 were located in the New York office. The Weeden board consisted of seven members, four of whom were Weedens. Yet it was still by the four Weedens, at informal meetings in the firm's apartment in the West Village, that our longer-term policy was determined.

Our Third Market revenue was growing nicely, but, for the first time in several years, it took second place to fixed-income trading. This was mainly due to the hiring of John Krause in 1970 and the decision to expand our traditional fixed-income trading into new areas. John was a municipal bond salesman, ex-marine, captain of his college football team, a popular leader. Frank was attracted to him and raised the idea that he would be a suitable CEO.

Alan was preparing for his 50th-year sabbatical and supported the idea. (Overlooked until later was the fact that John was a rehabilitated alcoholic, excessive chain smoker, had experienced a fractious divorce. He lived a very private life and was capable of outbursts of megalomania.)

Early in 1972, Alan and Frank recommended that John be made executive vice president. He would then take over as CEO in 1974 when Alan was to take his three children on a yearlong round-the-world camping trip. I was in New Hampshire campaigning for Pete McCloskey at the time.

Pete had graduated from Stanford the year before me, served as a Marine officer in Korea, and felt the same way as I did about the war in Vietnam. He ended up taking second place behind President Nixon in a three-way race in the Republican primary.

John came to the Hanover Inn and we spent the morning discussing what it would mean to the equity traders and salesmen having to report to John and what I felt about it, having been promised the job of CEO (at least by Alan). Surprisingly, even to me, I accepted it in good spirit and told John I would support him wholeheartedly. I was comfortable with my role as chairman and John's commitment to growing the company, including our equity business.

I had plenty to do, which kept me away from the stock trading desk: preparing testimony, giving speeches, traveling to Washington, and counter-punching against a full-court press by the New York Stock Exchange and its phalanx of members, associations and lobbyists.

One particular meeting illustrates the forces we were up against and the need to constantly work the halls of Congress. Fred Siesel had arranged for the two of us to meet with Congressman Robert Eckhardt, a Democrat representing Houston, Texas, and the second-most-important member of the House committee on securities industry matters.

We were allotted 45 minutes to explain our position. We arrived a few minutes early and waited while the congressman finished with another group. When the door to his chambers opened, out streamed eight men, headed by Lee Kendall, president of the Association of Stock Exchange Firms, which included a partner from a member firm (not surprisingly) headquartered in the Congressman's district. We exchanged the usual courtesies and then Fred and I joined with the Congressman in an in-depth discussion of the issues.

As we reentered the outer office, we were greeted by Don Calvin, vice president of the NYSE, accompanied by an equally large entourage of important people waiting to make their pitch.

In 1972, it was a time of growth and strong profitability at Weeden. Esprit de corps was high throughout the firm. The fixed-income desks were feeling their oats and the stock traders continued to chip away at the NYSE's dominance. The back office, now referred to as operations, had greatly expanded and included a group of talented managers who were incorporating the latest technologies and procedures for reducing costs. And better communications technology improved the real-time integration of the offices.

The family atmosphere continued despite our growth, with both generations of Weedens making their presence known in all our offices throughout the year.

There was no better time for expressing this "family" atmosphere than at our annual Christmas parties. It was a busy time for Jack, as he served as master of ceremonies in every office. As head of operations again, Jack was very popular and respected as one of the troops by everyone. I am sure that most all knew that he was gay, although, as was usual at the time, it was not discussed openly.

In New York, we were using the grand ballroom at the Downtown Athletic Club due to our increase in personnel. We had used the Tavern on the Green for several years until our overexuberant use of Silly Putty on their hardwood dance floor ended our relationship. We had a policy that no spouses would be invited. The main purpose of the party was the intermingling of departments and personnel in an other-than-business atmosphere. This policy had been in place going back to the Twenties, much to the consternation of my mother. She most probably suspected that it created opportunities for intimacy beyond a dance or two. She might have been right, as some of the skits implied just that. If they were correct, it started long before the Christmas party.

The skits were the center of attraction, and much time and creativity were put into them. No one was immune from being the target of their humor. Fred Siesel annually gave his "Karnak" routine, where he would tell the audience the answer and then ask if anyone could figure out the question. For instance:

Answer: "Name five big boobs." Question: "Alan, Jack, Don and Dolly Parton."

Fred's quick wit was always on the tip of his tongue, the best example of which was the 1975 May Day calendar. My only remembered contribution was singing, "If you choose your parents very carefully, you too can be chairman of the company" to the tune of "When I Was a Lad," sung by the Admiral in the "Gilbert and Sullivan" operetta HMS Pinafore.

Vera's move to Pond Brook Road made her daily life less complicated. She didn't have to worry about my schedule of late arrivals for dinner and trips out of town. Johnny was now in an English- speaking school. Tina, almost 10, was taking riding lessons at the local horse barn. Scotty was slowly being integrated into our family. A mother's helper from Germany to help out allowed Vera to come to the city occasionally.

Elizabeth and Frank were at school in Switzerland. My focus on market structure issues often took me to Washington and elsewhere. I made a point of coming up to Pond Brook every weekend, where I rested, found plenty of manual work outdoors, and read to the children in the evenings. They were the same children's books as before: Tolkien's trilogy, volumes of A. A. Milne's Winnie-the-Pooh, the ones I enjoyed. I thought of myself as a good family man.

My schedule was not so different from my father's during the 1930s. He was often out of town on business. When he was present, he was distant and uninvolved; I got an occasional reprimand or spanking when I resisted authority. Mother occasionally traveled with Frank, but we always had Gussie Eckstein, our live-in cook. I vaguely remember Mom reading to me, disciplining me and driving me to school when it rained.

There were no big discussions, no intellectual exchanges, little effort to expose me to the arts or music or museums. Vera had a much closer, hands-on relationship with our children, more involved in their activities and education. It was part of the package I hoped for when marrying her, and I was pleased that it was working out that way.

Meanwhile, my interest in the City Club of New York was growing. Early in 1972, I offered to finance a project I had had in mind ever since the Lower Manhattan Expressway (LME) was scrubbed from the city's plans in 1969. The purpose of the Expressway had been to reduce street congestion in Downtown Manhattan by taking the cross-town traffic off street level. The LME, while well-intentioned, would have been terribly destructive to a strategically located but underused part of Manhattan. Yet the problem remained, not just downtown but in the entire area running south from 59th Street.

I was also motivated by my experience at the San Francisco World's Fair in 1939 and the New York World's Fair in 1964. The San Francisco fair was held on a manmade island called Treasure Island, located at the midpoint of the San Francisco-Oakland Bay Bridge. One parked his private auto away from the fairgrounds and took a bus or jitney onto the fair site, where the only vehicles were electric, quiet and fun to ride in. Why couldn't the central part of Manhattan be the same?

With the board's agreement, I established the "Manhattan Auto Study" project under the auspices of the City Club. I engaged the urban-planning team of Peter Abeles and Harry Schwartz to do the study and make recommendations. In addition, I brought together a distinguished group of city planners, architects, economists and engineers to serve as its advisory board. I was involved at every stage of the study. It was my project from beginning to end.

The final report ran to 166 pages, took a year and a half to complete, and ended up costing $100,000. I consider it one of my better projects, even though it was quickly dismissed in the press as utopian.

I first called on Constantine ("Connie") Eristoff, then the New York City planning commissioner, to seek his cooperation. He smiled when I told him my idea, called it audacious, but agreed to help. I then went to the 12 other organizations with responsibility over some aspect of the problem (Taxi and

Limousine, Regional Planning, Triborough Bridge and Tunnel Authority, New York State Department of Transportation, New York City Department of Environmental Protection, New York Port Authority, Downtown Association, etc.). No one was looking at the problem holistically, nor were they even talking to one another.

The advisory board included such notables as Peter Bernstein, chairman of Bernstein-Macaulay; Percival Goodman, professor of urban design, Columbia University; Robert Heilbroner, chairman, Department of Economics, New School for Social Research; Dick Netzer, dean, Graduate School of Public Administration, New York University, along with nine other gentleman of similar stature. They contributed many good ideas after overcoming their initial skepticism that it would ever amount to anything.

We first collected the data residing in the files of the participating agencies, determined what was causing the congestion, and recommended ways it could be reduced with minimum cost and discomfort to local businesses, residents and commuters. Our recommendations were, as Connie had predicted, "audacious," but justified by the resulting economic and environmental improvement.

I spoke at the City Club in March of 1973:

"We began with the hope that if man can invent the automobile, he ought to be able to control it. This is not yet the case in Manhattan, where private autos, taxies, busses and trucks, parked and moving, inflict their noise, fumes and violence on the million pedestrians they daily inconvenience and endanger."

The main features of the plan were:

• Connect the Lincoln Tunnel at the Hudson River with the Queens Midtown by means of a deep tunnel, to be financed 90% by the Federal Highway Fund. We estimated this would remove 10,000 trips by trucks and 40,000 trips by autos from the local streets. At $6 per truck and $4 per auto, Monday through Friday, it would yield $55 million annually.

• Create underground parking facilities between the present shoreline along the Hudson River and the proposed new West Side Highway to be constructed along the end of the present piers, to be 90% financed by the Federal Interstate Highway Funds. We estimated that 120,000 spaces could be constructed, replacing the 114,000 off-street spaces presently available for commuters, residents and visitors. In turn, it would make those spaces available for the 75,000 autos registered in New York City and environs that are permitted to park on city streets. Cost of construction is estimated to be $800 million. At an average use of 100,000 spaces, Monday through Friday at $5 per auto, revenues would equal $125 million annually.

- Limit street parking during the business day to vehicles engaged in loading, delivery, pickup and emergencies.
- Require all presently exempt autos (75,000) to use off-street parking only.
- Introduce new forms of taxi use, eliminate cruising, and establish hack stands.
- Narrow traffic on Fifth Avenue and Madison Avenue between 42nd Street and 59th Street to three lanes, broaden the sidewalks, and introduce trees and benches.
- Provide jitney service cross-town servicing the Westside parking terminal, and uptown/downtown between 42nd and 59th on Fifth and Madison. The same could be done elsewhere if demand warranted it.
- Place tolls on all bridges connecting Manhattan with the outer boroughs.

Many of the proposals ran up against special interests that saw the changes affecting them negatively: the businessman who wanted to park in front of his store, the taxi driver who was used to cruising, the doctor and diplomat wanting to park anywhere, anytime. There were the New Yorkers in the outer boroughs who didn't want to pay a toll when driving to Manhattan. The Westside communities objected to the parking lot as being disruptive and intrusive.

The study found little support and was quickly filed away in the bowels of the Planning Commission. In my dreams, I can still envision trees, gardens and benches along a quieter and pleasanter Fifth Avenue.

Joel Harnett was chairman when I was president of the City Club. I became close friends of Joel and his wife, Lila, a couple that represented the best of New York City culture. They lived at the corner of 57th Street and East End Avenue. They grew up in Brooklyn—Jews of modest background; smart, lovers of the arts, active politically, energetic. They had no children. Joel had been the executive director of Look magazine until it went out of business after the war. He then founded his own publishing company, Media Horizons, focusing on the communication and computer industries. I was asked onto his board, whose makeup was mostly friends of Joel's: we were five bagels and a donut.

Lila was a regular contributor for Cue magazine, was on the board of the Whitney Museum and for a time was director of the New York State Art Council. Their cooperative was filled with early 20th century art, including two works by Edward Hopper.

In 1979, Joel ran as the good-government candidate in the Democratic primary for mayor of New York. There were six others vying for the honor:

Abe Beame, Mario Cuomo, Ed Koch, Percy Sutton, Bella Abzug and Herman Badillo. Ed Koch ended up beating out Mario Cuomo; Joel received 1% of the vote.

Their apartment at 57th was a short walk after squash at the Racquet and Tennis Club on Park and 53rd. Vera was spending the weekdays on Pond Brook Road. I would have a drink or two, maybe dinner, and talk about all sorts of interesting subjects. Joel and Lila were intrigued with Weeden's struggle with the NYSE, and I was fascinated with their knowledge and passion for the arts. Their interests were quite different from those of my parents, whose formal education was more limited and whose focus was on the present, business and local activities.

When I decided to write the story of Weeden and the NYSE in 2001, I sought out Joel for advice. By then, Joel and Lila had moved to Phoenix and founded the highly successful shelter magazine Phoenix Home & Garden. He suggested I involve Gary Avey, who earlier had been editor of Arizona Highways and at the time was the publisher and editor of *Native Peoples*, a monthly magazine featuring the art and culture of Native Americans.

The two of them were very helpful in editing and reorganizing my early drafts. In 2006, Joel died of prostate cancer. I had continued to visit Joel and Lila in Arizona, with Pat, until his death. Along with my Uncle Norman, I rank Joel among those who were truly good, kind and generous.

The early 1970s found the NYSE still determined to eliminate the Third Market: first by pressuring our customers not to deal with us; then by encouraging the SEC to restrict us; and, finally, by lobbying Congress to legislate us out of business. We were winning the battle in the media; editorials from the *New York Times, Wall Street Journal* and *Barron's* commented that our competition was in the public interest.

The attitude of the SEC had changed with the publication of their white paper. The two Congressional studies on market structure were favorable and called for integrating our markets more closely with that of the public exchanges. Legislation was being proposed that called for centralizing the markets, including us, and using the new technology to gather, consolidate and disseminate market information. The year 1974 was to be the year for enacting Exchange Act amendments that would create a national market system and rid us of Rule 394. We were so confident in the outcome that Weeden made the decision to spend $2 million designing the prototype for a truly national market.

Our euphoria was a bit premature. In 1973, Jim Needham replaced Robert Haack as president of the NYSE. Bob had gained the ire of NYSE's membership, especially its chairman, Bunny Lasker, when he criticized the fixed commission structure. Jim's mandate was to come out fighting any change. In his initial speech made to the Bond Club of New York, he urged Congress to pass legislation to eliminate the Third Market. He printed the speech in its entirety in the *New York Times* and *Wall Street Journal*. Jim did not mince his words: "Third Market firms must be given the choice now of joining an Exchange or going into some other business."

Jim had contrasted the Third Market with the NYSE where business was done in a "fish bowl" and warned of a "domino effect" if the institutions continued doing their business away from the auction market. A bit later, he invited me to a private lunch in his office at 11 Wall Street. I brought along a getting-to-know-one-another present: a fish bowl stuffed with ticker tape and a set of dominos.

Jim had been described as "short, stout and pugnacious" by Chris Welles in his book *The Last Days of the Club*. I found him pleasant enough, with an Irish sense of humor. Some months later, we had another encounter, this time at the Bull & Bear Bar in the Waldorf Astoria. We had just attended a dinner celebrating the National Hockey League. Most of those gathered at the bar were from Wall Street and made space for us as we approached.

No one interrupted us during the two hours we stood, sipping top-of-the-line cognac, courtesy of Jim, while we struggled to find understanding – maybe even accommodation. As I vaguely remember, we were still struggling when they closed the bar and Jim graciously had me driven home to my apartment uptown.

G. Bradford Cook, who replaced William Casey as chairman of the SEC, confirmed the thrust of the white paper at a speech at the New York Financial Writers' Association. This did not deter Jim, who continued his bad-mouthing of the Third Market and lobbying for its elimination.

Hearings began in the House and Senate on legislation that would become the Securities Act Amendments of 1975. Meanwhile, the SEC began pressing the industry to design and implement a consolidated tape and a composite quotation system, the purpose of which was to make it easier for the public investor to see in one place all the trades taking place and all the bids and offers available in all markets.

These changes were not in the interest of the NYSE, and they made every effort to delay their implementation. I was a member of every committee designing these improvements to the market, and found myself becoming the most vocal voice representing the interest of the non-NYSE participants. Years later, Arnie Staloff, from the Philly Exchange, wrote me a nice letter saying: "If it were not for your dogged insistence on the sharing of revenues from the consolidated tape, most of the regionals would have gone out of business."

What was supposed to be the Securities Act Amendments of 1974 was delayed a year when a last-ditch effort by legislative friends of the NYSE introduced a bill giving the SEC full authority to shut down the Third Market. We were able to marshal the Justice Department, the Treasury Department and the SEC to change the language, making it almost impossible for the SEC to act against the Third Market.

The main argument by the NYSE was their fear that firms like Goldman Sachs would leave the Exchange. We presented testimony of Goldman Sachs' managing partner, Gus Levy, at another federal hearing that "his firm was not likely to leave the NYSE." In response to our quoting him, Levy wrote Senator Williams, chairman of the hearing, "I feel it is very important to inform you that Mr. Weeden's reference to my statement, absent a proper analysis of what I know I meant by that statement, is, in my mind, most misleading."

I mention this only to throw a barb at Gus Levy, for whom I had great respect but who had no time for me. At a social gathering in New York, it was reported to me that when I entered the room, Gus turned to the group around him and asked in a depreciating tone, "Who let that guy in?"

The Securities Act Amendments were enacted in early 1975. Fixed commissions were eliminated by May 1. A consolidated tape began operation in June, and a composite quotation system was agreed upon. The only issue remaining for a national market system was how to tie the markets together electronically. Congress left it to the SEC and the industry to work out the details.

A National Market Advisory Board (NMAB) was appointed by the SEC, composed of representatives from the industry and users (bank trust departments, insurance companies, mutual funds and small investors). The issue was whether or not to create a central limit order book (CLOB). The NYSE well understood that their advantage over the other markets was their possession of limit orders. These are bids and offers slightly away from the market held on the specialist's book. This accumulation of interest was a strong incentive for investors to send their own limit orders to the NYSE. A central repository of all limit orders (CLOB) from all markets would eliminate this advantage.

The committee met for two days every month through 1976. Debate over a CLOB was the primary focus of those two-day meetings. Don Stone and I were the leading protagonists. Don was a partner of Lasker, Stone & Stern, a specialist firm on the NYSE. Don and I knew each other through the friendship he had with my brother Alan. We had co-roasted Alan on his 40th birthday in 1964. To insure that our friendship would survive our anticipated heated confrontations, we agreed to a tennis match, cocktails and dinner at the end of each first day. Today, Don and I, with Alan, still play golf regularly and talk about "those good old days."

As for a CLOB, eight of the 11 votes cast by the NMAB opted for one of four variations. The final decision was left to the SEC.

While I was arguing for a CLOB, my brother Jack was finalizing Weeden's prototype of a national market system that included one. The Weeden Holding Automated Market (WHAM) was installed on the Cincinnati Stock Exchange in 1976. WHAM provided equal rights to anyone or any exchange to act as a market-maker, the role Weeden already enjoyed. Over time, Merrill Lynch and PWJC experimented in making markets in a few utility stocks. Other regional stock exchanges participated. It was now called the Regional Market System (RMS), which morphed into the Multiple Dealer Trading System (MDTS).

To compete, the NYSE developed the Intermarket Trading System (ITS). While it lacked real-time execution between exchanges, it offered free access to their floor. It was strongly supported by the regional specialists dependent upon access to New York's markets and the offer of free access too good to turn down.

In 1981, by three votes to two, the SEC abandoned its commitment to a CLOB in favor of NYSE's Intermarket Trading System, relying on NYSE's promise to look into the centralizing of limit order information. It was Chairman William's concern that "Wall Street was not ready for a CLOB."

The reader might ask what difference did all this make to Weeden's business? As I wrote in my previous book:

"Was this just a further effort on my part to 'stick it in their eye' (whoever 'their' was)? Was I really in orbit, lacking all sensitivity to what the Street wanted? Needed? They certainly did not want further changes on top of what was already taking place. Even at Weeden we were going through a tough time, losing gobs of money. There were opponents to WHAM within Weeden as well.

"To me, it was very straightforward. In the same way we had felt it important to be part of Quotron, Autex and Instinet, I felt that with the impending Securities Acts Amendments, some kind of system that included a CLOB was inevitable, and I wanted to make sure Weeden was part of it."

My obsession with a CLOB has continued. In 1988, I wrote an op-ed piece for the *Wall Street Journal* titled "October Crash Proves Need for National Market System" that appeared on April 12, 1988. I made the argument that the 1987 crash would have been less severe if there had been a CLOB, allowing for all exchanges and over-the-counter dealers (including major block traders on the NYSE) to participate in stabilizing the rapidly deteriorating prices on the NYSE where the pricing was being determined solely by the undercapitalized specialists.

Then, in 2004, I wrote a series of letters to Bill Donaldson, chairman of the SEC, recommending a CLOB be implemented as part of Regulation National Market System.

My reasoning was based on the complexity and cost of the system being created without a CLOB and the fragmentation that would ensue. I was right on both issues. The present system is so complex and unwieldy that the SEC has lost control of it. As a result, a plethora of "dark pools" have been created by the major brokerage firms in which they cross customer orders without going to the registered exchanges. In addition, it has fostered the creation of high-frequency traders who take advantage of small time differences in reaching exchanges that allow for them to inter-position themselves between public orders.

The arguments for creating a CLOB have not changed, they've only intensified with the massive growth in volume and the wide variety of public investors dependent on a fair and efficient market. As for Weeden's present interest, the mood is "none of our business" and "we see no particular advantage to us."

At one time, the CLOB had the support of Congress, the NMAB and the SEC, but no longer. I am the only one still talking about one. When I attend the semi-annual meetings of the National Organization of Investment Professionals (NOIP), they good-naturedly address me as "Mr. CLOB."

The details in the previous section were helped by referring to my previous book. I have nothing in writing with details from my personal life: trips, vacations, family doings. This might appear to some as indifference or discomfort. Neither was my intention. Enough said.

By 1972, Vera was well settled into her life on Pond Brook Road. She would come into the city for social engagements and times when it was helpful for business. A succession of mother's helpers made it easy. In return, I came up from the city every Friday afternoon and returned early Monday.

The trips were long but relaxing, thanks to the club car. The train would depart Grand Central arriving South Norwalk, whereupon I would transfer to a single-car "Toonerville Trolley" that puttered uncertainly for another hour up the Aspetuck Valley to Danbury. It was a picturesque trip at a leisurely pace and helped me ratchet down from the fast pace of the Big City.

When I arrived, I was ready to rest and relax and not think about the business, the NYSE—or the family for that matter. I would take a couple of anti-allergy pills against the dust and pollen and wash them down with a stiff scotch and soda. When I arrived, everybody would be busy finishing their day of activities and preparing for the weekend. I was content to sit back, listen to their chatter and enjoy the interaction.

I found my relaxation in working outdoors: mowing the meadows (summers), cutting dead trees for butting and then splitting into firewood, or clearing the land of dead wood and brambles.

By 1972, the original cabin had had a series of facelifts which provided bedrooms for three children, a mother's helper and a master bedroom. My stone cabin was livable, but unused. I then built an attachment to our horse shed to house a full-sized kiln for Vera's new interest in pottery. There was a donkey in our meadow, followed by a horse. Tina and Johnny had developed a set of friends from school and the neighborhood. Scotty was newly arrived. Life was quite different from Park and 72nd.

Scotty was new to the family. We found him shy and apprehensive of his new parents, which was understandable after a year and a half of bouncing from one foster parent to another. His adjustment was aided by our cleaning lady from the city, Pearl Archer.

Pearl was from Jamaica, living in Brooklyn with her children. She would come up to Newtown with some frequency and give the place a good scrubbing. She was helpful in making Scotty feel at home; partly, I assume, because of skin color, but also because of her warm and gentle nature. She embraced Scotty, almost as one of her own. It eventually created a situation where he began to call her mother rather than Vera. I did not notice this problem until later, when it was one of the causes of our decision to reverse the adoption.

During these years, there were short trips to Europe on business and more extended ones during the summer with children. For several summers, Vera arranged for a house in Savognin, in the Grisons, a mountainous area in the southeastern part of Switzerland. Various relatives of Vera's would join us, and I would usually come for two weeks.

They were idyllic days: lots of hiking, playing together and reading. I continued to read to the children, with more-adult stories; short, well written, adventurous. I especially remember *The Old Man and the Sea*. We were lying in the soft grass near a small stream a short walk up the trail from town and overlooking the majestic snow-covered mountains in the distance. Everyone was crying at the end and I had a hard time getting through the last few pages.

We also continued our winter practice of visiting my friend Tom Wilson and family on St. Croix. Skiing in Vermont also became a habit and led to Vera's buying property outside the town of Northfield. It reminded her of Switzerland. I had no part in the decision but thought it a good idea. She had been the beneficiary of small amounts from the estates of relatives, which she kept in a Swiss bank account. To this day, I have no idea of the amount or which bank she used.

Those years were eventful for our family in a number of ways. In 1975, I decided to change my residency from New York to Connecticut. John Krause had successfully brought our equity trading under his wing, and the pressure to insure the permanency of the Third Market was behind me. Frank was entering his third year at Hotchkiss; Elizabeth had but one year remaining until her baccalaureate from the Lycée. The other three were in school in Newtown, Scotty having entered kindergarten. I sold our cooperative at 755 Park Ave. at a ridiculously low price even considering the fact that the city was being threatened with bankruptcy. I kept a smaller apartment in the same building for Elizabeth's use until her graduation. I then rented a modest one-room apartment on 60th between Madison and Lexington for use during the week.

Frank and Elizabeth were back from their schooling at the Ecole in Villars. Frank was active on the ski team at Hotchkiss and doing well. He had yet to meet the girl who became his obsession. Elizabeth had fallen in love with a man she met at Paxtons, a restaurant on the corner of 74th and Second Avenue. Tina was 13, older than her age and running with the wrong group at Newtown High. It wasn't long before Vera took her away from what she called "too fast a crowd" and placed her in Wooster School, a private school located on the edge of Danbury.

It was also Scotty's introduction to other children in Newtown—or, to put it a better way, "other children's introduction to Scotty." Strange as it seems, Scotty's blackness was almost unknown in this white middle- to upper-class town. This surprised me. Danbury, less than 10 miles away and long the center of the hat industry, had assimilated every ethnic and racial group that arrived from overseas and the Deep South. In its diversity it was a miniature New York City. Not so in Newtown. On the bus ride to and from school, Scotty became the brunt of catcalls and racial slurs that had Johnny defending Scotty verbally and sometimes physically. Naturally, this was quite upsetting to Vera.

On top of these incidents, there were other happenings that seemed more like a dagger to the very heart of what Vera felt was a generous and well-meant commitment. There was Scotty's growing view of Pearl as his mother and the visible display of it in front of her when Pearl came to Newtown. There were also a series of articles by African American commentators criticizing the adoption of their children by white families.

It wasn't long before Vera was asking, "Why am I doing this if there is no appreciation for my effort, not even a hug now and then?" I agreed.

Together, we saw that it was also becoming a source of tension within the family that our tenuous relationship didn't need. That it had been a bad idea became clear, but what to do about it? About the same time, Pearl suffered the loss of her youngest of six children from the sudden onset of meningitis. He was eight and the apple of her eye. Pearl almost immediately shifted the love for that boy to Scotty, and when approached about the idea of adopting him, she responded with tears of joy. The adoption occurred smoothly. All parties involved were either overjoyed or relieved.

I made one effort to see Scotty later in Brooklyn, but decided, along with Pearl, that it was not a good idea to continue any visible relationship. He was young enough to remember us as one of many changes in his life before joining a large and loving family into which he fit like an old shoe. We stayed in touch with Pearl after her husband left her and she moved south to live with her sister. Scotty eventually joined the Army, married, and had, I believe, a successful career in the military.

I have often revisited Vera's and my failed experiment in racial outreach. There were warnings from a Catholic placement service that turned us down, saying that it would not work out within our already large, tight-knit family and their judgment that our commitment was not strong enough to overcome the anticipated complications. They might also have been concerned about our not being Catholic and less-than-active church-goers. The adoption agency on 20th Street had been happy to offload one of their foster children who, at one and a half years of age, was no longer appealing to others looking to adopt.

The main question: Was it a bad idea from the very beginning, pursued for the wrong reasons with no discernible benefits and resulting in various degrees of damage to all concerned? It is easy to plead guilty to all of the above and admit to gross stupidity, arrogance and insensitivity. No one has ever said that to me, but I felt it as I might well be thinking the same if it had been one my friends doing the adopting. Nor has anyone ever said, "Nice try. The two of you were great for making the effort. Courageous!"

There was some fallout. By ending my liaison sooner rather than later, it redirected my thoughts and attention to Vera. It was a good lesson about the risks in trying to do "good." It most likely affected my father's view of my judgment and maturity with respect to running the business. And probably most important, Scotty finally ended up in a home with plenty of love and knowing he belonged. Certainly, Pearl was happy with the outcome.

With the need to protect my change of legal residency from New York to Connecticut, I began spending long weekends at what Uncle Norman had dubbed "Duck Hollow." My excess energy soon had me looking for physical challenges. I accelerated my plantings of hemlocks and purchased the railroad right-of-way that passed through the property. This gave us a total of 50 acres and a forest designation on 25 acres.

Then I had the bright idea of building a bigger house next to my little stone hut on the hill. We had expanded the original cabin below, but it still felt inadequate. I had no particular plan in mind. Vera had no objections while showing little enthusiasm. She did remark that it would keep me busy enough, which turned out to be a gross understatement.

My stone hut was in the right spot but hardly used. Fred Siesel was the only person to sleep overnight in it. He complained the next morning: "Never again. The birds made too much noise. They began at dawn. I couldn't get back to sleep." I asked, "How can you sleep living at 83rd and Lexington?" "Oh," he explained, "I'm used to it."

With some imagination and a lot of clearing, the view from the knoll to the rear of the property had a quiet beauty about it; the land sloped gently down to the brook, which slowly meandered through an arc of 70 degrees. Beyond was Mike Piskura's pasture where he grazed his milk cows. Alongside the brook ran the abandoned railroad bed, and in front of that was a large flat area with plenty of light.

The thought came to me that it could be made into a grass court like the one I once played on at the Piping Rock club. The house would be early New England; nothing fancy, rough-hewn, solid and cozy. And I would build it myself.

To this day, I remember the first shovel of dirt that began a three-year adventure. My nephew, Billy Weeden, and his wife, Diane, had driven up from New Jersey for the day. We walked up the road to the site where I had outlined the dimensions of the house. It was not yet noon and I was anxious to start the project. I shoveled the first clods of dirt to one side. Billy spelled me from time to time. We were making slow progress when we uncovered a large boulder. It was too big to move. I had a sledgehammer and meant to split it apart.

A few hard taps made nary a dent. Billy suggested we break for lunch. It was two beers and a full stomach later that I reluctantly agreed there was an easier method: Get a backhoe.

What a downer. I had planned to build the house only with tools available 200 years ago. My dream of replicating Thoreau's house on Walden Pond was not to be.

The next week, I was sitting on a Bobcat, digging a trench 28 by 32 by 3 feet for my foundation. After bracing the frame of half-inch plywood, I went to Lloyd's Lumber for my first yard of concrete. The bracing proved inadequate and the frame bulged badly. It reminded me of the Eiffel Tower.

The foundations required 20 loads of concrete. I would drive my Vauxhall station wagon five miles to Lloyd's Lumber. They would hitch up a small concrete mixer and fill it with cement, sand, gravel and water. My job was to get back ASAP and pour it into the molds before it hardened. No problems, except for one load that I couldn't get up the hill because of a heavy rain the night before. When I tried to back up, I jackknifed the load. I had to pour out $20 worth of hardening concrete and carry it up the hill in pails.

I had the misconception that any construction away from a property line need not have a permit. I was wrong. I called the Newtown building inspector. Would he mind coming out to take a look at what I had already done? I showed him a map of our property. I told him I had no drawings for the house and showed him the book I had ordered from the U.S. government on how to build wood-framed houses.

He was an old boy who had been doing this for a long time. He was very nice, and he alluded to this being an unusual situation—in fact, one he had never come across before. He OK'ed the site and the foundations but suggested I get some professional help going forward.

By now it was autumn, and cooler. I began to look around for downed trees that would serve as the beams to support the second floor. They would remain exposed and give the lower floor the feeling of an old New England home. I found several, including an ash long enough to span 32 feet.

The art of adzing a tree trunk is pretty simple. With the trunk, cleaned of all branches, resting on the ground, you create raised platforms on both sides, slightly higher than the trunk. Straddling the trunk, you swing the adze between your legs and slowly create a flat surface deep enough to give you a side the width you wish. In the case of my 32-foot ash, I wanted it to be approximately 10 by 13 inches. This size would meet minimum load requirements for the 30-foot span according to my "How to Build Wood-Framed Houses" manual.

An adze, according to my Oxford dictionary, is "an axe-like tool for cutting away the surface of wood." The blade is perpendicular to the handle and the blade edge is curled upwards at both ends. Using it requires concentration, as the swing takes the blade through your legs slightly below ankle level. It is a perfect exercise on cold winter days when the temperature is close to zero. I used some as beams and some as posts.

When pouring the foundations, I had inserted iron rebars inside the forms with about 3 inches protruding. They would batten down the 2-inch oak planks that would rest on the concrete. I wanted them to be deep and wide, so I went to a local lumber yard that collected trees from the area and would raw cut them into a full 8 inches. I used the same yard for all my posts, plates, baffles and beams, except for those I would be adzing myself.

The wood was newly cut oak. The posts were a full 6 by 8 inches, beams and plates were 4 by 8 inches and baffles were 2 by 8 inches. I notched the posts, plates and beams and secured them with 5/8-inch bolts. It became tricky when I was securing the second floor posts to the plate. It was heavy duty, and my son, Frank, helped when he was around.

I liked working alone, but there were times it made the job more difficult than need be, like placing the plate on top of the two posts so that the bolt holes lined up with one another. There was a lot of up and down the ladder, moving back and forth from one post to the other, and jiggling a heavy 4-by-8-inch, 10-foot-long plate while balancing oneself on a ladder. Still, it was out of doors, no one was around. I could work at my pace and stop when I wanted to. I loved it.

I had already learned through minor cuts and blue fingernails that you best stay focused when building stone walls or using a chain saw. The same was true here. Stay focused. That didn't mean, subconsciously, you didn't think about other things—like, in my case, market structure. Some good ideas popped up in the middle of a task where I really had to concentrate.

The kitchen and dining area were on the ground floor with the entire second level one big living room. Pella windows, floor to ceiling, covered the entire west side, with fireplaces on the east. The chimney was massive: 6 by 10 by 26 feet tall. The fireplaces were 4 1/2 by 3 by 3 feet deep, with a small fireplace nestled on the rear side. Each fireplace had its own vent. The stones of Roxbury granite came from the same abandoned railroad bed running along the edge of Pond Brook.

The footing for the chimney was 8 by 12 by 1 foot. I used galvanized iron fenceposts left on the property for reinforcement of the footing and throughout the entire chimney. If it had been designed as one, it would have made a great atomic bomb shelter.

The fireplace and the adzing began in earnest on the weekends as winter approached. Vera would pick me up at the Bethel or Danbury railroad station; an hour later, I would have changed to Levis, a Pendleton shirt and boots and be hurrying up to the site to plan the next two days.

Tina and Johnny were in school in Newtown; Scotty was now with Pearl. Frank was at Hotchkiss School in Lakeville and came down when he could. Elizabeth often came up with me on the train. She was back at the Lycée. We shared this final year in our apartment with a classmate of hers, a Czechoslovakian girl named Leah.

Elizabeth still insisted that she wanted to marry Neil Leibowitz, the man she had met at Paxtons, as soon as she turned 18.

Neil was 10 years older, designed handbags and was the spitting image of Omar Sharif. While I judged him favorably, I arranged for her to spend the summer at Sun Valley Lodge, where she would have a job and could practice her jumps and twirls on the outdoor skating rink. I thought the exposure to a Western atmosphere and a group of young people closer to her age might change her mind. She returned still resolute in planning to marry Neil.

As I pursued my idea to build my own house, Vera had come up with one of her own adventures. She had heard that the American Bicentennial, the 200th anniversary celebration of Independence Day, would include an assembly of Conestoga wagons emanating from every state in the Union and converging at Valley Forge by the Fourth of July. One of the caravans would start in Maine and be joined by wagons representing New Hampshire, Vermont, Connecticut, New York and New Jersey. Its route would take it through the middle of Newtown.

Vera planned to join it with her own junior-size, homemade replica of those enormous wagons that helped settle most of our country. Tina, Johnny and Peachy, our poodle, went along as well. It was a memorable two weeks, even for Peachy. I admired Vera for taking on the uncertainty and challenge involved, not to mention the very American nature of the venture. The children took to the idea wholeheartedly; Tina was 14 and Johnny 10.

Earlier, as 1975 came to a close, I was spending two days a month on the National Market Advisory Board. I was also wrestling with the NYSE members on the Consolidated Tape Committee and writing letters to the SEC on esoteric matters such as "net" vs. "gross" reporting on the consolidated tape. More important was the SEC's continuing acceptance of NYSE's Rule 394. Our frustration with the SEC is seen in my letter to the SEC dated August 14, 1975:

As Luck Would Have It

"... it is hard to believe that more than ten years are needed for the New York Stock Exchange to learn to live without Rule 394."

It was another 20 years before Rule 394 finally faded away. But worse than that is the fact that the CLOB, the main point of discussion of the National Market Advisory Board, still eludes SEC support as of this writing (2017).

These years had been "heady" ones for me, in more ways than one. My outside activities had gone well beyond Wall Street. My run for Congress led to the City Club, which led to the Manhattan Auto Study, which led to meeting interesting people and opportunities to voice my ideas in public. There was a dinner with Senator Ted Kennedy at his home in McLean, Va. A few experts on transportation matters had been gathered to express their views to the senator. As the only non-expert, I felt way over my head but still willing to voice my opinions.

This led to my appearance before the U.S. Senate's Subcommittee on Antitrust and Monopoly, where I commented on a proposed "Industrial Reorganization Act." As a trader on Wall Street, I saw no harm to shareholders in General Motors spinning off their bus and locomotive divisions. I also thought separating GM's auto business from its mass transportation business would encourage capital investments and government assistance at a time when reducing our reliance on foreign oil was of national concern. I even recommended breaking up GM's various auto divisions to increase competition, similar to the breakup of Standard Oil Corporation where, as a windfall, the stockholders made out like bandits.

Later, I testified before the newly created Federal Energy Administration. I criticized their "Project Independence," a $3-per-barrel tariff on oil as a public relations gimmick that would go nowhere in today's world of interdependence. Rather, they should focus on ways to conserve energy. "Rename your agency the Federal Energy Conservation Administration," I suggested. I then took the opportunity to make a plug for the work done in the Manhattan Auto Study, whereby thoughtful planning of auto, taxi and truck movement could reduce the use of gasoline and diesel while improving their efficiency.

In 1974–75, the country was in the midst of a sharp decline in the economy, high inflation and mass unemployment, all triggered by a sharp rise in the price of oil. In testimony before the U.S. Senate Committee on Commerce, I called for a graduated tax on gasoline at $.05 a gallon per year for 10 years; use the revenue to provide a rebate of $500 to all U.S. resident purchases of cars that get 20 miles or more per gallon and cost no more than $3,000; and encourage the scrapping of old unsafe gas-guzzlers by adding a sizable bounty from the gasoline tax to the normal $50 charged by the scrap industry. I recommended progressively higher excise taxes based on vehicle weight and horsepower.

In March 1975, I was again on the soapbox before the U.S. House of Representatives, Subcommittee on Energy and Power, calling for a four-point program of graduated gasoline taxes, small-car rebates, bounties for scrapping cars, and weight and horsepower taxes. Representatives of the American automobile industry vehemently opposed any requirement for raising fuel consumption per mile or building smaller, more efficient vehicles.

My ideas made sense then, and still do. I enjoyed being on a soapbox even though few were listening. All that came of it was a distraction from the day-to-day business of Weeden.

Weeden Holding Corporation reported record profits for the year ending September 30, 1976. It was the first annual report in which John Krause was listed as President and CEO. Our revenue and profit increases "took place in bond market activities." We had begun to trade government bonds and had received "recognized dealer" status by the Federal Reserve.

Our bond department also began sponsoring and marketing bond trusts. This involved acquiring a portfolio of suitable bonds, selling them into a newly created trust and making it available to brokerage firms to place with their customers. This is a very profitable business when interest rates are stable or falling as you earn a markup when selling into the trust as well as a commission when selling out of the trust to the broker. When interest rates began to rise late in the following year, this activity became an albatross.

Brother Jack had recovered from his hepatitis and was building out our new subsidiary, Dexter Securities. Its business would be servicing the non-member broker dealers and involved opening several small offices. It was also responsible for marketing our automatic execution system, WHAM. With a full year of negotiated rates behind us, we found that our Third Market business was down, but not as much as we had feared.

I was feeling very good about the state of the company. My role as chairman allowed me the luxury of leaving the day-to-day operations to others. When the NMAB concluded its work in September, I found myself having little to do; there was no longer the need to lobby, cajole, lecture or fight anyone on market structure.

I began spending more and more time at Duck Hollow building my house. I would alternate between adzing, framing and building the chimney. It was the kind of work I liked to do. I couldn't wait to get up to the site.

My weekends stretched out to three and four days. Slowly I began to master each of the jobs, honing my use of time and methods as I went along. As winter approached, I bundled up more warmly, ignoring the early snow showers and sharp winds. For the most part, I worked alone. Occasionally, Frank was at home and would help.

Vera seemed content doing her thing. She now had a working kiln, which was used by her and those in her pottery group. She continued her sculpturing and began to carve and paint duck decoys. Tina was attending Wooster School. Johnny had his friends in the neighborhood.

Winter turned into spring. The house began to take shape. Framing the lower level was almost complete. The chimney was poking its head up slowly. The concrete was no longer freezing between the stones. The granite tailings along Pond Brook were harder to find. My Rube Goldberg scaffolding was a crazy quilt of construction; adequate for hauling up 30-pound stones but scary enough that no one offered to spell me.

The oak posts, plates and baffles were now hardened from the winter exposure. All attempts to hammer a 20-penny nail into them produced bent nails and frustration. As spring turned to summer, I gained a full-time employee in Frank, who began his education in how NOT to build wood-framed houses. In a year or two he would use what he had learned to build a house of his own in Vermont.

High summer, and the first floor framing was now complete. The chimney had grown noticeably taller. It was time to place my adzed beams as the main support for the second floor. The work became more complicated and, I have to admit, more dangerous. A lot of effort was being done on ladders 8 feet off the ground.

The first beam to be cradled into place was my signature 32-foot ash, notched with 5/8-inch bolt holes that would secure it to the plates and posts 30 feet apart. Frank and I, using a rented Bobcat, lifted one end of the beam and settled it on top of the nearest plate. Frank's job was to slowly push the other end of the beam forward toward the opposite plate.

At some point in its travel, its weight would shift to the forward end and the beam would tip down. To prevent it from dropping too far, I had jerry-rigged two posts to catch it when it reached the horizontal. This allowed Frank to gently push it into place.

The operation was delicate and intense, with a lot of shouting and directing on my part. But we got it done. Anyone with a 16-year-old son would understand that I was very pleased with the way Frank handled the Bobcat and, even more, the way he handled the shouting of his excitable father. His confidence on the Bobcat was such that one evening, I came home late to find him using the backhoe by floodlight to finish digging out the 10-foot hole for our septic tank, the Bobcat leaning precariously on the edge of the hole.

The two of us became old hands at this business and quickly framed up the second floor with store-bought lumber. Then we tackled framing the roof. This was also tricky, because the roof was lopsided, causing the plates upon which the rafters would sit to be at different heights. An even more difficult problem to solve: how were we going to lift and place the crown plate, a 2-by-10 that was 34 feet long, which would rest 16 feet above the second floor?

Frank and I did it with help from my nephew, Bill, but I can't for the life of me remember how. I keep going through all the possible ways we might have held it up there while we attached rafters, but I can't remember which it was. What does remain vivid is the three of us standing at different spots around the top of the second-floor framing, balancing ourselves while lifting rafters into place.

Vera watched from a distance while asking from time to time, "Will it ever get done?" I finally realized there was still too much for me to do myself. I located a local builder who was willing to take on the task of translating my ideas onto paper, costing it out and then doing the actual construction. I would be responsible for finishing my area and he would do the rest.

There were still jobs inside "my area" like electrical and plumbing where I needed a licensed professional; or in the case of drywall, it was best done by a team working together. I installed the floor-to-ceiling Pella windows and laid 1-inch oak planks of various widths on both floors. This required screws, screw holes, sanding and two coats of polyurethane. In the kitchen area I laid down a Marimekko print plus four coats of polyurethane.

The roofing became a family affair. I used 24-inch-long, half-inch-thick cedar shakes from British Columbia to cover 1,500 square feet, plus another 1,500 on the front end of the house. Six-inch boards of knotty pine were nailed onto the underside of the rafters and insulation inserted in between. Frank helped with the shakes while Tina coated the knotty pine (rough side) with polyurethane. She painted while standing on two 10-inch planks resting on two tie boards 10 feet above the second floor.

A stupid incident occurred when a 25-foot pine tree fell the wrong way onto one of my newly installed windows. The wind had tipped the tree back onto my chain saw, snapping the tiny remains of my cut. I could only watch as its branches hit the window, bending at contact. Luckily, there was nary a scratch.

The family took occupancy in 1977. I asked the building inspector to come and make it legal. He insisted I put a post in the middle of my 32-foot ash beam if I wanted his approval. He said he was surprised it had gotten this far, which I took as a compliment. I wondered what he told the men at his favorite bar.

Early in 1977, dark clouds began to form on the horizon for Weeden Holding. Citing a 20% decline in the stock market, we reported a loss of $2,230,000 for the fiscal year ending September 31, 1977. John Krause's focus on the bond market was partly to blame, but I must share responsibility. When "May Day" 1975 arrived and minimum commissions were eliminated, the profitability of our Third Market trading suffered but hardly collapsed. Still, we should have changed our model and reduced our overnight inventory until we figured out how to operate post May Day.

A memo from Fred Siesel showing that we were equally profitable when carrying smaller positions was ignored. John Krause was new to running our Third Market. If a major change was required, I was the one to initiate it. Unfortunately, I was one who was calling for "full steam ahead."

Jack was busy rolling out Dexter Securities and WHAM. Alan, recently returned from his sabbatical, had not yet re-involved himself with the day-to-day activities of the firm. His office was still at 25 Broad Street in New York City, while Weeden's entire trading activity had moved to Jersey City. At 84 years old now, Frank was spending his time with the Alameda Swim Association. Reese Harris, retired officer of The Manufacturers Hanover Bank, and John Krause were the only other members on the Weeden Holding board.

Expansion had continued in our bond dealing. Excluding short-term governments, our ratio of bond plus stock inventory to capital was eight to one at the end of September. This was a 50% increase from the year before, all of which occurred in corporate and municipal bonds. This exposure placed us close to the regulatory limits imposed by the NASD and put us at considerable risk if something untoward happened. Of course, something untoward happened.

Other factors contributed to the unfolding crisis. In October, we acquired two high-quality research firms, William Reeves and Wainwright Securities, increasing personnel by 20%. We then lost control of accounts payable after switching to a new computer system. This made it difficult to know our costs and our daily capital requirements.

As this was unfolding, John Krause and I began a two-week trip to Japan to visit our newest shareholder, Nomura Securities. They were the largest Japanese brokerage firm and became a 3% owner of Weeden through their ownership in Wainwright Securities. Seeing the possibility of doing business together, John and I wanted to meet their management team.

With our problems escalating, John cut short his visit and returned to New York. When I arrived back a week later, I was greeted with an additional problem: John had been falsifying his expense reports. The amounts were significant enough that John tendered his resignation just before Christmas. The last week of 1977 found Weeden without a CEO, uncertain whether it was in compliance with the minimum capital rule and with a large bond inventory facing a rise in interest rates.

The board's first priority was electing a new CEO. The board consisted of five members: four Weedens and Reese Harris. The urgency caused by our uncertain capital position precluded the normal search outside the firm. There was agreement on the board that only a Weeden would be considered.

The discussions had a flavor of Abbott and Costello's "Who's on first?" routine. Alan suggested that the three brothers re-create the troika, with Alan as CEO and all three having an equal vote. I argued that the critical nature of our problem required a single decision-maker who was willing to make decisions quickly and decisively. In my mind, I was the only one able in the family. Frank, troubled by the impasse between Alan and me, offered to come back temporarily. When that idea was shot down immediately, Frank suggested that Jack become CEO, which was the last thing Jack wanted.

It was the last day of the year. We were again gathered without having reached a decision. Finally, Reese turned to Alan and asked whether he thought the firm could survive under the conditions that prevailed. Alan didn't think so. I said that we could but it wouldn't be easy. The vote was Frank and Alan voting for the troika. Reese joined Jack and me to make me CEO.

We entered 1978 a divided family, not knowing the firm's capital position and the outlook for higher interest rates.

I went back to my apartment on 60th Street, phoned Vera and swore off smoking and drinking until the crisis was over. I had never been a CEO, but I was eager to try and confident, as usual, in my ability to do the job.

On January 2, 1978, we still were unable to determine our capital position. On September 30, 1977, overnight loans were in the vicinity of $270 million with capital of $30 million. Inventories were down somewhat in the interim, but our losses could well have put us out of compliance. Our year-end capital position was due to the NASD on the 10th of January. The NASD reluctantly agreed to give us until Monday the 20th to make our report. This began a 24/7 effort to figure out just where we were. Sunday evening, the board was told that, most likely, we would be reporting negative capital at year end. I went back to my apartment thinking we would be forced to close our doors the following morning.

The irony was that our efforts to reduce inventory had paid off handsomely, particularly our positions in stocks, most of which had instant liquidity. Unfortunately, the NASD could not be expected to take that into consideration.

When the phalanx of NASD regulators marched into our conference room in coats and ties, they were greeted by our operational people sporting T-shirts with the words "WELCOME NASDIES." After their refusal to see the humor, Jim Avena, in charge of New York operations, pushed across the table a foot-high set of documents sufficiently confusing to delay any decision until our inventory reduction was further along.

While inventory reduction continued, Jack was engaged in high-level entreaties at the NASD explaining that, despite significant losses, we had more than corrected the anticipated negative capital numbers and were fully in capital compliance.

Another critical problem arose in late January, when the research/institutional sales group at Wainwright Securities announced their concern about our ongoing viability. They demanded salary and employment guarantees. I explained the situation to Jack and Frank during dinner across from my apartment. It was an uncomfortable dinner, with Frank troubled by the direction things were taking while aloof as far as offering any solutions.

It was clear to me that I was on my own. It was also clear that Frank had no intention of providing any of his windfall from the purchase of Quotron to shore up our diminishing capital base. I hardly blamed him, but have never forgotten it.

Jack and I went back to my apartment and talked about possible solutions. We agreed that we couldn't give them the guarantee they were demanding. We also knew that Pete Morley, their president, was looking for an answer before a 7:30 a.m. meeting with his group. We decided I would meet with Pete and Bob Myers find out how long they thought it would take them to become profitable; then it was up to me to make a decision— one that could be letting all 125 people go immediately. We called Mike Jeffers, our lawyer, and were told I could take that step if necessary. It was now after midnight.

The meeting was friendly but right to the point. Pete made it clear that it would take nine months at best to reach profitability, as the nature of their business had changed. Their preeminent position in providing institutions with 50- to 100-page research papers was no longer in vogue. We estimated they would lose $1 million to $2 million in the meantime. I said our capital situation could not support that kind of loss. I asked Pete if there was any chance of someone else buying them. His answer was no, because of the changes mentioned. This made my decision easy. I told him I would join him when he told his team they were no longer employed by Weeden.

As Peter spoke to the group, one of the salesmen left the room to accept an offer from Merrill Lynch.

On January 31, Leonard Sloane reported in the *New York Times*:

"Weeden & Co. reports that it will probably abandon its traditional role as a 'third market' dealer to concentrate on other aspects of securities brokerage and trading. Its parent company, Weeden Holding Corp., reported a loss of $6.1 million in the first quarter ended December 31, '77. Weeden Holding president Donald Weeden concedes that negotiated broker's commissions were a major factor in the decision."

As it turned out, our ability to reduce our stock inventory along with a rebounding stock market postponed that decision. Our problem was our large, sticky inventory in bonds while interest rates continued to rise.

The next six months of my life were cogently summarized in an article that appeared in the August 28th edition of *Newsweek*:

"Just two years ago, Weeden earned $7 million. Since then, it has lost $19.5 million. To make ends meet, it has chopped its staff from 790 to 170, closed eleven of its thirteen offices, ended its once lucrative government bond business, sold a stock clearing subsidiary and liquidated Wainwright Securities, an elite research house that Weeden acquired only last year. A tentative merger with a smaller third market house, Jefferies Co. of Los Angeles, offered some hope for Weeden, but last week the deal fell through."

The turndown by Jefferies was the last of several efforts to find a merger partner, which included the largest specialist firm on the NYSE, Spear, Leeds & Kellogg. Everyone I talked to was courteous, even complimentary, with Spear, Leeds and Jefferies seriously tempted. But both found us too big to swallow, even with my aggressive downsizing. Throughout this period, I was constantly in touch with my brothers, father and key personnel on what should be done. But I was where the buck stopped, and I ended up making the key decisions.

It was not fun, having to unwind a firm which had been in business for

As Luck Would Have It

over 55 years. Some of my very good friends in stock trading resented being let go; the London office in particular couldn't understand the need to close. An exception was our municipal dollar bond department, which was still making good money because they could short bonds easily. But when Bear Stearns showed interest, there was nothing I could offer to keep them from leaving as a group. I found myself at the end of the day mentally pooped and ready for bed. I would go to sleep immediately but wake up two hours later with my head full of ideas and concerns about what to do next. I got a lot of good reading done.

The media had plenty to say about me during this time, as summarized in the same article from *Newsweek*:

"Weeden's old foes put most of the blame for the firm's troubles on Donald Weeden, 48, one of three brothers who run Weeden. 'Don's an idealistic and nice guy,' says the head of one big brokerage house, 'who clearly didn't know how to run a business.'"

I continued trimming personnel and inventory after Jefferies turned us down, but the losses continued and were draining capital. This made it harder and harder to continue on our own. I found a buyer, Control Data Corp., for our Automated Trading System (WHAM), which netted us $500,000, and Frank put up $150,000 to buy our real-time inventory control system. Two of his grandchildren (sons of my brother Bill) had helped design the system and were willing to operate it as a stand-alone company. Those infusions helped, but I still needed a white knight to bail us out.

In August, I was making a speech at an industry conference in Palm Springs (109 degrees on the tennis court) on the value of a CLOB. While there I met with partners from Wedbush, Noble, Cooke, a brokerage firm in Los Angeles that did a lot of clearing for others. They showed some interest, but it went nowhere.

Back in New York, I received a telephone call from Jon Bulkley, president of Moseley, Hallgarten & Estabrook, a Boston-based member of the NYSE. He said they were interested in us as a publicly traded corporation with a significant tax loss carry-forward. They saw value in our major status in municipal bond underwritings but had no interest in our Third Market activity. We began serious negotiations in September and arrived at an understanding, though not firm, based on our respective capital at closing. At the time, the ratio was 63/37 in favor of Moseley.

In early November, our municipal bond department made a bad inventory decision that cut into our capital and raised concerns with some members of the Moseley board about whether a trading firm like Weeden was right for them. Jon called me after their board meeting and asked if we could meet early the next day. I suggested breakfast at the Racquet and Tennis Club at 7:30 a.m. I was convinced it would be a meeting similar to mine with Pete Morley, only in reverse.

I knew that Jon wanted this deal, but Fred Moseley, their chairman, was against it. I spent most of the night figuring out what to say in reply to Jon's telling me the deal was off. When we met and had settled at a window table looking east over Park Avenue to the Seagram's building, I opened the discussion by suggesting that we not wait until the close (January or February) for determining the split, but agree on one now and eliminate uncertainty. I then proposed a 76/24 split, being to their advantage of almost 10%. Jon thought for a moment and said, "That's not what I came here to tell you, Don, but I think it is attractive enough that I can sell it to my board. As far as I'm concerned, we have a deal."

We finished our breakfast, and I went to the office to explain the proposal to Jack and Alan and then the others on the board. Jon called me the next morning and said his board had approved the deal. That evening I enjoyed my first cigarette and scotch in nine months.

On February 19, 1979, Moseley Holding and Operating Companies were merged into Weeden Holding and Operating Companies, respectively, with Weeden's name being added to theirs. A 70% ownership of Instinet was distributed the day before to shareholders of Weeden at the rate of 2.2 shares for every share of Weeden. Alan, Jack and I became members of the Moseley board.

The Third Market.
The 8 billion dollar stock market competition built.

Volume Figures—Year 1970 (Source: SEC)	Dollar Value of Share Volume	Share Volume
New York Stock Exchange	$103,063,237,117	3,213,069,300
American Stock Exchange	14,266,040,598	878,535,705
Third Market (Including Weeden & Co.)	**8,020,839,000**	**210,067,000**
Pacific Coast Stock Exchange	4,985,958,460	164,975,312
Midwest Stock Exchange	4,827,578,648	145,506,407
Weeden & Co. (Third Market Volume Only)	**2,888,724,066**	**70,341,946**
Phila.—Balt.—Wash. Stock Exchange	2,628,687,150	76,931,512
Boston Stock Exchange	892,415,194	24,592,423
Detroit Stock Exchange	145,052,473	4,984,805
Cincinnati Stock Exchange	45,679,006	1,000,086
National Stock Exchange	43,215,441	11,925,891
Salt Lake Stock Exchange	6,255,090	5,800,192
Spokane Stock Exchange	4,606,316	8,336,598

Maybe some institutions and brokers
know something you don't know.

Weeden & Co.
specialists in competition

Ad in *New York Times,* 1970.

When the *blue* chips were down.

The fourth quarter of 1973 was one of the most unsettled in stock market history. First the Dow Jones Industrial Average went up 50 points...then it plummeted 214 points...then rose again 67 points. During this difficult period, Weeden & Co., as market maker, bought and sold more than 50 million shares* of those 262 stocks that are traded both by Weeden and on the New York Stock Exchange. Here are the details:

Volume Leaders

Stock	WEEDEN Volume	N.Y.S.E. Volume	Weeden Volume Compared to NYSE Volume %
Texaco, Inc.	1,419,000	6,869,600	20.7
Exxon	1,184,600	4,941,400	24.0
Kresge, S.S.	1,128,300	4,697,500	24.0
General Motors	1,074,000	9,053,600	11.9
Federal National Mortgage	977,900	5,440,100	18.0
Mobil Oil	974,400	3,292,000	29.6
Alcan Aluminum Ltd.	908,400	3,540,300	25.7
Ford Motor	902,300	5,291,200	17.0
International Paper	844,500	3,563,700	23.7
First National City Corp.	835,400	5,526,700	15.1
Sears Roebuck Co.	826,700	2,498,500	33.1
Continental Oil	779,200	4,410,000	17.7
Gulf Oil	733,200	8,295,600	8.8

The firm of Weeden & Co. ranks among the leaders because of our ability to offer best net price. We invite institutions to check our market directly or through their brokers prior to executing an order.

Weeden & Co.
specialists in competition

Full-page ad in *New York Times*, 1972.

Full-page ad in *New York Times,* 1973.

Don speaking at Securities Industry Association conference
with presidents of Midwest, American and New York Stock Exchanges
Michael Tobin, Ralph Saul, James Needham.

Recognition of Weeden family contribution to expanded
Men's Swimming Pool Complex, February 1974 (left to right):
Don's brother Bill, mother, father, brother Jack,
Stanford official, Bill's wife Patty.

Institutional Investor cover article.

Chapter 15

MHEW, 1979–1986

I remember the time my flight instructor put the aircraft into a spin and said "You have control, Weeden." In 1978, my job was to stop our spiraling losses before we crashed and burned. Despite my efforts, our capital had spiraled down from $24 million to $4 million and we were still losing money. The deal with Jon Bulkley leveled our wings and allowed Weeden to make a safe landing.

Moseley got what they wanted and a little bit more. Of our two remaining businesses, the municipal bond department would be integrated into Moseley's retail activity, with Alan as co-head; and our Third Market trading would remain as a stand-alone department.

The merger was not perfect. A number of Moseley's key salesmen covered the same accounts as Weeden. Board members were concerned about our risking their capital. We viewed Jon's intentions to keep our Third Market as temporary. His lawyers advised that Moseley would lose the $28 million tax loss carry-forward if they dropped our Third Market business too early.

Not surprisingly, our Third Market activity began returning a profit and remained profitable whether the market went up or down. Our institutional customers continued doing business with us; they were indifferent to the change. We were enjoying our independence. Soon the Moseley board members began to appreciate our presence. I had time on my hands. The equity team knew their jobs well. They didn't need my daily oversight, except when a problem arose with the MHEW management. While I was taking it easy, Jack and Alan were embarking on their own voyages that would accomplish equal, if not greater, returns.

Jack began using his expertise to solve problems arising between Instinet and their clearing agent, Securities Settlement, also a subsidiary of MHEW. Eventually, he left Moseley and went to work for Instinet full-time. There he performed a critical role (one similar to mine) in keeping Instinet afloat until help arrived.

Alan was never happy with his role at Moseley. There was little for him to do in a department focused on selling 10- and 15-bond lots to retail accounts. Alan left to work full-time for the Weeden Foundation when its assets had grown to over $20 million. This occurred from a contribution by Frank and Mabel when Quotron was sold to Citibank. It was something Alan had a long-standing interest in and the passion to do it well. For the next 30 years, under his direction (and later that of his oldest son), the Foundation gave away upwards of $50 million to environmental- and population-related projects. Alan and Barbara had amassed sufficient assets to enable him to spend all his time on the Foundation without pay.

After Jack's move to Instinet, Bill Lupien joined the firm as CEO. He was a specialist on the Pacific Stock Exchange who also understood the way OTC traders made their markets. He initiated a change in Instinet's model that incentivized them to show bids and offerings over Instinet anonymously that were inside the publicly displayed quote. The institutions using Instinet would execute against them anonymously. Slowly, the volume of trades expanded to the point where Instinet was viewed as a viable electronic exchange. In 1986, I was still on the board when we sold Instinet to Reuters for $120 million. The sale netted Weeden shareholders, who still had their Instinet shares, a very handsome capital gain. In 2007, Instinet was sold to Nomura Securities for $1.2 billion.

In a funny way, I was the brother who ended up at loose ends. Our trading continued to operate with little oversight from me. I was still in charge and the one who carried the name. Lou Barail looked after our daily needs and interacted with MHEW operations. My primary role was as a member of the MHEW board and occasional visits to clients.

I found myself mulling over what had happened at Weeden—how we got into the pickle we did and what could have been done to prevent it. What first comes to mind is the fact that we were still being run as a family firm. Except for a retired banker, Reese Harris, and John Krause, the board of directors consisted entirely of Weedens. This proved shortsighted and, most probably, exposed us to litigation from disgruntled shareholders who saw their stock plummet from more than $50 to a mere $2 per share after our merger. True, they had received 2.2 shares of Instinet for every share of Weeden, which eventually rose to $25 per share, but that happened only five years later and many shareholders had sold their Instinet long before.

"If they had put me in charge earlier, it would not have happened." This thought went through my head, but not seriously. At the time I felt I was doing something more important and made no effort to challenge the decision to groom Krause for the job. On the other hand, during the discussions on who should take over, I argued that Weeden's core business would have my full attention.

I wanted the challenge, confident in my abilities when faced with a crisis. I argued that I had taken on the job of turning around an unprofitable dollar bond desk; I had established a new office in London; I even promoted myself head of our stock trading desk without asking permission. There was Alan's remark to Vera that also motivated me: "Your husband has little chance of getting a job anywhere on Wall Street." Vera took the remark seriously. During the summer of 1978, she planted a vegetable garden in anticipation of my becoming unemployable.

"Six years in the penalty box" is the way I describe our time at MHEW. Our division did well right from the get-go. But management never got over their concern that our Third Market risk-taking would eventually get them into trouble. Part of my job was educating the board members about our business and making them comfortable with us. Several times Jon Bulkley alluded to the "too good a deal" we had negotiated with him at the outset; he even proposed that we accept a lower percentage of the profits. I explained that it was a poor way to recognize our success and that it would not be acceptable. If anything, our group should be included with those receiving options. Nothing happened either way.

When Lou Barail tragically lost his life in an automobile accident, I felt Jon Bulkley might replace me with Fred Moss, who had responsibility over all trading activities except ours. I was viewed as the spiritual leader only, no longer necessary. For the next couple of weeks, it was touch and go, but management concluded that my presence was more important than they realized.

Our department went on as before, but several of us were now thinking we would be better off on our own. I had some informal discussions with C.J. Devine & Co., a government bond house and a large OTC trading firm, both independent and wanting to expand. Each showed interest, but how to structure it to everyone's satisfaction was difficult.

It was about this time that Chuck Kelly came up with an idea that eventually provided the capital for us to leave Moseley. Chuck's law office was across the street from the Racquet and Tennis Club, and we often played squash together. This would be followed by cocktails at the bar, where I would tell him about our success at MHEW as well as our unhappiness under their management. Chuck looked at our record and wrote up an eight-page proposal for leaving Moseley and going on our own. He thought $10 million in capital should be enough to get established, and he began showing the proposal to some of his friends in Minneapolis.

The effort went along rather smoothly, considering our history, size and risks. I was introduced to several of the scions of Minnesota business: John Driscoll, part of the Cargill family that owned the giant commodities firm; Ted Weyerhaeuser, from the family who founded the timber company of the same name; Ben Jaffray, CFO of Cargill and with family connections to Piper, Jaffray and Co., the largest local brokerage firm in Minneapolis;

and Joe Bennett, whose grandfather discovered iron ore under the Mesabi Range in northern Minnesota. Chuck was close to all of them through his family connections. They met with others on our team and were willing to commit to $5 million. The rest was easy. Morgan Guaranty Trust loaned our principals a total of $3 million based solely on their past experience with Weeden & Co. and a promise to pay it back in five years.

Only four others in our group were privy to my thinking. I was concerned that Moseley would challenge our leaving. I assumed the other 20 in our group would ask to be included once we announced our intentions. In fact, that possibility was held over our heads while a friendly exit was negotiated. Moseley agreed to our use of the name Weeden & Co. and allowed us to remain until the end of the year. We offered them 10% of the company at closing on the same basis as other investors or a five-year option at a price that would increase over book value by 10% each year. They declined to invest initially while accepting the five-year option.

On December 31, 1985, we ended our relationship with Moseley. On January 2, 1986, we began doing business under the name Weeden & Co., Inc., located on the 19th floor of 180 Maiden Lane.

There were two revealing experiences for me as we organized the physical and management transition. The first involved location. I thought I had understood from Bob, Barry, Steve and Tim that they wanted to keep the costs as low as possible. I knew of a building on Sixth Avenue and 23rd Street where a firm was desperate to sublease. The five of us went to look at it: low ceilings, full of small cubicles, lacking a large open space, in a neighborhood that was totally non-financial. But the price was right.

Very little was said as they looked the place over. As we left, we stopped at the coffee shop across the street to talk it over. As we sat down, we noticed at the next booth a street bum slumped over, asleep. Bob Weppler took one look and exclaimed, "Let's get out of here!" We settled on a brand-new building, class A facilities overlooking the South Street Seaport, with a top-of-the-line rental.

The other involved the composition of the board. Chuck was in favor of the major outside investors holding a majority of seats. I broached the idea to the team. Their reaction was quite strong; they wanted control. All four wanted to be on the board. The result was a board of nine; Chuck plus three investors from Minneapolis, and me plus four. I would be the intermediary between employee/investors and the outsiders.

While the name Weeden and its long-standing reputation were important in obtaining outside funding, our performance during the Moseley years and the fact that all the key producers were putting up capital was even more critical. We were no longer thought of as a family firm. I would represent continuity to the Weeden culture and Street recognition while continuing the limited role I played while at Moseley.

I was again dividing my time between New York City and Newtown. Tina and Johnny were attending Wooster School in Danbury, Frank was going to Wesleyan College in Middletown, and Elizabeth and Neil were living in Queens close to the Throgs Neck Bridge.

Tina had begun piano lessons at home from Howard Tuvelle, a concert pianist on the faculty of the Western Connecticut State College in Danbury. Howard was a robust fellow, instantly likable, rather rotund and prone to smoking large cigars. On one of his weekly visits, Howard asked whether we had gone to the concert celebrating Charles Ives' 100th birthday. Neither Vera nor I recognized the name. The next week, Howard brought us a copy of Henry Cowell's biography of Charles Ives, written the year before Ives' death in 1954.

Thus began my relationship with Danbury's most famous son and my 15 years with the Charles Ives Center for the Performing Arts in Danbury. My involvement became something of a love affair as I read additional biographies and found Ives to be the kind of man I most admired: entrepreneurial, creative and independent, and a man with extraordinary talent both as a composer and businessman, a combination which set him apart as one of the few modern-day American Renaissance men.

Howard encouraged me to join the group that, in 1974, had organized a successful concert of Ives's work, attracting 8,000 to the Danbury State Fairgrounds, with Leonard Bernstein and Michael Tilson Thomas conducting the American Symphony Orchestra. With $25,000 remaining after expenses, they wanted to create a permanent site to honor Ives and his music.

Through the efforts of June Goodman, chairman of the state's Council on the Arts, legislation was passed setting aside 40 acres of recently acquired land adjacent to Western Connecticut State College's Westside campus for use by the newly formed Charles Ives Center for the Performing Arts.

At my first meeting, I found considerable differences among the board members on how best to honor Ives. One group was only interested in playing his music, another wanted to emphasize his support of American composers, while the largest group saw the Ives Center as providing a diversity of music presented in an informal somewhat bucolic setting congenial to the lifestyle and music of Ives. The result was three independent efforts to raise the $12 million estimated to build an indoor/outdoor stage with facilities for teaching, practicing and accommodating performers.

It turned out that, whatever the purpose, the local corporations had little interest in giving. Neither did any of the Danbury families whose fortunes had been made from the now-defunct hat industry. "For music, you go to New York City. Danbury has its State Fair."

Several board members resigned and the idea seemed doomed.

Meanwhile, my fascination for the man continued to increase. I came to see Charles Ives as the quintessential American whose music reflected his heritage and upbringing: born in a blue-collar town encased in rural New England.

Charles Edward was a ninth-generation Ives whose ancestors came to Connecticut shortly after the Pilgrims landed. His grandfather founded the Savings Bank of Danbury. His father, George, formed a marching band during the Civil War, one recognized by Lincoln and Grant as the best in the Army. It was from his father that this eager son, gifted with perfect pitch, learned to play numerous instruments beginning at the age of four. George taught him composition and a unique understanding of how sounds travel, change and interrelate.

Charles wrote his first song, "Variations on 'America,'" at the age of 13, and he played the organ for the First Congregational Church at the age of 15. After his father's death, Charles went on to study composition at Yale University, where he also had time to play on the varsity football and baseball teams, write songs for his fraternity's musicals, and play the organ every Sunday at the Center Church in New Haven (where he would insert a few dissonant chords, occasionally, to wake up the congregation). In 1906, with his friend Julius Myrick, he founded what became, by 1920, the largest and most creative life insurance agency in America. He retired in 1929 a millionaire and gave freely throughout the Depression to out-of-work composers. In 1947, he was awarded the Pulitzer Prize for his Second Symphony.

I had never listened to the music of Ives. My upbringing was limited to the popular dance tunes and songs sung around a campfire. After reading his life story and listening more than once to his more popular compositions, I began to realize their unique quality.

I agreed with the critics; they were experimental, controversial, cutting-edge, dissonant, atonal and hard to listen to. But the music was more than that—it was about America: its history, its people, its land, its rural life, the urban centers of hard-working immigrants. It incorporated the songs sung at church gatherings, the quiet murmur of the river and the New England woods, the patriotism expressed in band music on national holidays, and the ragtime emanating from the Southern black sharecroppers.

At the same time, there was another Ives: a successful entrepreneur selling life insurance, a populist who designed the first estate plan for the common worker, and an anti-war progressive who expressed his ideas in writing along with his music. Much of his work was composed while commuting from Scarsdale and later after moving to Redding, near Danbury. There he lived a quiet and modest life with his wife of 35 years. He was that rare American whose talents are measured at the highest level in both worlds of art and business.

In 1980, I wrote a memo to the board questioning our ability to raise significant funds. I recommended we take a more modest approach: clear part of the 40 acres, build a temporary stage adjacent to the central pond and present a series of concerts to showcase the possibilities of the site. The $25,000 in the bank plus another $50,000 should cover the costs of a series of four concerts. I was willing to put up half the shortfall. The board agreed and asked me to put it together for the summer of 1981.

Volunteers came and cleared the land adjacent to the pond. My son Frank constructed a temporary stage suitable to carry the full weight of the Hartford Symphony Orchestra. Jim Sinclair's New England Orchestra played a concert of Ives' compositions, followed by an afternoon performance by the Hartford Ballet. The series went smoothly and attracted a healthy audience. It was spoiled only when a thundershower rained down during the intermission of the Hartford Symphony Orchestra (some wag called it "pure Ivesian"). I was in Levis and cowboy hat making a pitch for contributions at each of the performances. Among the notables gathered were the mayor of Danbury, Joe Sauer; and former Connecticut Lieutenant Governor Clark Hull and his entourage, which included a rather attractive young divorcée, Patricia Cawley Gulliver.

Financing was difficult and the site went dark for three years. Undeterred, we engaged an architect to design a stage that would rest on the pond. It would contain 1,500 square feet with four pillars holding the roof, allowing for a 40-foot opening to the audience. I invited Beatrice Brown, conductor for the Ridgefield Symphony Orchestra, and Skitch Henderson, who had recently formed the New York Festival Orchestra, to visit the site and comment on our plan. Both liked the idea of placing the stage on the pond—"very Ivesian"—but Skitch, thinking of bringing his orchestra to play here, said it was too small. "Ya gotta make it bigger." We ended up with the opening 54 feet wide and providing 2,200 square feet of stage, about the size of Carnegie Hall.

Back at Pond Brook, my grass court had turned into a disaster. I had spent a good bit of effort in clearing, leveling, planting and nursing its growth. The special grass seed from Oregon had taken well. I had completed two cuts before the winter closed in. Frank had completed a storage place for racquets and court equipment out of pressed concrete (it is all that remains). Early the next spring with the final melting of snow, I discovered the grass was brown and dead; the culprit was a field full of Japanese beetle larvae that had eaten the roots during the winter. I rolled up the dead grass court and put it out of my mind.

Funding for our stage was still lagging. The price of National Semi-conductor shares had meanwhile increased handsomely and the Center was now registered as a 501(c)(3) non-profit organization. I decided to use some of this continuing windfall to start construction of the stage. I had finished reading the fourth biography of Charles Ives and was into his personality and mannerisms. Some even said I was beginning to look like him.

Construction began during the winter of 1983, which turned out to be one of the longest and harshest in recent history. The placing of the piles and construction of the flooring in subzero weather was a challenge to Bernard J Dolan Construction Company in Bethel, which had taken on the task of completing it by the fall of 1984.

That was also the year that the Danbury State Fair closed after operating since 1821. Its popularity had drawn visitors from throughout the Tri-State area. I thought our Center for the Arts might replace it with a "Musical Fair America." We might even attract music lovers living in and around New York City, who regularly constituted 50% of the audience at Tanglewood. Danbury was halfway between New York City and Lenox, Massachusetts, with four convenient exits off Interstate 84 and 684.

In addition to performances on the main stage, we would set up mini stages around the site where smaller acts and individual performers could perform simultaneously in between the larger acts. On the paths flowing from one stage to another would be located vendors offering food and gifts, mimicking what one experiences when going to a state fair. We would keep the trees, shrubs and other natural growth plus add new plantings for color and diversity. I wanted to keep the feeling of a New England outdoor setting.

I became totally immersed in preparing the site. I thinned out the trees to improve sightlines, created pathways leading to each new stage, and resurrected the existing stone walls. I even created new walls from stones collected farther afield.

"Musical Fair America" was solely my idea. I had an enthusiastic board that went along, but, as with the stage construction, I ended up providing most of the funding and became responsible for our shortfall in ticket sales.

We picked the end of September, when the Danbury Fair was normally held. It was the time known as Indian summer, when the weather turned warmer before the onset of winter.

I enlisted Phil Schacter, from my campaign days, to manage the details. The two-day program was prodigious. The schedule went off without a hitch, but the attendance was embarrassingly small and ticket sales fell woefully short of break-even. The weather didn't cooperate. The whole weekend was colder than normal, with periodic showers.

There were good reviews in the local papers, congratulations from many and condolences from the few who knew what a financial disaster it was.

Despite this beginning, the Center has had a summer season every year and is now thought of as a permanent feature of Danbury. One year, Danbury was chosen "City of the Year," edging out others of equal attraction due to having an active Center for the Performing Arts. I resigned the chairmanship in 1992, while remaining on the board for a few more years.

In 2009, the city took responsibility for the site and created a Charles Ives Authority. A new board was appointed by the mayor in cooperation with the university. It has a full-time professional manager. Attendance over the course of the summer season often exceeded 50,000. Various ethnic groups use the site for weekend events, and the university puts on one or two concerts a year. I am delighted with these changes and briefly served on the Authority's board to give its new members an historical perspective.

In 1983, I drove to Saratoga on the weekend of Father's Day, ostensibly to check out their art festival. In fact, I went to visit Evelyn Muller, who had a summer place on Lake George. She was the same Evelyn Grey I had been engaged to in 1953. She had reentered my life two years earlier when I received a call from her asking whether I remembered her. Of course I did.

My immediate reaction was cautious interest as to why she called. I thought that fire had long gone out, but we soon found there were more than a few embers still smoldering. Evelyn was as vivacious and attractive as I had remembered. She was also divorced from her husband, who had become an alcoholic. Her two children were grown and out of the apartment on East 86th Street. It was easy to renew our romance.

We began seeing one another periodically and then regularly. We would have dinner at her apartment or go out to restaurants in the neighborhood. Our relationship returned to the passion and intensity remembered from 30 years ago. While marriage was never discussed, it was expected that Vera and I would eventually part, after the children were out of the house and independent, and that Evelyn and I would then marry.

On that weekend in June of 1983 in Lake George, Evelyn took me to dinner at the country club, where she had many friends.

On my return the next weekend to Pond Brook Road, I was confronted by Vera, who, having been asked by Tina, wanted to know where I had been on Father's Day. For reasons not fully understood by me to this day, I was quite forthright in my explanation. A discussion ensued, not without tears, the result of which was my promise to end the intimacy with Evelyn, although ceasing to see her entirely would take some time.

My explanation included telling Vera who it was. When I told this to Evelyn, she was infuriated and didn't want to see me again under any conditions. She felt exposed as being a husband stealer, a thought that hadn't entered her head until then. That meeting was the last time Evelyn and I saw each other. From having in my mind that we would eventually marry to suddenly not seeing her ever again was hard to accept initially. Slowly, I found that I was no longer missing her. I began to wonder whether the relationship was ever very deep. Was it merely renewing a youthful memory that never fully rekindled?

I don't know and never asked what effect my admission to an affair had on Vera—whether it was merely confirmation of what she suspected or a complete surprise. We spoke no more about it, and our relationship during my weekends at Pond Brook remained unchanged.

For the remainder of 1983 and into 1984, I was focused on getting the "Ives" site ready for Musical Fair America. There was a lot to do and many volunteers ready to spend late afternoons and weekends sprucing up the 40 acres in preparation for our grand opening in September. There was the offsite effort to raise money. June Goodman, Joan Ward and Ed Goldberg diligently combed their Rolodexes, political and business relationships, and friends to supplement my sales of National Semiconductor shares. Ed spoke before the local real estate board and Pat Gulliver, representing Davis and Hoyt, volunteered to follow up with personal appeals to her fellow Realtors.

That is how Pat and I met again. A phone call, thanking her for her help, was our initial contact. Then June Goodman brought her to the site where volunteers were clearing the seating area of brambles, poison ivy and small stones. Her beauty showed through the mascara running down her cheeks and the eyes seemed to show interest in the guy with the chain saw clearing trees. I hoped she would come back again, but several weeks passed and she never reappeared.

Phil Schacter and I were eating dinner at the local Chinese restaurant when Pat showed up to order some takeout food for herself and her daughter. I waved hello and returned to my conversation with Phil. I didn't even get up to renew my invitation. As I watched her leave, I suddenly jumped up, telling Phil I'd be right back. I ran out to where she had just closed her car door. I said, "You said you'd be back and never have. I would really like to see you again." She promised she would, and she did. This time she wandered onto the site in her tennis outfit, having just come from playing tennis. I wasted no time and blurted out an invitation to have lunch. She agreed. The Oasis restaurant was nearby. We had a couple of drinks, ate some food and began exchanging stories about ourselves.

It was the usual "get to know one another": family, work, leisure time activities. I learned that Pat Gulliver, née Cawley, was born and raised in Danbury. Most of her family went back four generations in the area. I learned that she had been divorced for six years, had three daughters all out of college, and lived in Brookfield with one dog and two horses on 11 acres of land.

Pat talked about her marriage and divorce, and I was matter-of-fact about my situation with Vera. We must have both concluded before lunch was over that a relationship had begun that might well develop further. We parted with an understanding that we would see each other again soon.

Pat's beauty became secondary as I learned more and more about her interests, her talents and her accomplishments. Her views on most issues were similar to my own. A profile emerged of a wonderful, thoughtful person, full of common sense, passion and compatibility, with whom I would be happy to spend the rest of my life.

"Musical Fair America" came and went. Pat and I were seeing each other when we could. These rendezvous were infrequent and carefully planned so as not to create attention at home or within the community.

In October, Tina and Jacque Roux were married quietly in Newtown. They would visit Vera on the weekends. I enjoyed Nick (Jacque) and wanted to get to know him better. I suggested we take the canoe out on the lake despite a chill in the air and gusty winds. Vera objected strongly, arguing that the winds created a dangerous condition. A further confrontation occurred when we returned safely and I expressed my pleasure at having shared a male-bonding adventure with my new son-in-law. It must have been one of many times that my hyperactive ways intruded upon the peace and tranquility Vera had sought when moving to Newtown. The time I was spending on the Ives Center also added to her irritation.

At the same time, Elizabeth's marriage was falling apart. During Neil's extended trips to Taiwan, overseeing the manufacture of the Betesh line of knockoff handbags, he became involved with a woman in Taipei of questionable reputation. Elizabeth tried to save the marriage, including visits to a psychiatrist alone and with Neil. I agreed to pay for the sessions. Elizabeth told me that much of their problem was caused by the "cold upbringing" she had experienced from her German/English/Swedish parents, as opposed to the warm, loving atmosphere Neil enjoyed from his Jewish mother and father. I figured the therapist was Jewish, but I merely said to Elizabeth: "Think whatever you want to if it will help put the marriage back together." I liked Neil and hoped their differences could be resolved. Unfortunately, they couldn't.

Winter came and went; spring flowed gently into summer. The Ives Center was dominating my weekends with concerns about the site, financial problems and the normal personality issues of a board. Pat had joined the board and we were seeing one another more often. Eventually, I did something that was especially irritating to Vera—not egregiously so in my mind, but sufficient to her that she didn't want me coming up on the weekends: It was too much for her. "I don't want to see you for a while. I will let you know when I feel differently."

Whether she put it exactly that way, or whether it was implied in her voice, I can't remember. But it didn't take me long to assume that she wanted me out of her life. I walked around the property, thinking about how I should react. Finally, I concluded that this was the time to make the break; it was her decision to all but end the marriage. I packed up some papers, clothes, and odds and ends and drove my Subaru back to New York City. While leaving, I told Vera that I would call her when I was willing to come back. I never did return, except to retrieve a few personal things.

My father had died the previous November at the age of 91. He often said that he might live forever, but a long-developing cancer of the prostate suddenly metastasized into the bone and his death came quickly. I had flown out from New York and was staying at our home on St. Charles Street when it happened. I watched from outside his room while he went through the last moments of resistance. It was my first experience of dying up close.

The *New York Times* writer Walter Waggoner gave Frank the lead obituary on November 29, describing him as "a Leader in Founding 'Third Market." After describing the Third Market, he told of Frank's birth in San Francisco, growing up on sailing ships captained by his father, and forming in 1922 his own securities firm dealing in municipal and corporate bonds. He highlighted Frank's interest in the new technology that was changing the collection of market data and communicating it to the public.

Early 1985 found me separated from my wife of 30 years and plotting to leave Moseley. It was unfortunate that my father had died just a few months earlier, since he would have approved of both moves.

For tax reasons, I maintained my primary residence in Connecticut. Pat was willing to have me stay with her, but it seemed prudent to find a temporary address that didn't disclose our growing relationship. I naively believed that Vera would soon be suing for divorce. As the year progressed, I moved in with Pat. Vera and I met, at her request, at the Ives Center. It was not a pleasant meeting. I was surprised but not swayed by her entreaties for me to return.

By this time, I knew most of Pat's family and was familiar with the environment in which she grew up. A Weeden Foundation meeting in California was an opportunity for me to introduce Pat to my mother and to my brothers and their wives. While I was separated from Vera, I was still married, but nobody seemed troubled by it or showed special concern for Vera. Mom fell in love with Pat from the very beginning – no shattered glass of cognac — and showered her with presents each time we came to California.

From there, I wanted Pat to see Yosemite. We stayed at the Lodge and then, as a lark, I suggested that we hike up to Merced Lake. "It's not a bad hike. The scenery is unbelievable." She was amenable, but it almost ended the courtship.

We began at Happy Isles a little after 8 o'clock. It went very well until just below Nevada Falls. The trail became quite steep and sometimes slippery. At the top of the fall, Pat mentioned that her boots were too tight and she made the first of several changes from boots to tennis shoes and back again. As the trail climbed above the tree line and the temperature rose, Pat's enthusiasm began to wane. I assured her the worst was over, having forgotten that I was only 14 when I had last skipped easily up the 14 miles and 4,000 feet. There was talk of turning back. "We have come over halfway," I misled her. "Turning back would be foolish." This assurance kept her going for a few more miles. As the miles became endless, I held out the ultimate encouragement: "Think of that ice-cold gin and tonic waiting at the Merced Lake Camp."

It was six o'clock when we limped into the camp. The last mile or so I thought it prudent that Pat take the lead. Seating her down under a panoply of giant Douglas firs, I hastened to the dining hall for the promised cocktail. Lemonade? Yes! Alcohol? No. Insult was added to injury; there were tents for men and others for women, but nothing in between.

The courtship was saved by a day of rest, a short hike to a quiet lake with towering granite cliffs at one end, a sandy beach, a cloudless sky and no one to bother us except for a lone brown bear wandering along the opposite shore. As an encore, the next year I arranged for horses to take us up to Evolution Meadow, situated at 9,600 feet on the John Muir Trail and nestled below Muir Pass.

The new Weeden & Company's move to 180 Maiden Lane took place over the year-end holiday. It was flawless. We conducted our business as though nothing had changed. Client inquiry remained normal. The mood was festive; the future looked bright. From the 19th floor we could gaze directly down upon the newly reconstructed South Street Seaport, with its shops and restaurants and open spaces, and across the East River to Brooklyn Heights. I purchased a telescope and tripod, anticipating a summer-long viewing of youthful office girls sunning themselves below.

I finally decided to initiate divorce proceedings. I argued incompatibility and thought the process would be straightforward, involving only the distribution of assets. Vera hired a tough-minded lawyer from Bridgeport who took the case from negotiating a settlement into a court proceeding. At one point, her lawyer told my lawyer that he wanted to call Pat as a witness. I countered by saying there were people along Pond Brook Road who might provide similar testimony under oath. The request was quickly withdrawn. My own approach to the proceedings was benign—to put the best light on a long marriage that finally ran out of steam.

During this Christmas vacation, Pat and I invited our respective children for a week on St. Croix. The interactions between children and prospective in-laws went flawlessly, as did later interactions among all our children.

Chimney constructed by Don containing three separate fireplace flues; fireplace in upper main living room, 1986.

As Luck Would Have It

Chapter 16
Love and (Re)Marriage

On April 21, 1987, my divorce from Vera was final. The next day, Pat and I were married in a grove of maples at the Ives Center, less than a stone's throw from where we first met. Our three-year courtship had been one of passion and discovery. I found myself married to an extraordinary woman. The ensuing years have been a wonderful, near-to-perfect relationship, despite the fact that we are both strong-minded and independent spirits. Much has to do with our shared view of the world around us and both of us being healthy in mind and body.

I was 56 and Patricia Gulliver née Cawley was 49 when we married. Pat had been married to Bob Gulliver for 18 years and divorced for nine. She was the daughter of John and Marie Cawley (née Young). Her early upbringing was neither "Cinderella" nor that of a normal family. Her father was a strong Irishman, popular and well known in Danbury, not least because he was the local federal tax commissioner. Unfortunately, he was marked as an alcoholic with a volatile disposition. Soon after Pat was born, she was handed off to Marie's older sister, Ersilia Baur; the reason given was her mother's health and John's social life. Another sister, Gloria, also placed her two boys, Ed and Billy, with Ersilia. Gloria had had a whirlwind life touring the world as a singer and dancer until complications from tuberculosis took her life.

It was into this complicated but congenial family atmosphere, including Ersilia's own daughter, Barbara, that Pat's father often appeared, day or night, demanding the return of his daughter.

Alcoholism was a problem of Marie's two brothers as well. As Pat tells it, Danbury was full of alcoholism; it existed just down the street and in many families important to Danbury's hat industry.

In this environment, Pat learned to be careful in her relationships, to keep her thoughts to herself, and study people closely so as to avoid trouble. This ability to analyze people's intentions and observe their character is remarkable. I have found her insights very helpful in my business dealings, as they are far sharper and more on the mark than my own.

I also discovered that she was smarter than I am. Our IQs are the same, but her memory is extraordinary. She won a number of spelling bees in school and knows the lyrics to songs from the Fifties forward through the mumblings of Bob Dylan to the latest tunes. When she came to Russia with me in 1993, she had studied the language for six months and was able to converse easily with people on the street. She reads literary fiction constantly. Bob Beshar, another voracious reader, would discuss with Pat recent novels they had read and compare them with books read years before. She was equal to Bob in remembering characters, plot, style and how the quality of writing compared with other authors.

Most of all I, found her feelings about people stronger and deeper than mine. Her sense of fairness, decency and behavior toward others was demonstrated in the early Sixties, when she became a member of the NAACP and marched with them in protest of racial discrimination. I found out later that when she was elected president of her high school sorority, she insisted on changing their bylaws to allow membership to blacks and Jews. These were not the qualities I had focused on that hot day in July at the Ives Center. They became the cake, and her beauty became the icing.

Pat was blessed physically. She was an attractive child who blossomed into quite a beautiful teenager. At 18, Pat was invited by Minute Maid to be on their Rose Bowl float in Pasadena on New Year's Day. That experience exposed her to talent agents for Hollywood. Soon she was at MGM making a screen test from "Come Back, Little Sheba," after which MGM offered her a contract. They thought she might eventually replace Lana Turner.

For the next two years, Pat alone, and then with husband Bob and their daughter, Tricia, took up residence in a beach-side apartment in Malibu. As Pat describes it, the acting work was intense, with classes, lessons, rehearsals and screen tests. There were courses in voice and diction, how to smile in front of a camera, and how to walk across the room with style. Her singing lessons went very well, the dancing not so well, and her acting skills, learned in high school plays, showed promise. Then she was cast as the ingénue in the last of the Andy Hardy movies, "Andy Hardy Comes Home." As television began to take over MGM, she was screen-tested for "Father of the Bride."

It must have been an exciting time for someone just turned 20. Before Bob and baby arrived, there were the evenings attending movie premieres and dining at Ciro's or the Mocambo or the Garden of Allah, usually in groups that included Fernando Lamas, Budd Schulberg and Mickey Rooney. It was MGM's way of having her seen, noticed and talked about in the Hollywood gossip columns.

For the premiere of "Gigi," MGM provided her an evening dress, styled her hair, applied her makeup and made sure there were photographers available when she arrived at the theatre. She made visits to the VA hospitals and other charity appearances arranged by MGM ito gain exposure for their latest starlet.

It was a memorable experience for Pat, but it was difficult for Bob, who was left to attend courses at a community college. Then another baby came along, and it became widely known at the studio that Pat was married. MGM's vision of their next sex goddess faded rapidly, and Pat and Bob returned to Danbury. Pat had wanted to make it as an actress but found that MGM was more interested in her as a sex symbol. That part of Hollywood had been distasteful from the beginning, so it made the return to a more normal life less disappointing than it would have been otherwise.

Back in Danbury, Pat spent her days as a hometown wife, active in hospital events and cake sales. Eventually, she and her friend Carol Hoyt sought out part-time modeling opportunities in New York City and began posing for commercial photography. They soon were traveling to Mexico for Corona Beer and taking trips to the Caribbean on behalf of the cruise ship industry.

Bob was unsuccessfully pursuing an acting career. Over time, he turned to the same bottle as did Pat's father, ending a marriage of 18 years and three daughters. Enter yours truly, parading around at the Ives Center wearing genuine Levi's and a rumpled cowboy hat.

The period of 1986–87 proved a watershed as well with respect to my ongoing role in the business. My responsibilities arising from the crisis that befell the prior Weeden—the avoidance of bankruptcy through merger and the obtaining of capital for a new beginning—were now behind me.

In the new Weeden, my active contribution diminished as others stepped forward and assumed the role of guiding the firm. Led by Barry Small, Tim McDonald and Bob Cervoni, the firm experienced a period of growth and profitability that for several years returned over 100% on capital to its unit holders. In 1994, we moved the firm to Greenwich, Connecticut, to avoid the unpleasant trip into Manhattan and take advantage of Connecticut's low taxes.

In 1995, Barry Small replaced me as president and CEO while I continued as chairman of Weeden Securities Corp. I am now chairman emeritus while still active as a board member.

Mom had been advised that flying was not good for her heart, but after Pat and I were married, she decided to make one last trip east to visit Weeden & Co.'s new office at 180 Maiden Lane. She had already shown her pleasure over the revival of the name by investing $400,000 on behalf of the Weeden Family Trust, which she and Frank had established to benefit her grandchildren and future Weeden family members. She said the next time she spoke to Frank, she would tell him that Weeden is in business again and seems to be doing well.

Mom passed away in January 1986 at age 91. Frank had died four years earlier. She kept his ashes on the top of the bureau in his bedroom. Most evenings she would pour herself a martini and sip it in the big chair facing the bureau and have a quiet conversation with Frank. She was happy with her "boys" and would bring him up-to-date on the many grandchildren visiting from time to time.

Shortly before her death, she was admitted to the Alameda Hospital and I flew out from New York. As soon as I entered her room, Mom looked at me and asked cryptically: "Are you out here because you think I'm about to die?" My explanation that it was a sudden meeting called by National Semiconductor didn't fly. She died two days later.

I was closer to Mom than to my father. She was my protector and disciplinarian. When I was young, she read to me, drove me everywhere and reviewed my report cards. She was a no-nonsense mother and seldom emotional, even to the point where kisses were dry and quick. She managed to keep the house immaculate despite its constant use by four sons and their pals from the neighborhood. She defended me when I got into trouble and sometimes had to apologize to the neighbors when mischief occurred.

She would sit at one end of the dinner table and Dad at the other, four boys in between. Most of the conversation was about swimming while she watched that our elbows remained off the table and we finished chewing before speaking. She kept track of those of us who called on her birthday and those who didn't. One of the last things I remember was her besting me at dominoes and placing my 40 cents into her change purse full of prior winnings.

Mom always appeared elegant and well dressed, except when tending her garden, when she would be clad in blue denims and a kerchief. She was graceful and poised in public and worried whenever the scale showed over 108 pounds. Mom traveled a lot, taking trips with her children, grandchildren and lady friends. Frank was happy to stay home, having done plenty of flying on business.

Their marriage lasted 67 years. You might say it lasted 71 years if you include the four years when Frank was resting on the bureau. It was a marriage that almost didn't happen except for the persistence of Frank—in an interview shortly before her death, Mom explained how they met.

"There was this man sitting across from me on the ferry boat that took us from Alameda to our work in San Francisco. He kept peeking over his newspaper at me and then hiding behind the paper when I looked up. My friend Myron told me that his name was Frank Weeden and that he would like to meet me. I told Myron I had no interest in meeting that dandy and 'You can tell him that.' Well, he did finally manage to meet me, and we were married the next year."

Mom was devoted to Frank and gave him a great deal of leeway in how he acted. I never thought Frank a "dandy," but he did like women and was quite flirtatious with the young mothers of the children learning to swim. Dancing was his specialty and Ginger Rogers his favorite movie star. Mom insists that he never cheated on her, but in their later years together she became increasingly annoyed by his ignoring her while spending all his time with his Alameda Swim Association.

Mom's lack of formal schooling limited her range of knowledge and intellectual curiosity. She enjoyed opera, her garden, her family and sight-seeing during her travels. The politics, history and local people were not mentioned in her long and descriptive letters back home.

Mom insisted on treating all of her sons equally. Alan made that difficult for her; Jack made it easy; I gained some special favor as the youngest; while Bill, as her doctor in her later years, eventually was appreciated more than the rest of us.

Mom's death completed a series of changes in my life. I had now lost both parents; there was my divorce and the demise of our family-led firm. The business relationship with Jack and Alan ceased while our friendship remained close. In the new Weeden, employees became partners. Above all, Patricia was now my wife. My love for her continues unabated.

New pavilion on pond at Charles Ives Center, Danbury, CT, 1984.

Poster for first performance in new pavilion, 1984.

Don building his stone walls, Charles Ives Center, Danbury, 1985.

As Luck Would Have It

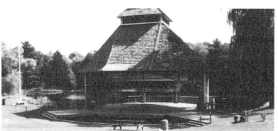

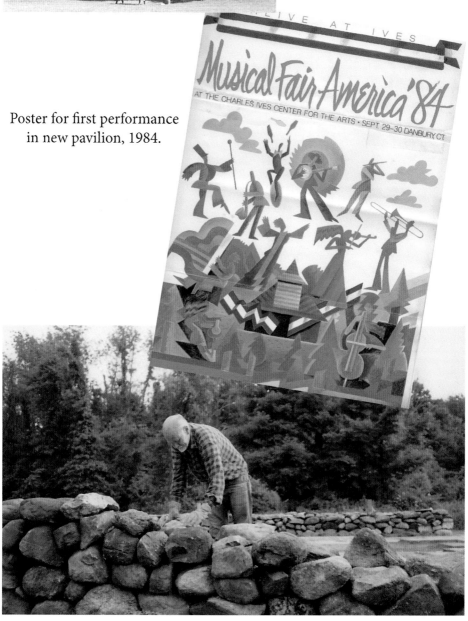

As Luck Would Have It

Pat at Glacier Point with Half Dome in background, 1985.

Pat on the trail up to Merced Lake from Yosemite Valley, 1985.

Campsite McClure Meadow, Evolution Valley, elevation 9,600 feet, 1986.

Don relaxing at McClure Meadow, 1986.

As Luck Would Have It

First meeting of Mabel and Pat,
1236 St. Charles Street, 1987.

Marriage of Pat and Don by Judge Nahley,
Charles Ives Center, Danbury, April 22, 1987.

Don and Pat.

As Luck Would Have It

Epilogue

After 30 years of marriage, Pat and I still live at the same address, sleep together in the same bed and have successfully integrated our respective families into one. We have maintained our love for each other undiluted by age and familiarity. Those years have been filled with challenges at home, adventures abroad and long vacations on beautiful St. Croix.

This is an appropriate time to end this memoir and begin a new book, one covering the next 30 years, from 1987 to ... whenever. Pat will be my leading lady; others will have major roles. There will be new players, successful ventures, awful failures, good times and tragedy. Meanwhile, I will digest what I've written and think about whether or not I got it right.

Thank you for taking this journey with me.